JESUS MARY JOSEPH

The Secret Legacy of
Jesus and Mary Magdalene

JESUS MARY JOSEPH

The Secret Legacy of
Jesus and Mary Magdalene

Ariadne Green

Palm Leaf Press

Jesus Mary Joseph: The Secret Legacy of Jesus and Mary Magdalene

For further information, please contact:

Palm Leaf Press
209 San Marino Ave.
Vallejo, Ca. 94589

Photo and Cover Design by Marka Lewis

Jesus Mary Joseph: The Secret Legacy of Jesus and Mary Magdalene
Ariadne Green

1. Title 2. Author 3. Non-Fiction/Spirituality/Gnosticism
Library of Congress Registration Number: TXu 1-874-496
ISBN: 978-0-9766862-1-7

ACKNOWLEDGEMENTS

I want to thank my editors, Toni Robino and Doug Wagner, and all those in my life who kept their promises to me, especially my daughters Vianna and Nitsa, my late mother, Val, and Aunt Stella. To the six astrologers, Thomas Wigglesworth, Ruby Grace, Harriet Witt, Marka Lewis, Lynn Bradford and Robert Hand whose remarkable interpretation of the charts of Jesus and Mary Magdalene proved invaluable, I am forever grateful. And finally, I want to thank Mary Magdalene for setting this book on its course.

COVER PHOTO

The cover photo is of a stained glass window at Holy Rosary Church, Paia, Hawaii. It depicts what Orthodox tradition tells us are the Sacred Heart of Jesus and the Immaculate Heart of the Virgin Mary who were bonded as mother and son and whose unmitigated love and compassion for humanity was best expressed through devotional images such as this one. However, I have reassigned this image to the two it more aptly belongs — Jesus and Mary Magdalene — because it poignantly depicts the strongest of all bonds, the eternal bond between Divine Complements and Twin Flames, hence — Twin Hearts.

Cover photo and cover design produced by graphic design artist Marka Lewis.

TABLE OF CONTENTS

Introduction...1

Chapter 1: Son and Daughter of God.............................9

Chapter 2: The Twin Soul Legacy
            and Mystery of the Bridal Chamber...............27

Chapter 3: A Destiny in the Stars..................................51

Chapter 4: The Aquarian Hasmonean Princess.................67

Chapter 5: Divine and Complementary Partners...............77

Chapter 6: The Exile of the Guardians of the Grail...........89

Chapter 7: The Thomas Code......................................123

Chapter 8: The Inheritors of the Grail..........................140

Chapter 9: Da Vinci's Last Testament...........................168

Chapter 10: Expectant Mary Magdalene........................196

Chapter 11: Gnostic Mary Magdalene: Petites Heures......220

Appendix I: The Story of the Twin Centered Rose...........270

Appendix II: The Gospel of Thomas.............................275

References...290

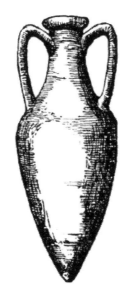

She
While the king was at his table,
my perfume spread its fragrance.

My beloved is to me a sachet of myrrh
Resting between my breasts.

My beloved is to me a cluster of henna blossoms
from the vineyards of En Gedi.

He
How beautiful you are, my darling!
Oh, how beautiful. Your eyes are doves.

_____

Song of Songs

INTRODVCTION

"The truth is not hard to kill and a lie well told is immortal." — Mark Twain

In my second book, *Divine Complement: The Spiritual Terrain of Soul Mate Relationships*, I wrote a significant chapter titled *Sacred Bride and Bridegroom* offering historical, as well as mythological understanding to the premise that Jesus and Mary Magdalene were Divine Complements and married. Since that time, so much more was revealed that I am compelled to bring the new discoveries and research into this book.

My quest for Jesus and Mary Magdalene's true legacy did not originate because of my Greek Orthodox Christian upbringing. In fact, I hadn't studied the New Testament in depth until I began researching and writing on the topic of Jesus and Mary Magdalene and the Gnostic gospels. Growing up, I never doubted the fantastic stories of Jesus Christ that I had been given by the Greek Orthodox Church and clung to my grandmother's heart, whose love for the Church and its doctrine was without question. I was somewhat entranced by the rituals and traditions of the Church, especially the Easter week ceremonies celebrating the Christian mythos of the death and resurrection. Good Friday services were especially memorable in that the entire congregation marched in procession with lit candles in hand around two city blocks following the "Epitaphio", a tomb decorated with spring flowers and rose pedals strewn across a painting of Jesus' body that lay in its well. The adults lamented in song while the children played with the flickering flames of the candles that dripped wax into paper cupcake holders.

Later in life, I became even more entranced with the flame, the flame of spiritual illumination and its gnosis. As a dream expert, my dreams as well as the dreams of others have been a constant source of spiritual revelation and wisdom, illuminating the mysteries of the soul, the archaic record and evolution of humanity's consciousness and, when my own, in mentioning my personal psychological evolution. In having listened to over a thousand dreams a year over the course of twenty years, I have also learned a great deal about dreams that communicate more than what is in the storehouse of the subconscious. Those dreams I recognize as heaven sent communications.

On those special and rare occasions, it was through my dreams that I received communications from the divine, from Mary Magdalene guiding me towards the path of research for this book and Jesus whose abiding love lifted me into the fullness of his love through a dream that to this day is an indelible memory. It was through that particular dream with Jesus that I was first introduced to the fact Jesus and Mary were twin souls and Divine Complements and that they had a remarkable story to tell, one very different than the one told by the architects of Christianity.

The dream that stimulated over ten years of research for this book was no ordinary dream. I was on the English Channel standing and gazing into the rippling waters when I looked up to see an obelisk rising high out of the center of the channel. The obelisk resembled the Washington monument and I thought its placement odd, to say the least. A woman was heroically climbing it, nearing the top. When she reached the apex, her exuberance at having accomplished the feat was evident. She stood up arms over her head as if summoning applause. Suddenly, invisible hands handed me a rolled map. The map spread open before my eyes, encompassing the entire visual plane. It was from the 1st century and charted only a portion of Western Europe, Gaul and Britannia. I surveyed and studied the mountainous region of the Pyrenees, the waterways and other topographic features. As the dreamer, I was not cognizant of the secret being disclosed, but only knew the map must be significant. Within a moment, I was lifted into a heavenly plane by a volume of love that was beyond anything I have ever experienced. It was Jesus sitting with me now and I was enveloped by the transcendent energy emanating from his heart. His hair was only a half-inch long and he was clean-shaven making his facial features stand out. His face was soft, beautiful and inviting. He wore a tunic of woven woolen fabric so soft to the touch that it offered me comfort to rub it between my finger and thumb. All the while, my heart was open in response to the love he had for me. He said only one sentence: "Ariadne, we must go back to Nazareth." I awoke with a start.

This initiatory destiny dream was meant to begin me on a long path of discovery through the legends of the South of France and Great Britain to discover an astonishing hidden legacy, pieces of a post-crucifixion history yet to be completely uncovered and thoroughly researched. The obelisk in the center of the channel, a profound clue, had a two-fold meaning. Firstly, I identified it as Cleopatra's Needle, an ancient Egyptian monument to the Sun God Ra that has stood in the City of Westminster in the United Kingdom since it was transported from Egypt and erected there in 1878. Its origins were the ancient city of Heliopolis, Egypt and it was constructed in about 1450 BC to flank the sides of a temple alongside its twin pillar. The obelisk is thought to be symbolic for the petrified ray of Aten, the sun disc, and the hieroglyphics carved on its sides celebrate victories and pay homage to Horus, a Son of Ra, and to Ra himself. The city of Heliopolis, however, was the most important clue in unraveling the intended message of this portion of the dream because it disclosed the first destination point of Mary Magdalene's journey into exile after the crucifixion. This fact will be discussed in the chapter, *Exile of the Carriers of the Grail*. Secondly, the woman climbing the obelisk was demonstrating the ease with which I could ascend into a heavenly dimension to commune with my guide, Jesus, who like the Sun god Horus was once proclaimed the Son of God.

The dream was also an invitation to travel to Israel and when the opportunity presented itself, I was on a plane. The town of Nazareth also had a two-fold meaning in the dream. Firstly, as it turns out, the town of Nazareth did not exist at the time of Jesus and, therefore, was a poignant reminder of the many fictitious and mythologized facts that fill the New Testament. Secondly, what I discovered on my travels to Nazareth was more a personal message than a clue to unravel about Jesus and Mary's legacy. It was a message about personal redemption. There was much more to discover in Israel as I walked the ancient magical and meaningful trails following in Mary Magdalene and Jesus' footsteps. So many of my experiences were transcendent and life altering.

The first biography of Jesus Christ, the Gospel of Mark, was written in about 65 AD and like the other three canonical Gospels, Luke, Matthew and John, it is considered an authoritative testament

of the three short years of Jesus' ministry in Judea and Galilee. By
definition a testament requires witnesses, however, none of the four
gospel writers were amongst Jesus and his disciples during his
ministry which was some thirty years before Mark ever put his quill
to papyrus. It is assumed that the historical accounts about Jesus
and his ministry before Mark were likely passed down through oral
tradition, a word of mouth transmission of stories about a spiritual
master who had touched the hearts of many and who created such a
stir in the community that his followers multiplied by the hundreds.
But what historical proof exists that the Gospels actually relayed an
accurate account of Jesus' ministry, life, death and resurrection?
Little. And as you will read in a later chapter, the Canonical
Gospels only offered a corrupted version of Jesus' authentic
teachings. Yet, Christianity has presented the four canonical texts as
the unquestionable truth, purporting them to represent God's word.
To consider them otherwise is a heresy.

The glorified image and projection, of this God Man, Jesus
Christ, who ministered only for a brief period and sacrificed himself
to redeem humanity, is that of a mythological figure bearing
similarity to the gods of the Hellenistic era. The sharp contrast is
that the mythological Jesus was not paired with a Divine
Complement or consort as was Mithra with Anahita, Osiris with
Isis, and Adonis with Aphrodite. As it turns out, the Orthodox
Christian version was a purely fabricated image that had little to do
with the actual legacy that Jesus and Mary Magdalene intended to
leave, one in which God and Goddess were united together
initiating others into the mystery of the Kingdom within. The
pseudo-myth of Orthodox Christianity served a handful of
patriarchs of the church who used it to create a world religion, a
religion that has been perpetuated because most of the truth was
suppressed; only a few fossils remain concealed in legend and
revealed in the art of the Renaissance by artists who were privy to a
secret tradition.

One thread of truth that can be drawn from the Christology of
the Church is that Jesus resurrected, re-birthed his consciousness as
Christ, while he was alive and was one of the wisest spiritual
teachers to have incarnated on earth. But he did not die on the
cross, as I believe I will hermeneutically prove as we examine the
"great secret" held by a group of 12th century Cistercian monks in
France, a secret hinted at in the most famous of all the Grail

romances — *La Queste del Saint Graal*. This "great secret' is so shocking that the interjection, "Jesus Mary Joseph" used as the title of this book, I deem appropriate. It best describes my own shock and disbelief after discovering the truth as well as hinting at a portion of the secret.

As we will see, what Jesus accomplished in his long life would not have been possible without the love and constant reflection of his equal and Divine Complement, his beloved Magdalene. The second thread of truth that we can derive from Christian mythos is that there was a mythological basis to his life and Mary's, but one with an altogether different mythological theme than that of a dying God. It is his story and her story woven together that form a new image and more authentic history of Jesus Christ, one that the chapters of this book are meant to illuminate.

There have been many recent contributors, some scholars, others who lack scholarship but who possess insight none-the-less, who have presented significant pieces to the huge mosaic that constitutes the real legacy of Jesus and his passionate companion, Mary Magdalene. Many like Margaret Starbird, Karen King, Elaine Pagels and the late Laurence Gardner, just to name of few, have put forth substantial research in the areas of theology, medieval history, Renaissance art, and Gnosticism and have done much to help us discard Christian dogma that rendered Mary Magdalene a sinful prostitute and to raise her to the station of Jesus' Divine Complement and even his wife. They have given us new ground to stand on and much to continue to digest.

This book is not meant to revisit topics that have been thoroughly researched and discussed, such as Priory of Sion, Rennes-le-Chateau, the Shroud of Turin, and Templar/Masonic links. Instead, I offer substantially new research centered on Jesus and Mary's relationship as Divine Complements, their travels, their teachings and a Gnostic tradition that survived through the Middle Ages. The research substantiates others' discoveries and nullifies some. I will leave to you to decide what rings true your heart.

Those familiar with my book Divine Complements Forever will recognize I have included the chapters on the astrology of Jesus and Mary Magdalene and the Bridal Chamber mystery in this book. In actuality those chapters were written for this book and I included them in Divine Complements Forever to support that book's premise with two beautiful examples, Jesus and Mary Magdalene.

The premise of this book is that Jesus had a profound destiny to fulfill when he incarnated in Judea in 7 BC. His destiny was to fall in love with a goddess, his twin flame, to realize his inborn god-like potentials as Christ and alongside his Divine Complement to light the path of spiritual enlightenment for many. That destiny was inscribed in the memory of his soul and charted in some detail at the moment of his birth.

Because my own spiritual emergence was catalyzed and followed a mythological plot, the myth of Ariadne and Dionysus, I began exploring the possibility that Jesus and Mary Magdalene destiny plan had also followed a mythological blueprint, one that would have determined their fate and brought them together for their profound mission. Themes like the virgin birth, the place of birth of Bethlehem, the love between a god and goddess, the wounding of the god, the rescue by his consort and finally the resurrection, all pointed to several myths of the Hellenistic era. The most similar to Jesus' story was the Adonis and Aphrodite myth, in which Adonis meets an untimely death and is rescued and resurrected by his goddess consort, Aphrodite. The mythological plot culminated in not only the resurrection of a god, but in the reunification of God and Goddess as divine lovers and partners. This reunification was integral to the salvation plan and reconciliation of the fall, something that the pseudo-myth of Christianity had revised and corrupted.

We will travel beyond the mythic projections of Jesus and Mary Magdalene as merely legendary and mythological archetypes, images that have stuck with us for centuries. These images exude a variety of qualities and attributes, some fairly positive and others preposterous. As we will see, no more preposterous is the portrayal of Mary Magdalene as a penitent sinner whore dwelling in the desert or in her cave in St. Baume for 33 years, languishing in sorrow endlessly with only the hope of ascending with angels at the end of life. Or the image of Jesus, a simple illiterate carpenter, who by divine design was immaculately conceived and grew up to become a celibate Rabbi who performed miracles, was proclaimed the Son of God, and martyred at the age of thirty three to save us from sin. Even some of the more modern images brought to light in recent years may prove to be little more than wishful thinking. They are idealized projections out of deep need to redefine the couple as perfect complements, who never argued, lived simply and harmoniously amongst a community of Essenes and traveled to such places as India to minister tenets of a mystical school based on more ancient traditions—all theories lacking evidence. Instead, Jesus and Mary Magdalene were two distinct personalities, very human, who were both born to be mystics and spiritual teachers. First and foremost, they were bound by a promise to each other, a stellar promise to always honor the love infused in them since the beginning of creation and to cherish their everlasting bond. The tenets of their teachings were meant to initiate and enlighten their disciples to the mysteries of the Kingdom within, the inborn potentials of the god-self and mystery of the *bridal chamber*. This mystery represents the Holy Grail, a secret God potential based on a tri-unity factor hidden deep within the heart of our spirit. And it was their quest to realize it first and then to minister the secrets to their community as "gnosis" (knowledge).

From the cup that held the blood of Christ that was carried to Gaul by Joseph of Arimathea to the "Sangrael", decoded as "Sang Rael" (blood royal) the meaning of the Grail conjures up many images. Whether the Grail is a dish, cup, magical alchemical cauldron or lapis stone, its power is what is significant and its quest paramount. And while many have tried to define the quest in a variety of ways, they seem to have missed the most straightforward description, one put forth in *La Queste del Saint Graal*:

> "It was written that The Quest is not a quest for earthly things. But it is to be the search for the deep secrets and confidences of Our Lord. And for the great mysteries which the High Master will openly show to that fortunate knight whom he has elected to be his servant. To him he will reveal the great marvel of the Holy Grail and will show him what a mortal heart could not conceive nor the tongue of an earthly man could utter."

And it is the deepest secrets of the High Master that this book will explore, not only the more authentic teachings of Jesus in a Gospel that I believe he penned but the secret legacy of the Grail carriers who embarked on a journey to Egypt, Gaul and finally Britannia, continuing to gather disciples throughout those regions who they initiated into the mysteries of the Grail.

The discoveries about the lives of Jesus and Mary Magdalene are of such a controversial nature that I'm sure there will be those who fail to embrace their authenticity and, as a result, may fail to embrace me. I'm also sure many questions will arise as to what additional proof exists. In response, I offer a passage from the Gospel of Thomas:

> They said to him, "Tell us who you are so that we may believe in you." He said to them, "You examine the face of the heavens and the earth, and yet do not know what is in front of your face nor do you know how to discern this present time."

Many of the true facts about the post crucifixion story and the relationship between Jesus and Mary Magdalene have been right under our noses, just beneath the surface summoning us to use a critical mind and intuition to discover the secrets. It's in this present time in humanity's evolution, evidenced by the number of books on the subjects of Mary Magdalene and the "sins" of the Gospels, that we're meant to finally bring together pieces of the truth from a variety of sources. In this way, we can hopefully discard the myths and what we've been conditioned to believe about Jesus Christ, his mission, his ministry and, even more important, the woman whom Jesus was said to have loved more than his other disciples – Mary Magdalene.

CHAPTER ONE
Sons and Daughters of God

We are all sons and daughters of God — DIVINE.

Of all the famous Divine Complements (soulmates) in history, Jesus and Mary Magdalene have fascinated me most. Although, most of us were taught and conditioned to believe only one of them was divinely born with a destiny to light the path of salvation and offer hope for reconciliation of the fall, the other (Mary Magdalene) was as important to the total picture of our legacy from God.

As twin flames, Jesus and Mary arrived at a time in history when reconciliation of the fall was a long awaited event for the cultures in the Mediterranean regions. The prophesies of Daniel and Isaiah, as well as the mythologies of the region, all pointed to a divine savior who would unite the people and offer them the promise of better times, the milk and honey of an abundant life – a paradise restored. In the mythologies of Mesopotamia, Sumer, Egypt, and Greece, twin Gods and Goddesses separated by fate were reunited through the resurrection and rebirth of the divine born masculine archetype who had met a tragic and untimely death. Whether it was Adonis and Aphrodite of the Greeks, Tammuz and Ishtar of Sumer, Mithra and Anahita of Persia, Osiris and Isis of Egypt or Adam and Eve they were the celebrated masculine and feminine twin lovers conquering death and consummating their love after a long separation. For most of these cultures, rites and rituals celebrated the God and Goddess and reenacted portions of their mythology honoring and supporting their reunification. As fertility rituals, they demonstrated each culture's deep understanding of the God/Goddess inborn potentials. These cultures projected supernatural powers onto their deities and offered animal sacrifice as appeasement to ensure a fruitful harvest.

While the Jews were looking forward to the promised Messiah, who would reign as King David had centuries before, the Persians and Medians awaited the incarnation of a deity, Mithra, a solar hero, whose feminine counterpart was Anahita, the water bearer. For the Zoroastrians, the Saoshyant or "savior" would fulfill their hopes for the reign of a good and ideal king, someone who was as benevolent as Cyrus, who had united Persia and Media and liberated the Jews in Babylon in 539 BC.

Jesus incarnated with his destiny map clearly defined, a mythological map that would be illuminated to him throughout the course of his life. This underlying mythology was the Adonis and Aphrodite myth, a Hellenistic myth that began circulating in the regions of the Mediterranean about 300 years before Jesus' birth, setting the stage for his incarnation alongside his Divine Complement, Mary Magdalene.

The Adonis myth's theme of birth, death and resurrection is one of psychological rebirth, spiritual emergence and reconciliation of the division and separation we have come to know as the "Fall". Adonis and Aphrodite, god and goddess archetypes, are the characters in a romantic plot of heroic proportions questing to preserve their love and lives together. They can be viewed as Divine Complements who embody the godly attributes of the masculine and feminine intelligence – Aphrodite as the Goddess of Love and Adonis, the solar fire driven masculine spirit. The gods and goddesses live within each of us as powerful archetypes that drive our personalities and our fate. But for those like Jesus and Mary Magdalene, whose destiny it was to fully embody their divinity, these archetypes catalyzed a profound journey toward self-realization resulting in a spiritual emergence and the cognition of the unity of their souls as Divine Complements.

The Adonis and Aphrodite myth unravels as a narrative of Adonis' birth, maturation, passion for conquest – and consequently his untimely death – and his rescue from the underworld and resurrection through the efforts of Aphrodite. To summarize the myth, Adonis is half mortal and half god birthed out of a myrrh tree, symbolic of the tree of life and primordial perfection. Aries, the initiator and a dark rival, disguises himself as a wild boar and attempts to kill Adonis at the very moment of his birth, but before he can, the Goddess Aphrodite rescues and delivers him to the Goddess of the Underworld, Persephone, to raise and protect until he reached maturity. Once he emerged mature, Aphrodite became Adonis' consort and lover. Adonis' un-tempered passion for the hunt, however, was a worrisome issue for Aphrodite, who frequently warned him of the dangers of hunting wild beasts. Aphrodite's worst fears materialized when one fateful day Adonis set out to hunt the same wild boar that nearly killed him at the time of his birth. The beast pierced Adonis with a mortal wound. By the time Aphrodite arrived, Adonis had succumbed to death. Armed with vengeance, Aphrodite descends into the underworld determined to resurrect her beloved Adonis. She relinquishes everything (all earthly possessions) including her sword to gain entry into Hades. Battling Persephone for the right to resurrect Adonis, she succeeds by gaining the sympathies of Zeus the patriarch of all the Gods and Goddesses who works out a compromise in which three quarters of the year Adonis would return to the land of the living and one quarter he would spend in the underworld with Persephone.

As a symbolic narrative of the psychological and spiritual emergence of a hero, the myth presents a progression from birth to maturation of the masculine psyche that requires a feminine complement to resurrect his soul and true purpose, in order to fulfill his destiny. The myth speaks of an unfortunate fate, a confrontation with death representing the psychological peril that the male psyche faces when operating separately from his feminine complement. His independent forward-thrusting ego must be sacrificed in his descent into the underworld. Stripped of his earthly identifications he succumbs to the power of the Death Goddess, Persephone, and re-emerges reborn to his spirit to reclaim his authentic self, a divine God holding the strength of spiritual maturity. Both human and divine he is reborn to stand alongside the Goddess of Love, Aphrodite, having achieved a new consciousness – embracing the importance of his spiritual union with his feminine complement.

Jesus' soul carried with it a mythic blueprint for this psychological transformation and spiritual awakening. He was awakened and enlightened through the catalyzing circumstances of his fate, his persecution and crucifixion, resulting in near death. The event forced him to psychologically die and dismember his personality so that he could rise in consciousness to realize the fullness of his spiritual mission. This process was synergized and supported by the bonds of intimacy with his Divine Complement, Mary Magdalene. His crucifixion did not result in a literal death, but instead an escape into exile, the details of which we will explore in another chapter.

Jesus' blueprint for spiritual emergence was imprinted deeply in his soul's DNA, unfolding through a synergistic balance of his masculine and feminine sides. His life unfolded from beginning to end as an evolutionary plan offering him the opportunities to grow in his consciousness, to touch the enlightened potentials of his soul and to ultimately initiate into the mysteries of the sacred marriage to be anointed within the Bridal Chamber of his heart. This initiatory transformational process resulted in the resurrection, a rebirth of his soul transforming his consciousness into the divine human form – a God manifest on Earth, God's worthy choice to light a spiritual path for humanity. It was for him to realize completely so that he might illuminate the path for us all – the path on which we might discover our authentic selves and achieve spiritual redemption, honoring God and God's spark of love within us.

Of late, several authors, including Freke and Gandy (2004), when examining the mythological similarities to biblical history have questioned whether Jesus actually existed. These authors are purporting that Jesus was probably nothing more than an archetype fabricated by Christian Orthodoxy to fulfill a messianic vision and to promote a religious ideology that denied the inner mysteries of Gnosticism and other self-realizing traditions like Buddhism. Although it's probably true that the Virgin birth, the December 25th birth date, the birthplace as Bethlehem, and the arrival of the three kings or Wise Men were borrowed motifs, some from the celebrations of Adonis and those of Mithra, probably inserted to paint a convincing picture of Jesus' divinity, there is little doubt that Jesus was a living, breathing man performing a profound spiritual and political mission. The reconstructed-myth theory of Freke and Gandy arises out of ignorance and misunderstanding of the origins and function of mythology and results in throwing out the baby with the bathwater.

As a public dream scripted into the collective consciousness of humanity, a myth could be realized by any soul whose destiny it was to fulfill its blueprint for awakening and prophecy. Myths contain metaphorical and symbolic elements, patterns and forces of archetypal energies that drive the human soul and spirit forward through evolution. The more important themes in myths reconcile the forces of good and evil and repair the division of the split soul. Therefore, the life of the individuating hero would contain elements of his or her mythology. With this in mind, we begin to understand that it was the complex destiny of the "living Jesus" to fulfill a soul/spirit/human mission and to be an example of a divinely born world-redeemer. Mythology drove his spiritual and personal quest for higher truth, the sacred marriage and the rebirth of his divinity. And it undoubtedly illuminated the mission God had sent him to accomplish. What was creatively put in front of him were the necessary spiritual and heroic tasks and tests that would resurrect his consciousness to embody his divinity and illuminate his spiritual political purpose. Unfolding and manifesting in his life were elements found in the mythology of Adonis and Aphrodite, the underlying myth that also pointed him toward Mary Magdalene, his goddess of love.

Jesus' quest for the sacred marriage was an individualized plan that awakened him to his androgynous nature and reconciled any shadows cast on the masculine and feminine aspects of his soul. In the consciousness field of his creative destiny, women played as important a role as did his male brethren, the Apostles. Women were light-bearers illuminating for him the definition of his feminine soul. From them he gained an intimate understanding of the feminine aspect of God and the goddess within his own psyche, a part struggling to emerge and contribute to a balanced intelligence, yin and yang. Three women named Mary accompanied him most days of his ministry offering support, respect and a constant reflection and reminder of the importance of the role of women to his mission. The third Mary, Mary Magdalene, whom some have referred to as his favored disciple, clung to his side, not as a grateful saved harlot from whom seven demons were cast out, nor a mere follower, but as his sacred bride to whom he was bonded in love and friendship. Although there is no mention of Jesus' marital status anywhere in the Gospels, neither is there evidence that Jesus was not married. The subject is never covered. The wedding feast in Cana however is well documented and offers enough material for almost anyone to at least wonder if it was Jesus' wedding, as there is a reference that would lead one to believe that he was the bridegroom:

> "…The governor of the feast called the bridegroom, And saith unto him, Every man at the beginning doth set forth good wine; and when men have well drunk, then that which is worse: but thou hast kept the good wine until now." – John 2, 8-10

This passage of John's account of the wedding feast is the last in the description of Jesus' miracle of turning water into wine. Within the context of the events described by John one could presume that Jesus was the bridegroom as he was the one solicited by his mother, Mary, to do something about the empty wine jars. As Henry Lincoln, one of the author's of *Holy Blood, Holy Grail*, has pointed out, if it wasn't his wedding, then why was he playing host?

Jesus' marriage to Mary Magdalene would have been one of arrangement as was customary in Judea at that time. A Hasmonean, Mary was a perfect choice because of her genealogy, connecting her to the Maccabees who had conquered Palestine a century before and whose aristocratic and priestly line was noble and would add substantial financial worth to the picture. Status was an important consideration in choosing the appropriate bride in all arranged marriages. Most times it was the main consideration. However, in this case the bloodlines were more important. From an early conversation with the late Laurence Gardner, author of *Bloodline of the Holy Grail*, it made perfect sense to me that Jesus and Mary's betrothal would have been a dynastic one aimed at forging a tighter bond between his kingly line of Judah and her priestly royal line of Aaron. With an aristocratic and wealthy lineage, Mary could have helped to support Jesus and his ministry. The marriage would have guaranteed a future succession of kings in Judea beginning with Jesus' offspring, assuming that Jesus himself would reign. So important was the dynastic marital contract to ensure the continuation of the bloodline of David that it seems very unlikely that Jesus would have been taken seriously as an unmarried Rabbi. The Hasmoneans had their own claims to the throne and it made perfect political and religious sense that a marriage to Mary Magdalene, also known in the gospels as Mary of Bethany, would have smoothed some of the dissention between the two families and rallied them together to bless the union.

Illuminating the obvious lessons, a fate that divided Judea, was being offered the opportunity to heal through a savior whose path was one of unification with God and one supported by his feminine counterpart in the image of Eve and the Goddess of Love. The condition of a division between the many sects not able to agree spiritually nor politically was the foreground of Jesus' spiritual and political movement. It was his personal political mission – perhaps more so than his godly mission – to unite them. Under the thumb of

Roman rule, Palestine and Judea had lost face and dominion over their own people. They were under the tyranny of Roman rule and puppet ministries of the Pharisees and Sadducees. The houses were divided, the cities were divided and Jesus' insightfully stirring the consciousness and conscience of his audience stated it so.

> "Every kingdom divided against itself is brought to desolation; and every city or house divided against itself shall not stand: And if Satan cast out Satan, he is divided against himself; how shall then his kingdom stand?" (Matt. 12:22-30)

I shudder to think what Mary Magdalene thought of the politics of her husband as he stepped out to demonstrate his more Godly authority amongst the Pharisees and Sadducees. A woman's intuition and wisdom might push her to warn against any action that would jeopardize their mutual mission of love. She would warn him undoubtedly not to cast love aside in favor of political conquest. With Adonis driving Jesus forward to light fires in the community, Jesus may have been ill prepared to meet the opposition he obviously met almost from the very beginning. We must remember that his ministry was newly born and it is reasonable to conclude that his spiritual awakening, new born identity and his profound spiritual vision had propelled him to take issue with the religious philosophies of the ruling high priests and to force the issue that he was God's choice arriving with a new mandate — a bold early move. His spiritual philosophy and view of God was a radical departure from the long legacy of spiritual puritanical fanaticism that was inlaid in Judaic spiritual customs and the religious doctrine supporting them. His charisma, altruism, wisdom and authority amongst all the classes likely angered and intimidated the elders.

From the biblical accounts, it is difficult to discern which elements of Isaiah's prophecies were emulated and staged by Jesus and which ones were added into the narrative later by the architects of the New Testament. Both occurred. Jesus was deliberately out to prove that he was the Messiah whom had been prophesized by Isaiah, planning to fulfill that prophecy by using every minute symbolic element he could to back up his claim. His royal blood, descending from the House of Judea as well as his dynastic marriage to Mary Magdalene lined up all his ducks in a row. And it is likely that he had his eyes set on taking his place amongst all the favorite Kings of Israel beginning with King David. Had Jesus adhered more to the underlying script of his myth, Adonis and Aphrodite, rather than pursuing the legacy of prophesies by Isaiah, he may have appreciated the value of his beloved Mary Magdalene in helping him to achieve a greater spiritual mission, one that would set the example of divine partnership and the equality of women.

In the same way that Aphrodite warned Adonis about getting too close to the wild boar, an archetype in Jesus' myth representing the Romans, Mary would have clung to Jesus' side guarding his life as Aphrodite had guarded Adonis. She would have tried to preserve and demonstrate the love she had for him at all costs in hopes that he would be inspired by it. She would have supported his aims while tempering his passion with caution. The personality of Mary Magdalene will be more thoroughly described in another chapter, but what needs to be underscored here is that she was driven by the underlying myth of Adonis and Aphrodite as much as Jesus was and that she came to embody the example of Aphrodite, the goddess of love. We might imagine fate presented them with a mountain of troubles to confront at times, ones that had to be set aside when they were meant to express the communion of their marriage. How they did it is an unknown. Their personal egos and individual aims would have had to be put aside to recognize that through sacred partnership they could achieve a great deal more then if they were divided or separated. With the grounded power of their love and commitment to each other they could better serve their community and mission. Afterall, it was their destiny to faithfully serve a divided community as a united front.

Did Jesus honor the role of women in his life when among him were men who rendered little status to the role of women? His best friend, Peter, was critical of women, if not a complete sexist, especially in regard to Mary Magdalene. In Saying 14 of the Gospel of Thomas, a gospel omitted from the New Testament, Simon Peter was quoted as saying, *"Let Mary leave us, for women are not worthy of life."*

It would be a challenge for any enlightened man living in a patriarchal society that dictated a subservient role to women to speak in favor of a woman's divinity and to attempt to elevate her status in men's eyes. Fate must have presented Jesus with many supreme tests to prove his wisdom and fairness toward women. He would either have to conform and uphold the views of the men around him or challenge the status quo. On the surface, as portrayed by the Gospels, there seems to be little evidence that he passed all the tests, considering that the Gospels paint Jesus as a patriarchal son who referred to God only as Father and had little to say about women as a whole. He had to mature and individuate from the oppressive patriarchal male influence on his psyche. There's evidence that he did to some degree.

Jesus' response to Peter's statement above was colored with sarcasm:

> "I myself shall lead her in order to make her male, so that she too may become a living spirit resembling you males. For every woman who will make herself male will enter the kingdom of heaven." (Saying 114, Gospel of Thomas)

If we interpret this passage literally, without noting the sarcasm, it would amount to a misogynous statement that the feminine soul isn't worthy of life. Instead, the saying mentions that Mary's soul is as much masculine as feminine. Jesus is also asking Mary to have the courage and boldness to stand up in the face of opposition, like a man, and if she does, she, too, would be worthy of entering the Kingdom of Heaven.

Jesus' many radical departures from Judaic tradition in the role of rabbi are evidenced in much of Scripture. He was an enlightened teacher, and it therefore seems reasonable to think he had other things to say about the status of women. Peter was a reflection of male supremacy serving Jesus as an antagonist. I'm sure Jesus became enlightened enough to know that Peter's reflection was indicative of a long legacy of inequality, one he, himself, would have to heal from to have an enlightened relationship with Mary Magdalene and one that honored God's feminine face.

From the Gospels, it's evident that not only were women among his disciples and part of his audience as invisible servants, but they were on the front lines. After all, who was in the foreground beneath the cross at the Crucifixion? The three Marys were still beside him and for a very important reason. Jesus had something to realize during that horrific event: that God had arrived at the cross as the three faces of Mary, a goddess of love. As it seems, all his male disciples but John had abandoned him. In his enlightened mind, the Marys reflected God's image, and their compassionate presence must have comforted him in the fact that God had not abandoned him. As Jesus said, *"The kingdom is within you and it is outside you."* He was well aware of the fact that his life was a stage, with actors, male and female, playing their roles to help him solidify insights that would advance his soul and elevate his consciousness. The supposed final scene of his life was ending as he was surrounded by women he loved and who loved him. He was to embrace them as his salvation.

The heroic task of a world redeemer is to step forward, discard the legacy of community and offer a more God-given example of equality and higher truth. And for Jesus it would have been paramount to honor women, perhaps even more vehemently than men, as he came as the Son of Man to offer himself as an example of God's creative intention – an intention of equality of the sexes and of equal partnership. After all, if he came to mend the separation and to raise his own beloved in his heart as his Eve, he would have to offer an example of a man who supported the equality of women. In a statement that's usually misinterpreted, straying from its historical implications of the status of the feminine, Jesus redefined God: "*Whoever blasphemes against the Father will be forgiven, and whoever blasphemes against the son will be forgiven, but whoever blasphemes against the Holy Spirit will not be forgiven, either on earth or in heaven.*" – Saying 44, Gospel of Thomas.

Although Orthodox Christianity usually quotes a similar passage in Matthew and defines the Holy Spirit as the inborn aspect of God in the Son, the more appropriate definition of the Holy Spirit, one used by Gnostics, is that of the Divine Feminine – God the Mother. If this dramatic statement is really what he said, we can be assured that Jesus recognized that God's feminine expression needed to be honored above even himself because it had been the most defiled and degraded image of God. The insult, degradation and injury to his own Divine Complement, Mary, sparked by jealousy and ignorance, undoubtedly burdened Jesus' heart and made it necessary for him to speak out in such a way as to shame his disciples into feeling some level of reverence for the feminine. His consciousness had been awakened, and he was now to awaken others.

The keys to the Kingdom lie deep within the spirit and the soul—the spirit that holds the divine spark of God and the soul that reflects the fabric of God's complex creations. Jesus' true teachings, like those found in the Gospel of Thomas, pointed to an inner kingdom that he described in a variety of ways in his parables – for example as a small mustard seed, a tiny un-awakened seed of consciousness with huge potentials, or as a measure of leaven that multiplies loaves of bread. The four canonical Gospels offer a rewritten and corrupted version of the majority of Jesus' most important teachings. Therefore, we must look to the Gospels of Thomas for deeper understanding of Jesus' greatest teachings of the mysteries. In the Gospels of Thomas, there are numerous hints of secret teachings regarding initiation into the Kingdom of God through a path of unification. One such mysterious saying appears to offer an understanding of the necessity of healing the condition of split soul in order to realize the Kingdom of God. Thomas 106 reads as follows: *"When you make the two one, you shall become sons of man, and when you say, 'Mountain, be moved!' it will move."*

Saying 22 offers a lengthier and more defined description:

> "When you make the two one, and when you make the inner like the outer and the outer like the inner, and the upper like the lower, and when you make the male and the female into a single one, so that the male is not male and the female not female, a hand in place of a hand, a foot in place of a foot, and an image in place of an image, then you shall enter the kingdom."

What's described here is a complete metamorphosis of the individual beyond any enlightened awakening, one of unification of the divine aspects of the soul and one resulting in the rebirth into one's god/goddess nature so that the hand becomes the instrument of God and one's image moves from human to the divine form. This is exactly what Jesus had accomplished to become the Son of Man, Son of the Light or Son of the Bridal Chamber. It was the path he consciously took and the path he lit for his disciples, one that embraces the inner, the outer, the masculine, the feminine and one's own power to perform the miracles of God. It is a realization accomplished only through the deepest initiation in the Bridal Chamber of the Stellar Heart and one in which the individual must come into conscious contact with the signature that God implanted in the hearts of man in the beginning.

The soul-to-soul and spirit-to-spirit connection and realization between Jesus and his twin complement, Mary Magdalene, must have been momentous, rewarding him with the recollection of the deepest memory of his soul's beginnings. To return to the root of unified consciousness as an individual soul with God and in deepest spirit-to-spirit communion with one's twin soul is an ultimate realization, setting one on the course of healing the split and separation within. The reconciliation of the fall is what Jesus came to embody, and what he had to offer was a demonstration of deepest affection and love, for his beloved Mary Magdalene – perhaps more important a purpose than his political quest to claim his messianic inheritance.

It's evident that Jesus valued the sanctity of marriage as well as having the deepest understanding of the lasting soul-to-soul communion between Divine Complements, the Stellar Promise. In the Gospel of Mark 10:1-16, Jesus says,

> "But from the beginning of creation, `God made them male and female.' For this reason a man shall leave his father and mother and be joined to his wife, and the two shall become one flesh.' So they are no longer two but one flesh. What therefore God has joined together, let not man put asunder."

Jesus gave the Pharisees more than they asked for when they asked him about divorce. He reveals enlightened knowledge of the deepest connection between a man and a woman created by God at the beginning of creation, suggesting that it be honored as a lasting promise. *"And the two shall become one flesh"* remarks strongly on the condition of unity as a bond merging the consciousness of two until they are, as a metaphor, "one flesh." His choice of words was deliberate, pointing to a merging of spirit and body. He didn't say that they would merely live in the same house and share expenses. He said it twice: *"And the two shall become one flesh"* and, *"And so they are no longer two but one flesh."* Why? Because he wanted to reveal the underlying nature of the bond between a couple, one that points to our original legacy from God, the Stellar Promise – the eternal unity between twin flames. Would a man who was celibate or unmarried make such a statement? Not likely. Jesus understood the bonds of relationship because he was a married man who had touched the twin-flame signature in his heart and had intimately connected with his beloved through the body, flesh to flesh.

From the Gospels, we know very little about Mary's life except that she was sister to Martha and Lazarus and traveled alongside Jesus. From Lawrence Gardner we could conclude that she was a woman of means and that her wealth supported Jesus' ministry. Her royal blood and lineage connecting her to the aristocratic and priestly house of Aaron would have afforded her a spiritual upbringing as well as perhaps a stronger sense of God than most in her community. Her destiny, of course, was to serve Jesus as his wife, lover, companion, confidant, adviser and perhaps even antagonist when pressures mounted.

As with all young women struggling to form their own identities while facing strong pressure to conform to parental expectations and societal obligations, Mary probably had to struggle to discover her worth as a woman. The status of women in Judea, even among aristocratic families like hers, was low. Women were expected to selflessly serve the patriarchs of their families as well as their extended community. They seldom were allowed outside the range of their parents' watchful eyes. Affluence in Judaic society had its own set of obligatory responsibilities, and it's likely that Mary and her sister were forced to endlessly serve their extended community. Although well-educated, young women were regulated by Judaic customs that imposed a great many limitations on their behavior. They were forced into their stations in life and expected to be grateful and humble servants. She and Martha were probably cast in Cinderella roles early.

The fairytale myth of Cinderella emerged several times during my research of Mary Magdalene, and I thought it a fitting myth in describing Mary's image and psychological peril. Bred to serve, Cinderella feels used, defeated, ashamed and depleted of her worth, no matter how much she has to offer intellectually and how much her brilliance shines. Her only hope is to be honored for who she'll become to a man. Mary was probably groomed for her prince, and there was a happy ending. The glass slipper was meant for only her to wear, and she drew a great reward in stepping into her destiny with her Divine Complement: the lover she deserved. The suppressed and degraded womanly shadow followed her, however, not only in her lifetime but also throughout her legacy.

To fully appreciate Jesus' destiny as the Son of Man, we must conclude that Mary had arrived with a destiny that would have complemented and punctuated her beloved's and one that would offer him a reflection of an equal partner. Her reflection offered him a glimpse of his least integrated potentials, those that would help him to further develop his feminine side, the intuitive, emotional, earthly aspect of his soul. He would have to integrate her qualities into his own personality to some extent to fully embody both the masculine and feminine aspects of his own androgynous soul. Because Divine Complements offer each other a complementary reflection, we might imagine that Mary's talents supported Jesus' ministry. She was probably as eloquent with words and as articulate a teacher in her own right as he was. As a disciple, she would have been expected to propagate his teachings and assist him in his ministry. It was to become her ministry also.

If Jesus came to light the way to repair a split that caused our separation from God's Kingdom, Adam and Eve's fall, then Mary Magdalene arrived as the clearest representative of the legacy of Eve – a woman scorned, ridiculed and made sinner, yet one who was as divinely created in the image of God (as Goddess), just as Jesus was divinely created to embody God. As a remarkable image of the feminine born of God, Mary's nature could be compared to that of Aphrodite, who arrives on Earth out of the sea of her creative potentials in celebrated innocence and passion. The names Mary and Aphrodite, in fact, both mean "myrrh of the sea." Like Eve's, Aphrodite's image has been tainted by the shadow of shame cast on women's sexuality and on her status among men. Therefore, the deepest of Mary's wounds would have been projected back at her by those who may have criticized her most: the disciples who sought Jesus' abiding love, loyalty and recognition. Their opposition and envy of her intimate understanding of the thoughts, desires and intentions of her beloved must have been personally humiliating and would have created tension in her relationship with Jesus. Yet they would have strengthened her character and her commitment. We know she continuously served Jesus' mission alongside him, evidenced by the number of times she appears in the Gospels as one traveling with him.

The divine destiny of Jesus and Mary Magdalene was meant to fulfill the Stellar Promise. Their incarnation was the clearest example of two – God and Goddess – embodying their divinity and marking the path for all of us. Their mythology, the Adonis-Aphrodite myth, was an intricate piece of an evolutionary legacy and was meant to serve the consciousness of all of humanity by offering the blueprint for the reconciliation of the fall. Their commitment to be together throughout their incarnation fulfilled

their promises to each other and to God. They were to fill the cup
with their enlightened wisdom and offer it up to humanity.

The Awakening of Adonis- 1900 - Painter: J.W. Waterhouse

HYMN SABBATH BRIDE

Rabbi Isaac Luria, the Ari Zaal – 16th Century
I sing in hymns to enter the gates
of the Field of holy apples.

A new table we prepare for Her,
a lovely candelabrum sheds its light upon us.

Between right and left the Bride approaches,
in holy jewels and festive garments.

Her Husband embraces Her in Her foundation,
giving Her pleasure, squeezing out his strength.

Torment and trouble are ended.
Now there are joyous faces and spirits and souls.

He gives Her great joy in twofold measure.
Light shines upon Her and streams of blessing.

Bridesmen go forth and prepare the Bride's adornments,
food of various kinds all manner of fish.
To beget souls and new spirits
on the thirty-two paths and three branches.

She has seventy crowns and the supemal King,
that all may be crowned in the Holy of Holies.

All the worlds are engraved and concealed within Her,
but all shine forth from the "Ancient of Days."

May it be His will that He dwell among His people,
who take joy in His sake and sweets and honey.

In the south I set the hidden candelabrum,
I make room in the north for the table with the loaves.

With wine in beakers and boughs of myrtle
To fortify the Betrothed, to strengthen the weak.

We plait them wreaths of precious words
for the crowning of the seventy in fifty gates.

Let the Shekhinah be adorned by six Sabbath loaves
connected on every side with the Heavenly Sanctuary.
Weakened and cast out the impure powers,
the menacing demons are now fetters.

CHAPTER TWO
The Twin Flame Legacy in the Bridal Chamber

The mystery of the Bridal Chamber, where twin souls unite, is hidden in the dimension of our spirit, concealed yet knowable as a dimension of the heart.

Our spirit, for the most part, is considered a mystery, as are the nature and origins of our spiritual connections with others. Those entering our lives whom we consider our closest friends or lovers seem familiar to us not only because we get to know them intimately through human bonds but because we have touched a memory and a mysterious connection to their soul. Their entrance into our lives seems orchestrated by a higher power, holding the promise of a divine purpose, and we bond again, reacquainting ourselves with the connection. The relationship can take on the color of a meant-to-be reunion, having something otherworldly about it, divinely planned, soulful and godly. Many call this mysterious connection "spiritual attraction" or "spiritual chemistry" because it overrides logic and overpowers us with a love that seems difficult to explain in ordinary terms. It is indeed hard to resist.

Matches are made in heaven as well as on Earth. Soul mate theory, the notion that there's one person in the world we were born to be with, has been described and expounded on in the discourse of philosophical ideologies and incorporated into the marital components of religious traditions around the world. For instance, the Talmud, the authoritative book of Judaic rabbinic discussions, suggests that there is one authentic soul mate meant for each soul, a *basherte*. Those who adhere to Judaic tradition believe that 40 days before a male child is born, a voice from the heavens announces the one to whom the child is meant to be betrothed; God is the ultimate matchmaker, and it's the family's responsibility to honor and help fulfill God's plan.

For thousands of years, couples in India have been betrothed through arrangement. The caste, status and financial dowry of the bride and groom are primary considerations in arranging a good match, one that will be blissful as well as regarded suitable to the families' status. In consideration of a match, an Indie family will normally consult a priest/astrologer who compares the couple's natal astrology charts. They evaluate the compatibility of the couple, looking for the planetary signs that point to a soul-mate connection. In India, synastry, the art of compatibility forecasting, is called *jataka vicara* or *kundali milan* and is a well-established marital custom that evaluates not only the complementary aspects of each personality but the destiny and karma of each soul. If the match is compatible, the planets and the astrological constellations will reveal enough similarities and complementary qualities to assure the couple's parents that they've chosen wisely.

Ancient philosophers pondered deep and serious questions on the nature and origins of love and wrote extensively about fate, karma, free will and destiny as it relates to the human soul and to soulful lovers. Plato in *The Symposium* said it's the urge of every individual to find their other half, that one person who will complete them:

> "So ancient is the desire of one another which is implanted in us, reuniting our original nature, making one of two, and healing the state of man. Each of us when separated, having one side only, … is but the indenture of a man, and he is always looking for his other half."

Our Divine Complement (twin flame) offers us the reflection of our other half, the masculine or feminine aspect of our soul that is probably least expressed in our personality. They are also the one evolutionary partner to whom we are most spiritually connected and through whom we can learn more and more about the nature and true meaning of love with each incarnation. There is a legacy to this relationship that's of a divine origin and encompasses many lifetimes.

The creation of souls as stellar angels was a creative miracle that occurred long before the creation of Adamic Man and the physical reality we call earth. The human soul and spirit was birthed in a fluid of love, preceding time and space and the spheres of our known universe. We were created within an infinite realm of a divine source we know as God, in a paradise of milk and honey, a life-giving love and energy. It wasn't an earthly paradise but an otherworldly field of light and love that stretches through infinite space—beyond the beyond.

God breathed into existence a multitude of souls who reflected the essence of God's most beautiful expressions. We were all radiant beings of light harmonies that could move through the creative fluids of God's light, in continued communion with God and each other. As children set free on a playground, we were the joy in the Creator's eyes and examples of his/her power to love and put into form and existence beautiful souls as children, daughters and sons of light. What God conceived was a miracle of beauty, bounty, intelligence and love that could multiply beyond the beyond and spread love and creativity everywhere. Out of God's heart and in God's mind we were conceived in his/her image and essence. God made us uniquely creative, beautiful, intelligent and bold. We were all creatively perfect in the beginning.

Within God's plan was a beautiful promise, that each soul would be joined to a perfect stellar complement with whom he or she would be spiritually bound and forever unified. In the beginning, God created twin souls, not singular individual souls who had no one to play with. God created two together who would be the example of the love that God wished to be propagated everywhere and forever. Two who would be in communion with each other and with God always. The Creator birthed them along with other soul twins within huge soul groups—spiritual brethren.

The twin souls or "stellar twins" were linked through a beautiful template of love within the Stellar Heart, a significant masterpiece at the center of the fabric of the oversoul. Within this chasm of the Stellar Heart, stellar twins would be forever harmonized, no matter how far apart their souls might travel. The harmony of one was locked into the heart of the other in spirit and fused by love. And when creatively together in purpose and intention, they created a magnification of God's love everywhere they traveled.

Each individual soul was made of radiant harmonies that were different yet complementary to others'. Complete and whole within itself, each soul had both male and female aspects. Each soul was therefore androgynous. The unified creative intelligence of both male and female harmonies within each soul was a perfect intelligent design and a reflection of God's unified intelligence. The masculine angular, brilliant intelligence that was the active creative principle abounded with glory and higher intelligence. The feminine receptive, intuitive and emotional side was pure wisdom. These two light harmonies intertwined in a unified dance of everlasting creative intelligence in spirit form. They were equal in power and intelligence and yet different, the way colors have different hues and melodies have different notes. These harmonies were unified into a complex matrix and web of light that was crystalline in structure and made up the complete design of the Stellar Body — a God Suit.

Much like the intricate and individual design of a snowflake, the matrix for each individual soul was a unique coded design with distinct individual attributes and characteristics. Each soul was both god/goddess blooming with the radiant attributes of the individual matrix God had chosen for them. This unified essence is still locked indelibly within the oversoul DNA and within the human form as spirit.

Since the fall from grace, that moment we separated from God, we have been on an evolutionary course recapitulating a legacy of separation called *split soul*. Split soul was a division we chose to humble us, one that resulted in a continental divide between the masculine and feminine aspects of our souls, shadowing the image of our androgynous nature – the image of perfection God created us to be. It sequestered us from the knowledge of our divinity as god/goddesses and veiled us from the mystery of a unified intelligence, yin complementing yang. We relinquished our authentic power, the equal and synergistic balance between intuition and intellect, as well as most of the creative potentials that our unified intelligence could achieve. As a result, our experiences in life have been limited and reduced to what we can perceive with five senses and what can be constructed through the understanding of the masculine rational mind, an often-lopsided perspective.

In his teachings to his disciples, Jesus offered a mysterious description of the potentials of the oversoul, hinting at a unified intelligence that can manifest nothing less than miracles with a simple command. Jesus said,

> "When you make the two one, you shall become sons of man, and when you say, "Mountain, be moved !" it will move. — Sayings 105, Gospel of Thomas.

In this passage, Jesus says that when the two (masculine and feminine), become one (unified), one can become as he, a Son of God, someone with supernatural powers capable of creating miracles of manifestation.

Much like a blind person, we wander through life failing to recognize that those who enter our lives are bringing the reflection we need, and we fail to grasp the bigger picture – there's spiritual meaning to these relationships and a legacy, one that includes many incarnations through which we evolve toward spiritual unity. We also fail to witness God permeating and emanating in everything, and our view is therefore dull gray. We may think life is full, but for the most part, life is spiritually unfulfilling and devoid of wisdom and meaning. Our deepest unconscious yearning is to complete ourselves by seeking out a reflection of our other half in the men or women who enter our lives. Our psychological goal is individual wholeness, integrating a higher intelligence of balanced masculine and feminine attributes and talents. We must emerge reborn to our spirit, embodying the necessary authentic qualities to stand as an equal to someone who complements us.

Most of our favorite myths and fairy tales from childhood, like Snow White, Sleeping Beauty, the Little Mermaid and Beauty and the Beast remark on the spiritual/psychological quest for wholeness that culminates in the mystical union or sacred marriage. They often define the psychological dilemmas and difficulties that arise with the soul that's struggling to individuate and emerge from unconscious patterns of conditioning into consciousness and balanced unity. The reconciliation of masculine and feminine, and between Divine Complements, prince and princess, and king and queen, is usually depicted as an awakening out of the unconscious state through some magical romantic experience, as in a kiss that promises the happily-ever-after result: fulfillment. The prince quests for his princess, Sleeping Beauty, awakens her with a kiss and – poof! – the spell that repressed his feminine complement is broken. Cinderella must discard her rags and legacy of shame and magically transform to make it to the ball on time, where she will dance all night with Prince Charming, symbolically representing spiritual unity with her soul-match. The Little Mermaid, who lost her voice to the sea witch, must emerge from the undersea of the unconscious and trade her tail fins for legs (psychological maturity) and reclaim her voice as an equal partner if masculine and feminine are to stand united as equal complements and achieve greatness in the world. And Snow White, who's poisoned by the same apple that caused the fall of Eve, must cleanse herself of that legacy and return to "snow-white purity" (innocence). It's that kiss from her Divine

Complement that breaks the spell and revives her soul, and their sacred marriage reconciles "the Fall".

For most of us, however, the inner marriage of our internal bride and bridegroom is left un-actualized and our consciousness remains split until we are awakened spiritually.

Our Divine Complement enters our life, like a prince or princess, at that right evolutionary moment to answer our soul's call for reunion. By divine design and in divine time they greet us, shining the light on the more hidden potentials of our soul so that we may discover the disowned or repressed parts of our personalities and grow in intelligence. They prepare us for the sacred marriage, to unite our internal bride and bridegroom, the god and goddess within that carry unique attributes of creative brilliance and intuitive wisdom. Alongside our Divine Complement, our perfect match, we are spiritually and psychologically prepared and matured through assimilation and integration, learning from their reflection in the relationship mirror on a daily basis. And with their help we can rise to greater authenticity, seeing ourselves in a new light—as whole unto ourselves and needing them not to complete us but to fulfill our deepest desire for love and companionship.

Beyond serving the individuation process, helping us to reconcile the split between the masculine and feminine internal aspects, our Divine Complement is our most deeply connected spiritual and evolutionary partner. They are bonded with us because of a legacy we share; something called the Stellar Promise, the eternal commitment of twin souls. In the beginning, God created twin souls linked at the heart, and it's this connection that draws us together now to reconcile past failings and to touch again this mysterious lasting union.

The full-circle return to the consciousness of spirit, soul and material as undivided and linked intricately with God and with our twin complement is our ultimate spiritual goal. All spiritual paths and doctrines have had something to offer as paths of enlightenment, but the path of unification has been the least-traveled, remaining a mystery hidden just beyond our conscious understanding. States like cosmic consciousness, nirvana, and Christian revelation fall short of the experience of awakened tri-unity with God. The mystery of our tri-unity with God lies beyond accurate definition, ideas and most knowledge, held in an invisible place in the heart – the heart that is our root and at the root of our consciousness.

As the entrance to the dimensions of the God self, what we ordinarily refer to as our spirit, our heart is our awakener to the consciousness of the light and represents a temple of unity and love. Not the heart we generally check to see whether it's beating a steady rhythm but our Stellar Heart, the intricate and unique matrix center of our oversoul that hums harmonies and touches the consciousness of others. The Stellar Heart is best-conceptualized as a crystalline chamber resembling a radiant seven-pointed star. Like a bright star-cut diamond, it radiates and harmonizes light, a light that's intelligent, creative and transforming. This intricate matrix exists as part of the sixth dimensional spirit body (light body) and therefore is beyond most perceptions of the un-awakened mind. Its higher intelligence and brilliance exceed the workings of the biological brain and ordinary thinking functions. Even those accomplished in traditional meditation techniques, such as transcendental meditation and Buddhist practices, may not yet have touched the deeper dimensions of the Stellar Heart to realize the inborn potentials of the signature codes contained within. However, through heart-centered meditation and repose we can touch many levels of this divine intelligence and experience beautiful rays of colored harmony that infuse the heart. This light of God will flood our hearts with love and permeate our consciousness, heightening our awareness of the love that is at our core. God's light welcomes us into the Bridal Chamber, where it becomes an anointing fire of love that cleanses, purifies and transforms us at the deepest structure of our DNA.

The initiation within the crystalline chamber reveals mysterious dimensions of light where rays of colored harmonies initiate us into deep memory. The memory is really the imprinted legacy of our origins, and touching it represents a core realization. The rays of light arise from two sacred trinities imprinted as codes of light that are housed within the Bridal Chamber. The trinities of light are really two signatures. One unifies masculine and feminine intelligences, two unique polarities represented by two V's; one is inverted, and together the two create a mysterious **X**. The other signature unites us with another— our twin flame and Divine Complement. The signature of twin-soul communion is represented as two horizontal V's, **><**, moving closer and closer together. The arcane symbol **X** expresses both unification codes in a single symbol: male and female, spirit in matter as well as the unification of twin flames, V's on their sides facing each other to form the ><. Both codes have dwelled within us since our creation and represent the root of our consciousness with God.

There is some evidence to suggest Valentinian Gnostics of the 2nd century, whose tenets are considered by some to have been derived directly from Jesus' wisdom teachings, applied the symbol of the "X" in their initiations of the Bridal Chamber. The Gospel of Philip makes mention of a cross and says its power was understood by the Apostles. The verse reads,

> "But one receives the function of the [...] of the power of the cross. This power the apostles called "the right and the left." For this person is no longer a Christian but a Christ."

The cross that has both a right and a left would naturally be the "X" (oblique cross) and it appears the Valentinians understood it to represent the mystical marriage, the unifcation of opposites — masculine and feminine — taking place in the Bridal Chamber. Philip goes on to mention the cross again, identifying the cross amongst a number of spiritual gifts given by the Father to one who is about to be anointed in the Bridal Chamber.

> "He who has been anointed possesses everything. He possesses the resurrection, the light, the cross, the Holy Spirit. The Father gave him this in the bridal chamber; he merely accepted (the gift). The Father was in the Son and the Son in the Father. This is the Kingdom of Heaven."

The symbol **X** (oblique cross) continued to be used by Gnostics during the Middle Ages and can be found in many religious works of art of that period. It became emblematic for the Gnostic Church, the underground stream of Christianity, and was used to identify works of art pertaining to that tradition by Gnostic artists. An archaic symbol, it may trace back to the Paleolithic era, often found carved in on megalithic stones from a variety of cultures including Neolithic Druid. Interestingly, several "X's" are carved amongst the many symbols on the recently excavated *Magdala Stone* at the site of an early Jewish synagogue in Magdala near Galilee. It dates back to the 1st century and it is suggested that perhaps Jesus and Mary

Magdalene may have attended services at that very same synagogue. One of the many mysteries of Rennes-le-Chateau are the many "X's" that can be found carved on stones in the area. An ancient stone, which is now on displayed near the Mayor's office in Rennes-le-Château, was found nearby the Rock of the Magdalene and the Grotto of Mary and contains many clearly carved 'X"s. It is possible the x's on the stones are early remnants of the Mary Magdalene tradition of the Cathars in Languedoc and perhaps it was to signify her sacred marriage with Jesus, her Divine Complement, through the mystery and tenets of the bridal chamber. Simply put the "X" represented partnership and marriage.

In early Byzantine iconography as seen in Greek Orthodoxy, the "X" was often used in substitution for the Latin Cross (*crux ordinaria*). As Christ's cross, it derives its cruciform representation from the Greek letter "chi" standing for "Christ". The Church of Rome adopted the symbol as "Crux decussata" ("decussated cross") or "St. Andrew's Cross" and reassigned it as the badge of St. Andrew. It was symbolic of his martyrdom.

Many other archaic symbols (pagan and religious) and modern symbols, as well, point to the mystery imprinted in our Stellar Heart. Ancient trinity motifs, symbol forms such as the Druid triskele consisting of three conjoined spirals, the three-foil interlacing pattern of the Celtic triquetra, the French fleur-de-lis, the Judaic Star of David and even the Christian cross that forms a natural trinity at the top, continue to be part of a rich symbolic cultural art heritage. These symbols arise from the imprinted memory of our souls and have always been a part of our legacy. More often than not, their true meaning and interpretation have been lost or corrupted, as with the Christian cross, which had its meaning altered from "the manifestation of spirit into matter" into a symbol of Christ's crucifixion. Symbols like these stimulate our unconscious to ponder their greater spiritual meaning.

Symbols have always initiated us into the deepest mysteries within the soul, stimulating memory and transforming our consciousness. Those who meditate on symbols can testify to the powerful initiation they can produce. Initiates in the ancient pagan mystery cults, for instance, used their symbols in ritual to create divine magic. They possessed a spiritual awareness of the creative design in nature that their symbols often signified.

Triskele   Star of David

Sacred Heart   Volcom TM

Roxy TM

Cross at Rennes-le-Chateau

The trinity has been our most used and lasting symbol, probably because it points to the hidden imprinted signature in our hearts. Although the design motifs vary, they all represent the power of the number 3, a meaningful numerical value signifying spiritual power, and one that points to the mystery of our tri-unity with God.

The collective symbolic world is everywhere we look, and every day we're reminded of a world with meaning. We needn't venture far to meet up with a few trinity symbols used as emblems or as part of a company logo design. The Mercedes-Benz emblem, for example, forms a perfect trinity within a circle, reminding our subconscious that our tri-unity with God is at the center of the whole of consciousness, and the Mitsubishi Lancer trinity emblem stands as a three-foil signature of power. If we look further, we may notice that the BMW emblem holds a mystery of its own, replicating the signature >< in blue and white – the deepest code within the Bridal Chamber uniting twin souls. More well-defined and stylized images, like the Volcom™ and Roxy™ emblems that are popular surfwear-company logos, symbolically capture the defining features of the Stellar Heart with amazing detail. Volcom's black and white rendition of a crystalline stone has an intricate geometric trinity at the center. Like the yin-and-yang sign, it symbolically unites dark and light, masculine and feminine. The Roxy logo, an even more remarkable example, is a rendering of a heart split in two within another heart. At the center is the signature code for twin-soul communion, (> <). Through this representation we're given an artist's vision of the division – split soul – and the elements in the Stellar Heart and the Bridal Chamber that reconcile their division. These logos undoubtedly were divinely inspired representations meant to stimulate our deepest subconscious memory. Their artists and creators were probably unaware of the deeper meaning but inspired by a divine source just the same. Like Druid priests who centuries ago carved triskeles on the sides of rocks, rendering their mystical understanding into symbolic expression, modern-day artists deliver the symbolic record of a collective imprinted memory through their divinely inspired art forms. These logo designs undoubtedly have emerged at this time to awaken humanity to the mystery within the Bridal Chamber and to point us in the direction of our hearts.

Like the quest for the Holy Grail, the initiation of the Stellar Heart takes us to the terrain of the God-self, producing transcendent experiences that point us to our lasting relationship with God. There are many stages of preparedness for this evolutionary leap, and they begin with an innocent desire to know God and to know the self through a quest for enlightened truth and direct experience of God's love. Those who answer the call to initiate and follow a long path of inner transformation may well retrieve a bounty of spiritual worth. This worth is the bounty of one's own angelic light; retrieving it is like unearthing the deepest treasure and the keystone that holds together all the pieces of the soul's existences – the Grail. We first must prepare, shedding the garments of our legacy of failings and the entrapments of conditioning and put on new garments of light. We must reckon with much grief and sacrifice a great deal to redeem our worthiness again. And we must view ourselves worthy of a full measure of our hearts' potentials – worthy because we've come far enough in evolution, humbled ourselves enough, let go of enough of our ego's identifications and the perceived separate identity from God. Spiritual and human redemption will make us worthy again to rise to the potentials of a unified consciousness and touch the light of our spirit as well as the spirit-to-spirit connection with our twin complement. Through desire, surrender, self-forgiveness, prayer and absolution, the veils may be lifted enough for us to be immersed in the experience of the true light of God, helping us to shed even more in order to begin a more difficult journey. Not many have succeeded at what's termed the transfiguration of the soul and complete rebirth to one's divinity – the birth of the Christ self, God Man. In fact, there's only one who may have achieved a complete transfiguration of spirit, soul, mind and body, and that was Jesus, although many have become enlightened to the cosmic self. Even though most could never achieve Christ consciousness in a lifetime, we all can enter the Stellar Heart to touch the light of God and awaken to the dimension of their spirit. And everyone can marvel at the intertwining color rays that make up the two signatures within the Bridal Chamber, the trinity of internal stellar complements, male and female, and the trinity unifying twin souls. It takes only a quiet meditation of repose to enter the Stellar Heart with intention to begin to visualize its dimensions.

Jesus, a "Son of the Bridal Chamber," as he was referred to in the Gospels of Philip, one of the lost Gnostic gospels unearthed in recent history, had obviously realized the mystery within the Stellar

Heart. The initiation mystery, eloquently described in Philip as an anointing with God's light culminating in a sacred inner marriage between bride and bridegroom, was taught to Jesus' disciples as a secret so sacred that it was reserved for the few who had proved their faithfulness to him and his mission. The initiatory secrets represented the keys to the inner Kingdom, unlocking the unity of the soul and spirit.

Of Jesus' teachings and initiations Philip writes,

> "The Lord did everything in a mystery, a baptism and a chrism and a eucharist and a redemption and a bridal chamber. [...] he said, "I came to make the things below like the things above, and the things outside like those inside. I came to unite them in the place." [...] here through types [...]and images."

Philip was describing a five-stage sacrament in which the initiate attains the consciousness of his spirit as unified with God. He is also referencing Saying 22 of the Gospel of Thomas in which Jesus describes the unification of opposites, "making the two one and the inside like the outside and the above like the below', a complete assimilation, integration and realization of the God-self — the Christ within.

Philip goes on to describe the anointing that occurs within the Bridal Chamber, the inner sanctum and consciousness platform that is realized through an initiatory meditation:

> "The chrism is superior to baptism, for it is from the word "Chrism" that we have been called "Christians," certainly not because of the word "baptism". And it is because of the chrism that "the Christ" has his name. For the Father anointed the Son, and the Son anointed the apostles, and the apostles anointed us. He who has been anointed possesses everything. He possesses the resurrection, the light, the cross, the Holy Spirit. The Father gave him this in the bridal chamber; he merely accepted (the gift). The Father was in the Son and the Son in the Father. This is the Kingdom of Heaven."

Jesus, the 'Nazarene', which means "truth-bearer," delivered profound meaningful messages and spiritual teachings through his parables, such as the "grain of the mustard seed" and "the merchant who found a pearl". It's likely that he never expected the majority of his audience to fully understand the mystery behind his words, though some scholars assume that those who congregated around

him must have understood him better than most who study the
Gospels today. Why would he speak in parables and never expect
the majority to understand? He was gathering his initiates, those
who might seek him out and question him further about the
mystery of the Kingdom within. Their quest to know and to be
forgiven would gain them entry to the inner circle as disciples,
where they were offered the keys of initiation to experience some of
what Jesus already undoubtedly had mastered.

In Mark 4:1, when asked why he spoke in parables, Jesus said to
his disciples:

> "To you has been given the secret of the kingdom of God, but for
> those outside everything is in parables; so that they may indeed see
> but not perceive, and may indeed hear but not understand; lest they
> should turn again, and be forgiven."

And in the Gospel of Thomas Jesus said, *"I disclose my mysteries to
those who are worthy of my mysteries"* — Thomas Saying 62

We can conclude from these passages that the worthiness of the
individual is at issue and that those who might humble themselves
by returning to him again and again would be blessed for their
sincerity and their quest to know with further teachings and
initiations.

We must further assume that Jesus' disciples had been initiated
into something extraordinary, a mystery that would humble and
enlighten them. Both the Gospel of Thomas and the Gospel of
Philip, considered to contain Gnostic principles and therefore
deemed heretical by Orthodox Christianity, mention the mystery of
the Bridal Chamber. Jesus makes reference to it in the following
two passages in the Gospel of Thomas:

> "Many are standing at the door, but those who are alone are the
> ones who will enter the bridal chamber." — Thomas saying 74

And,

> "What is the sin that I have committed, or wherein have I been
> defeated? But when the bridegroom leaves the bridal chamber, then
> let them fast and pray." — Thomas saying 6

It should be clear from these passages that the mystery of the Bridal Chamber Jesus refers to represents an inner sanctum of the heart where a sacred marriage unites him with God, not a temple outside himself in which he would have to fast, pray and await the revelation of God. Jesus intimated that he was not separated from his spirit but fully anointed as a son of the Bridal Chamber, embodying God's intelligence as a bridegroom.

To shed more light on the mystery of the Bridal Chamber, we can look to the following passages the Gospel of Philip, which unfortunately has a bit of the Coptic text missing because of the destruction of the papyrus.

> "..Christ came to repair the separation, which was from the beginning, and again unite the two, and to give life to those who died as a result of the separation, and unite them. But the woman is united to her husband in the bridal chamber. Indeed, those who have united in the bridal chamber will no longer be separated."

And,

> "The holies of the holies were revealed, and the bridal chamber invited us in ... Those who are separated will unite ... and will be filled. Every one who will enter the bridal chamber will kindle the light, for ... just as in the marriages, which are ... happen at night. That fire ... only at night and is put out. But the mysteries of that marriage are perfected rather in the day and the light. Neither that day nor its light ever sets. If anyone becomes a son of the bridal chamber, he will receive the light." –Philip, 84, 20-85

The holies of the holies represented the indwelling place of God, the Bridal Chamber, where God's light is experienced as an anointing fire that transformed the initiate, igniting the imprinted memory of the soul's internal unity and ending the legacy of split soul — the separation. This unity is described as a marriage and as I previous explained, it represents an imprinted signature of tri-unity, male and female joined by God's love.

Most scholars of Gnostic Christianity who have offered their interpretations of this gospel consider the Bridal Chamber to refer to a portion, if not the whole, of a ritual initiation that was outwardly performed rather than inwardly achieved. The ritual of the Bridal Chamber represented the five stages of initiation, perhaps ritualized by priests in Solomon's temple: baptism, chrism (anointing), Eucharist, redemption and resurrection.

There is evidence that the mystery of the bridal chamber ritual was known to the Pharisees. Saying 39 of the Gospel of Thomas reads,

> Jesus said, "The Pharisees and the scholars have taken the keys of knowledge and have hidden them. They have not entered nor have they allowed those who want to enter to do so."

The writer of the Gospel of Philip likens the bridal chamber to the "Holy of Holies" of Solomon's Temple in an early passage. This analogy suggests that the mysteries of the bridal chamber were known and ritualized at the Temple during Solomon's reign. We know that Solomon, who succeeded his father King David as King of Israel in 971 BCE, built his elaborate Temple of Solomon as a Tabernacle to God basing its structure on keys of esoteric wisdom, cosmology and philosophic principles. The domes, arches, pillars and carvings, many gilded in gold, all held symbolic meaning pointing to mystical secrets of initiation used for spiritual illumination. There were three main areas of initiation at the center of the temple: the Ulam, the porch of the structure described as a Cosmic Temple, the Hekal (Holy Place), and the Debir (Holy of Holies). They are viewed as three separate symbolic temples of transfiguration through which the initiate would have been spiritually transformed and awakened to the God-self. The Cosmic or Universal Temple, representing the universal harmony of all creation, was decorated with the Archons, the constellations and planetary rulers that influence a man's psyche and from which he must resurrect his divine light. The second arena of initiation, the Holy Place, was symbolically represented as the human body, the material level and the human form as a temple for universal spirit. Through its initiation man is purified, transformed and symbolically resurrected — reborn to his divine nature and spiritual power. The center most chamber, the "Holy of Holies," was considered the dwelling place of God and the Everlasting House. A 20 ft. cubic room lined in gold and inlaid with jewels, it metaphorically represented the heart. It contained three veils, the last leading to the bridal chamber where at the center the Ark of the Covenant was situated. Interestingly enough, the beautiful figures of the cherubim woven into the veil were images of angelic beings of the highest order, appearing as winged lions and bulls. Depicted also as male and female, they were given the characteristics of both men and animals, representing the unification of man's primal nature with the divine. The images of the cherubim, therefore, tie sexuality with spirituality. The high priest would pass through the veil and enter the Holy of Holies once a year, on the Day of Atonement, to offer blood on the mercy seat for his sins. Solomon also engraved the walls of the Temple with likenesses of the male and female principles in celebration of a mystery, one that joined masculine and feminine in unity. Within the chambers of initiation the mysteries of the sacred marriage were likely advanced, perhaps through ritual enactment of hieros gamos. Solomon's Seal, also known as the Star of David, represents further evidence of Solomon's mystical knowledge as a divine magician and priestly King. Emblematic for the unity at the heart, it unifies heaven on earth, male and female.

Passages in the Gospel of Philip seem to suggest that the water of the baptism and the fire of the chrism were experiences not attained in standing before the temple altar but were of the Bridal Chamber of the heart, an interior altar for the sacred marriage. The anointing was not with hot oil but with and of the light.

> "It is from water and fire that the soul and the spirit came into being. It is from water and fire and light that the son of the bridal chamber (came into being). The fire is the chrism, the light is the fire. I am not referring to that fire which has no form, but to the other fire whose form is white, which is bright and beautiful, and which gives beauty." —Gospel of Philip

In the light of consciousness (the day), the mystery of the sacred marriage is illuminated. The bride (water) and bridegroom (fire) of this marriage are imprinted balanced harmonies, yin and yang, male and female, two creative intelligences melded together as unified higher intelligence. The internal and eternal forces of their authentic qualities complement each other, feminine intuitive and masculine mental brilliance, and hold the key to the first initiation of the Bridal Chamber. Therefore, the bride of this union represents the feminine aspect of the spirit actualized by the initiate who has integrated the higher intuitive intelligence and feminine spiritual power into his or her consciousness.

The bride and bridegroom, as sacred lovers, also reflect the sacred spiritual connection between Divine Complements. Nowhere do we find a more beautiful example of the sacredness of divine lovemaking and devotion between two souls than in the Song of Songs, also known as the Song of Solomon, in the Old Testament. The poetic dialogue of yearnings and praises between the bride and her bridegroom deliver the reader into respect for the spiritual nature of romantic love and the spiritual bonds between two lovers, bride and bridegroom. The Song is thought to be associated with the ancient rite hieros gamos, a sacred sexual ritual with anointing and erotic lovemaking that was said to transform and uplift the lovers to their God and Goddess nature.

The following verse beautifully describes the preparation for the rite, one reminiscent of the anointing of Jesus by Mary of Bethany.

> "While the King sitteth at his table, my spikenard sendeth forth the smell thereof. A bundle of myrrh is my well-beloved unto me; he shall lie all night betwixt my breasts." — Song of Songs, 12, 13.

Within their bridal chamber, the bridal lovers were given the opportunity to transcend their humanness to touch the Divine and to unite in celebration of each other's divinity. This rite offered a transcendent path that was tied deeply to human sexuality and to the spiritual bonds that linked sacred lovers.

Margaret Starbird, author of *The Woman With the Alabaster Jar*, concludes that Mary of Bethany and Mary Magdalene, who are mentioned in the Gospels 14 times, are one and the same. Mary of Bethany's ritual anointing of Jesus as the priestly King at Lazarus's table would have solidified his claim as the Messiah, as well as spiritually prepared him for the sacred marriage. The practice of dumping the jar of perfumed oil of spikenard was part of the hieros gamos ritual, which would have prepared the King to enter into sacred communion with the Goddess. Early Jews may have revived the ritual based on a similar ritual performed in Canaan and Sumer, where sacred prostitutes, who were considered noblewomen, performed the rites. The dumping of the oil on his head was symbolic of the blessing of the phallus. Mary's wiping the excess fragrance with her long hair at Lazarus' table was a gesture that connected her deeply and intimately with him. It is not likely that anyone less than his spiritual spouse and one who was a high priestess of the temple would ritually anoint him in such a fashion.

Normally, the bridegroom's entrance into the bridal chamber would follow the anointing ritual. "Bridal chamber", in this case, referred to an exterior environment, a sacred bedroom rather than the interior bridal chamber within the Stellar Heart. Completing the ritual, the sacred sexual act was performed, representing the meeting of the human with the divine aspect of the feminine, an act that would spiritually transform the initiate.

Defined, the term hieros gamos is used to identify a divine lovemaking ritual between two divinities, one male and one female, between two human beings (under certain special conditions), or between a human being and a God or Goddess. The ritual would enact the reunification of the split soul of masculine and feminine, giving rise to the resurrected priestly King.

In ancient Mesopotamia, it was enacted as a ritualized public sexual union between the king and a hierodule ("sacred prostitute"). Human partners became divine by virtue of their participation in the ritual. It was thought, for example, that the priestess who took part in this ritual embodied the goddess Inanna, the Queen of the Heavens. The hieros gamos ritual ensured the wellbeing of the king, the prosperity of the people and the continued fertility of the land.

The only remnant of the rite, which the Orthodox Church included in the Old Testament, is in the Song of Songs. The Church included it despite its suggestive sexual language, believing that it was more accurately interpreted as a metaphor for Christ's love for his church. However, the poem, or "song", was obviously written as a chant between two lovers devoted to each other and in intimate partnership and therefore, could be better applied to Jesus' divine partnership with Mary Magdalene. Although many consider the Song of Songs to have been written to Solomon as a poetic narrative of hieros gamos, a tribute to the King, some have associated the poem with Mary Magdalene because of the verses remarking on a woman's dark face and garments, akin to the Black Madonna, whom Mary Magdalene was said to have embodied. For whomever the Song was written, it holds universal value as the song between any two sacred lovers consummating their love in a spiritual communion to touch the divine spirit of God within themselves.

Despite the fact that Orthodox Christianity did everything in its power to deny humanity the recognition of Jesus' Divine Complement, and to deny his sexuality, from the immaculate conception to a portrayal of Jesus as a monastic and celibate Son of God, it takes only a little research to find strong evidence that Jesus had embraced a sacred bride. The unification path of enlightenment would have led him to the reflection of the Divine Feminine in someone linked to his masculine soul and embodied in a woman who would have helped him to fulfill his destiny, as he would have helped to fulfill hers. That person was Mary Magdalene.

Revelation 21 reveals the return of the Lamb, Jesus, with his bride. She is dressed in fine linen, and although John appears to have interpreted her as the New Jerusalem being revealed to Jesus, she appears as the image of the Divine Feminine, summoning all to her splendor and to the Kingdom. The Orthodox Church has continued to perpetuate the interpretation that any mention of a Sacred Bride refers to Jesus' love for the Church, his bride. However, anyone who has traveled beyond the confines of this interpretation and into the mythic dimensions of the soul's labyrinth or explored the mythologies of the world has been met by the image of a feminine archetype, a goddess, who initiates the journeyer into her mysteries. The reconciliation of the split between her and the true masculine complement culminates in the sacred marriage and wedding feast, representing the fulfilling promise of God's abundant possibilities manifest on earth.

Without the Sacred Bride there can be no inner marriage or resolution of the fall, no nurturing of the heart, or abundant feast to fulfill our dreams. For the most part, the bride has been lost, discarded and abandoned and her image blackened and disrespected. The keys to the kingdom are locked away in her heart and until her wisdom is welcomed we are not redeemed.

A legend pointing to the 'lost bride', as integral to the solution and redemption of the world, is the Quest for the Holy Grail. As we have explored, it can be seen as a quest for spiritual illumination and immortality. The Grail is revealed only to one who is pure of heart and bold enough to seek its mysteries, as were Jesus initiations into the mystery of the bridal chamber. In the numerous versions of the legend of King Arthur and the questing hero Parsifal, the King is portrayed as having a mortal wound, symbolic of the suffering of his kingdom. The Grail reflects that which restores king and kingdom to health. Though its power is held in a chalice, cup or other vessel, it is clear there is a feminine holder who presents the chalice at the feast. She is seen as a young woman carrying the Grail in a procession behind a young man who is holding a blood-dripping lance. She passes it among the knights and the King at the table, and all feast on the bounty it brings forth. The young Parsifal, who is bewildered by the power of the Grail, fails to ask the question that will illuminate the Grail's mystery. As a result, the kingdom falls to famine and further plight, and it is not until he finds the Grail Castle again four years later that he gets his second chance to ask, "Whom does the Grail serve?"

Some have interpreted the Grail to be symbolically specific to the chalice Jesus used at the Last Supper and the cup that caught the blood of Christ at the Crucifixion, which Joseph of Arimathea later carried to Gaul. Still others suggest it represents the Sangrael, the blood royal of the direct descendants of Jesus. We should not, however, separate the Grail from the carrier of the Grail, the 'lost bride' and feminine complement, who if remains separated from her king the world would be left a wasteland. Her God-inspired wisdom is served to those who seek her out and welcome her to their hearts. Symbolically, the Grail represents unification with Christ, holding the promise of healing, immortality and fulfillment. The lost bride summons all in the "spirit of Christ" to recognize who it is the Grail serves — the consciousness of all.

The Second Coming, the reunification culminating in the wedding feast, represents humanity's ascension into the Kingdom of God, through which all receive God's salvation. It offers the same hope as that of the Grail quest and of the ceremonies and celebrations of Adonis, which held the promise that when Adonis returns, his reunion with Aphrodite would bring about a restoration of the culture. The imagery of all three mythological motifs points to the return of the resurrected God or King, not as a lone savior of the world, but alongside his feminine complement. Their unification represents the long-awaited Stellar Promise and reconciliation of the fall.

This mythic salvation plan is contained in each of us, hidden deep in the bridal chamber of the Stellar Heart, where the bride and bridegroom have always dwelled in perfect unification with God. As Jesus said, "The Kingdom of God does not come with your careful observation, nor will people say, 'Here it is,' or 'There it is,' because the kingdom of God is within you." (Luke 17:20, 21)

The Kingdom of God within the Stellar Heart holds the promise of everlasting life in communion with God. The legacy of human separation from the Bridal Chamber and the seemingly never-ending evolutionary spiral of duality that resulted from the fall are in their final chapter. Through God's creative push, we will all ascend through the Bridal Chamber of our stellar hearts, and reborn stellar angels—Christs and Christas. Jesus and Mary Magdalene continue to light our paths from the heavenly realms, guiding and supporting our spiritual growth and applauding each spiritual achievement.

Johann Michael Ferdinand Heinrich Hofmann (1824-1911)
(Christ at 33 and in the likeness of Jesus in my dreams.)

Jesus Christ
Natal Chart
March 23, 0007 BC
2:26 AM — LMT — 2:21:12
Nazareth, ISRL
32° N42° 035° E10°
Geocentric Tropical Koch True Node

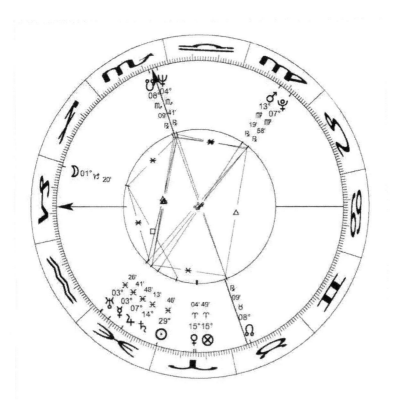

CHAPTER THREE
A Destiny in the Stars:
Astrology of Jesus

. Jesus did not descend and rise to become a perfect divine king. He descended and rose to become human.

We know that during the century of Jesus and Mary Magdalene's birth, great attention was paid to the alignment of planets and stars. Astrology took root in Mesopotamia around 2000 BC and spread to Greece and neighboring regions, culminating in the first personal natal chart with the familiar signs and symbols around 409 BC. Astrology was both a science and a philosophy, as it is today, for the people of the Mediterranean region, and at the time of Jesus' birth it was still practiced as a form of divination despite the fact that it was adamantly opposed by various Jewish religious sects who relied on prophecies rather than astrology. The reference in the Gospel of Matthew to a great star that rose in the heavens over Bethlehem at the moment of Jesus' birth, guiding the wise men to a manger in Bethlehem, was probably a tall tale embellishing the circumstances of the birth with a miraculous sign to confirm his divinity. What's more likely to have happened is that Magi from Persia had forecast a conjunction of Saturn and Jupiter that occurred three times in 7 BC and were looking toward the fulfillment of their own messianic prophecy. Looking up to the heavens, Saturn and Jupiter would have appeared close together in the constellation Pisces in March, May and September. This 'triple conjunction' is a rarity, occurring only every 973 years. The Magi were a noble group of Zoroastrian astrologer-priests from Persia and Medea who often functioned as both priests and governmental council advisers. According to the prophecy of Zoroaster, the divine-born king Mithra, "son of the light" also known as the "solar fire god", would incarnate in the coming era and bring hope of reconciliation to the culture. In the ancient mythologies of ancient Persia from the second millennium B.C.E, Mithras is protector of truth, the great liberator and warrior fighting the forces of the darkness. Mithra is often paired with his a consort, Anahita, the water bearer, a goddess ruling over all the waters of the earth and the source of the cosmic oceans. Associated with the planet Venus, like Aphrodite her Greek counterpart, she is a feminine archetype of beauty as well as fertility goddess.   Her constellation in the night sky is that of the water bearer, Aquarius, Mary Magdalene's sun sign.

The Magi would have seen this rare series of conjunctions as creating the optimum symbolic sign and circumstances for the birth of a divine king.   And they were undoubtedly eager to find him. Whether or not the Magi also expected the incarnation of Mithra's Divine Complement, Anahita, is uncertain, however the mythology, like that of Adonis and Aphrodite, promised reunification of both King and Queen—God and Goddess.

As far back as medieval times, astrologers have claimed to have constructed the horoscope of Jesus Christ.   The earliest example is a chart circulated by Jerome Cardan, a great European philosopher, mathematician and astrologer who in 1524 offered his calculations, chart and interpretations based on the birth date of Dec. 25 in the year 1 BC.   Cardan was immediately met with accusations of impiety.   A more recent astrologer/astronomer, Michael Molnar, offered the date April 17 in the year 6 B.C and based his theory on a rare and remarkable planetary alignment when Jupiter, Saturn, the sun and the moon would appear in the Northern sky briefly in close alignment in the constellation of Aries.   His theory received a great deal of attention for its well-researched premise and convincing arguments. In truth, countless astrologers have rejected the Dec. 25 birth date and based their calculations on other likely dates, several using the last of the three Saturn and Jupiter conjunctions, September 7 BC, with Bethlehem as the coordinate.   All the astrologers had their own reasons and evidence for their calculations and lofty conclusions.   There's little agreement on not only the month and the day but the year.   Some say it was 4 BC, others 6 BC and still others 7 BC. Was Jesus a Capricorn, a Pisces, an Aries or a Leo? And what about Mary?

As I began my research into the mythology of Adonis and Aphrodite, pulling out various elements of symbolic material from the myth and comparing them to Gospel narratives, the parallels became obvious.   The birth, death and resurrection theme as chronicled in the four Gospels of the New Testament are replicated themes, containing elements almost identical to those in the myth, the most obvious being that of a virgin birth. I became intrigued with the fact that the Greek god Ares, who in the myth was said to have disguised himself as a wild boar, had attempted to penetrate the womb of the myrrh tree where Adonis lay ready to be born. If Ares was the catalyst for Adonis' birth in the mythology, perhaps Jesus was born under the sign of Aries. I was certain that the myth had prophesied Jesus and Mary Magdalene's incarnation and wondered whether it had also offered a prophecy of the sign under which the Son of God would be born.

I continued to ponder the question innocently with no expectation that my hypothesis would ever be confirmed. Never did I think I'd be given the date as well as the time of Jesus' birth. But as the days went on, I saw numerous synchronistic signs, repetitions of the number 23 appearing everywhere my eyes wandered – on the digital readout on my clock, on license plates, in headlines in the newspaper. It took me the better part of three days to figure out that the number 23 related to the question I'd been pondering. Once it dawned on me, I inferred that Jesus' birthday must be March 23 because the sun's cycle in Aries begins March 21 and ends April 20th. I set out on a quest to discover the year and time.

The year was fairly easy to pinpoint because I found enough rational evidence in the research of authors such as Laurence Gardner and Henry Lincoln to narrow it down. Intuition drove me to the conclusion that the year was 7 BC, when Jupiter and Saturn would meet in the night sky three times.

The birth time was still necessary to ascertaining Jesus' ascendant, his rising sign. It remained a big question for several days, and I did more than ponder the question. I asked Jesus to give me the answer, thinking that if he'd wanted me to know the date, he would probably point me to the time as well. I set out on a vision quest to discover the hour and minutes, driving for miles looking for the right sequences of numbers on anything my eyes caught a glimpse of. At the end of the first day, I was thoroughly confused by a barrage of number sequences, and I thought it unlikely that I'd been given any real answer. I retired to bed that night asking Jesus for a dream, knowing that I frequently receive clues and guidance through dreams from the spiritual dimensions. But I awoke without dreaming so much as a clue and felt frustrated. I fixed myself a cup of coffee and sat on my lanai as I normally do every morning to enjoy nature and have a few peaceful morning moments. Looking into the neighbors' yard, I noticed a piece of heavy equipment sitting in the middle of the well-manicured lawn. Alongside the letters "CAT" printed on the machinery was a set of numbers near the bottom: 226. I assumed that the number identified the model of the equipment or that it was an identification mark to be used for inventory. Could this be the sign I'd asked for? The "sign" was parked, after all, just behind my own back yard and "painted" in numbers large enough for my eye to see clearly. I felt certain that 2:26 A.M. was the correct birth time and by the end of the day I had intuitively received many more confirming signs followed by goose bumps. Nearly six months later through a similar set of synchronistic signs, I was given the date and time of Mary Magdalene's birthday.

At that point, I had to solicit some expert help to construct the first set of natal charts.   The process through which these charts came into form was divinely steered from beginning to end. As with any divine mission, the process was not without its tests, errors (in this case miscalculations) and a great deal of frustration after discovering I was handed the wrong charts from the first astrologer, someone I had come to know and respect for his astute interpretations. But even the most accomplished astrologer could overlook the fact that BC dates must be calculated without a 0 year and that a very different calendar was used before the 1500's—the Julian calendar.   Modern astrology as a science is precise in calculating modern dates, however determining the exact positions of the stars and planets at the moment of Jesus and Mary's birth posed problems. There are variables such as the change from the Julian calendar to the Gregorian, Sidereal versus Tropical astrology, whether the 0 year is counted and the natural wobble of the earth (Delta T) to consider. Each variable alters the way the chart is calculated, therefore, the resulting natal charts would differ considerably. The first charts though interesting in their synastry between Jesus and Mary Magdalene proved inaccurate because of a miscalculation.

Fortunately, Robert Hand, the world-renowned astrologer, scholar, and author of numerous astrological books, rectified the errors in calculation. The charts that emerged were nothing less than astonishing, indicative of two equally powerful spiritual individuals—both mystics and revolutionary teachers—who undoubtedly had a mutual destiny to serve humanity. Each shone the light on the other's soul and complemented each other's strengths and unique traits, so much so that they would have blended perfectly for the divine mission that was laid out for them. Robert Hand's conclusion was that the charts are remarkably powerful, as well as similar, each with Neptune, the planet associated with enlightened consciousness, in a very powerful position. Jesus' Neptune was positioned directly at the midheaven and Mary's was culminating. He went on to describe them as revolutionary teachers whose ideals were likely a radical departure from the traditions of their culture and who would have stirred the consciousness of their community through the power of their words. Their aims would have been to selflessly serve as profound examples of spiritually enlightened masters and their motives derived out of a sense of duty and love for humanity. Mary was an Aquarian wise woman, motivated by humanitarianism and her partner, Jesus, an enlightened master who could charismatically change the world with the power of his words—a complementary match. Robert further commented that the synchronicity of the two charts presenting such an equality of power and similar purpose is at the very least astonishing and that they precisely fit the more recent image (the emerging archetypes) that Jesus and Mary Magdalene are thought to have embodied.

Realizing that further questions might arise as to the authenticity of the charts, whether they truly described twin complements with a mutual divine destiny, I decided to consult with several other professional astrologers, many of whom were close acquaintances or friends. Each contributed their insights to build a concise interpretation of the charts, pulling out important details and pointing out the more important aspects and planetary placements. What emerged was a composite picture of Jesus and Mary's more important traits, talents and abilities. Their interpretations also brought into view many of the fateful challenges they would have had to endure in fulfilling their divine destiny together. All were convinced the charts were authentic and divinely transmitted.

Beyond the obvious reason for revealing this important discovery, having pinpointed the date of Jesus' birth, my purpose in discussing the natal charts of Jesus and Mary is to offer further substance and evidence to support the premise that they were twin souls, each with a destiny map that would complement and punctuate the other. For that reason, I'm merely highlighting the interesting elements of their individual charts, offering a brief description of the character traits, temperaments and the qualities that would have been characteristic of their personalities and contrasting and comparing the two through astrological synastry. I've also added some details that emerged from my communications with Jesus and Mary Magdalene. I've refrained from trying to prove the accuracy of the charts through comparisons with Gospel narratives, except in a couple of instances, leaving it to the reader to investigate and ponder the parallels. Discussing all the aspects and elements of Jesus and Mary's chart synastry could, in truth, fill several books and therefore is beyond the scope of this book. Instead, I've included each of their natal charts for those who wish to make their own astrological interpretations.

The charts presented on the following pages were formulated by inputting the data into Solar Fire, a reputable astrological software. The results are also consistent with the calculations derived from several other astrological programs, including Matrix and CCRS. I want to add that I applaud any astrologer who might add to the interpretations set forth in the coming pages.

The Gods and Goddesses, as archetypal forces in the subconscious, help form the personality and award Divine Complements each a unique intelligence and a set of talents to complement each other.

The Horoscope Personality of Jesus

Jesus was born at 2:26 a.m. March 23, 7 BC, in a small town in the Galilee, not Bethlehem. His birth in the early morning hours of the Vernal Equinox would have been a momentous sign heralding a rebirth and renewal for the consciousness of the community. And in the year of a triple conjunction of Jupiter and Saturn, signaling to most the birth of a Messiah, the timing appears to have been perfectly orchestrated. Because Jesus' sun was at 29 degrees Pisces transitioning into the cardinal sign of Aries in a matter of only six hours, we should consider him as an "ingress Aries" rather than a Pisces. Born on the cusp, his sun was entering the first sign (Alpha) of the Zodiac, Aries, while at the same time leaving the last sign

(Omega), Pisces. Hence, new meaning can be derived from the proclamation, *"I am the Alpha and the Omega"* – Revelations 1:8.

With Aries as his stronger identification Jesus' natural temperament and personality would be characterized as strong-willed and head strong, yet still sensitive, a Pisces trait. The sun in a man's natal chart drives his personality and represents his strongest ego identification. Therefore, he would have been driven toward self-actualizing the spiritual warrior archetype, a compassionate strong leader. In Greek mythology, Aries was known as the god of war and went about conquering tribes, driven by a passion for combat. As an archetype, Aries represents "the warrior," pursuing his destiny passionately and seeing his spiritual mission as a conquest. Jesus' strongest suit was probably an ability to lead politically and spiritually. He would have been driven to leadership with a fire lit in his heart, the element of an Aries personality. With Aries fueling a strong sense of commitment and loyalty, Jesus would most likely adhere to his cause and the promises his soul made to fulfill the complex destiny before him. He would fully expect his disciples to remain with him and demonstrate the same kind of loyalty. With Mars conjunct Pluto in the ninth house, Jesus would have had to go to battle for his beliefs. Therefore, his position in the spiritual community would not have come easy and without taking its toll. This battle, as we know, was not to conquer lands but to conquer hearts by putting forth the highest ideals that he naturally would have expected others to follow. He was the way, and he expected his disciples to follow his lead.

As an interesting side-note, the biblical symbolism of Jesus as the "Lamb of God" could have been derived from the fact that Jesus' birth was in the sign of Aries, signified by the Ram of the Zodiac. Although the lamb has been traditionally interpreted to represent his innocence, gentleness, and self-sacrifice, the ruler qualities of the Ram more aptly signify passion, courageousness, and fearlessness–attributes describing someone possessing a fighting spirit and great determination.

A fire sign, Aries possesses the spark of initiative and the mental strength to conquer the worldview of others, often by shattering more traditional beliefs and, in Jesus' case, offering instead higher truth and divine principles, characteristic of an enlightened master (Neptune on the Midheaven). He probably possessed the fortitude and passion to fulfill a mission with greater conviction than most. As an ingress Aries, he would have armed himself with strong principles and conviction and aspired to greatness. He would have pursued his mission and goals in a direct fashion and in a confrontational style, with little hesitation or equivocation. With Mars in the 8th house, it would be difficult for Jesus to back away, put aside any of his principles, or back down by abdicating his position.

Ruled by Mars, the Aries personality is a masculine-thinking type whose ego is strongly identified with his masculinity. Jesus would have valued masculine traits and generally considered himself manly. If he was to become virtuous and with spiritual integrity, he would have had to shed the conditioning of a culture that saw men as superior and embrace women as equals. His destiny path would have led him to embrace 'the goddess within' so that his soul could evolve to balance and opportunities to appreciate the women around him for offering him examples of a feminine approach to life.

To complement his Aries identification, his ascendant (rising sign) in Capricorn would have made him appear fatherly, serious, even contemplative, defining him as a calming, secure presence for others to seek out and admire. His Capricorn stability would have tempered the fire of his Aries personality with caution and led him to deliberate before taking action. The natural tension between Aries and Capricorn would have taught him that Rome wasn't built in a day and that it would take considerable time and effort to succeed. His self-determination, temperament and fatherly persona all seemed to come together to structure his personality for the destiny he'd received.

Ruled by Saturn, Capricorn inspires others by defining and refining statements, making points clear. Others would naturally look up to him, perhaps even projecting the archetype of the King of Hearts onto his personality, as he was a loving and sincere patriarch who they would naturally wish to lead them.[1] Jesus would have been physically attractive and extremely charismatic, magnetizing large groups of people around him.

---

[1] The aspects in Jesus' natal chart that denote physical attractiveness are Venus in Aries and Venus square his Ascendant in Capricorn. Charismatic qualities are associated with Mars conjunct Pluto.

With Neptune at the midheaven, Jesus' spiritual side is brought into greater definition. His spiritual aspirations were pointed directly to the heavens, probably leading him to ponder the deepest spiritual questions and to be steered always in the direction of God for the answers.

With Neptune in such a strong position, Jesus would have awakened to his spiritual power early, likely through some type of transcendent experience—a spiritual awakening. From that juncture he would have used the revelations derived from other mystical experiences to formulate a body of wisdom and enlightening teachings, some of which still remain and are found in the more important sayings of the Gospels. His faith in God would have been strong, developed through spiritual practice, such as meditation, contemplation and prayer. His Neptunian mind would have thirsted for spiritual knowledge and he likely chose to study the more mystical occult traditions such as Qabbalism and the teachings of the great philosophers of the time.

Jesus' spiritual task was to ground spirit into matter and rebirth his consciousness to embody his divinity. With Jupiter conjunct Saturn in Pisces, it was easy for him to ground his revelations and divine communications with God into a spiritual doctrine of truth, an ideology that pointed to the 'kingdom within'.[2] In this way, he could initiate and inspire others onto the enlightened path he himself followed.

With a moon at 1 degree Capricorn to reflect his more unconscious feminine and emotional side, he was offered the balance of a highly practical feminine earthy sign adding even more Capricornean qualities to his nature, this time influencing the instinctual side of his personality. In the position of the moon, Capricorn can be likened to the Goddess Hestia—the tender of the hearth— known for her warmth, hospitality and generosity. The virtues that define Hestia are: mild, dignified, patient, stable, secure, welcoming and well-centered. Jesus would likely seek refuge and sanctuary during times of challenge or insecurity, finding stability and nurturance through marriage and with his mate. Jesus' natural tendency would be welcoming and generous towards others.

---

[2] The expansiveness of Jupiter conjunct Saturn in Pisces would also remark on his ability to manifest miracles

The feminine qualities of Jesus' personality would have been less actualized or even repressed until they could be reflected to him by one who mirrored his feminine side.[3] He would have strived to make his Capricorn qualities more conscious in order to integrate them into his personality and to become whole and balanced. From this reflection, he would learn to keep his emotions and the impulsiveness of his Aries personality in check, learning restraint and diplomacy to balance his tendency to barrel over others' points of view. He would also learn about the earthy goddess who sustains life with abundant possibilities and nurtures others emotionally.

With Uranus, Mercury, Jupiter and Saturn forming a quadruple conjunction in Pisces as very powerful psychic and spiritual aspects, Jesus would have displayed a highly developed intuitive side and profound psychic abilities.[4] A conjunction is when two planets occupy the same degree or are within $8°$ of each other on the zodiac wheel and signifies the merging of planetary energies to strengthen and balance the personality, mind and heart. The play of these planetary energies would have helped him to refine his clairvoyant abilities and bring the psychic side of life into meaningful definition. He would be empathetic and therefore compassionate, though less likely to identify with those who were suffering than to offer them solutions. His natural tendency would be to instruct rather than to console. Jesus would have been driven by a spiritual purpose, a strong believer with unshakable faith. He would possess a highly developed sense of himself as a spiritual master, seeking to perfect himself to match the definition he was given as the Son of God, ideally without losing connection to the human dimension. A planet position that points to his altruistic nature and sensitivity to others is Jupiter in Pisces. He wouldn't be satisfied following spiritual rules that were in opposition to the principles of love. His empathy for the suffering of others would have evolved towards unconditional love and compassion as he matured spiritually.[5] Therefore, unconditional love would be what he would have stressed in his teachings. His tendency to focus his compassion and

---

[3] Sun square Moon would force psychological growth, the assimilation of the feminine traits of his partner.

[4] Neptune in Scorpio on the mid-heaven would also afford him psychic gifts.

[5] Neptune in Scorpio trining Jupiter in Pisces would have made Jesus extremely empathic.

efforts on the downtrodden, the meek and the poor would have been strengthened through his relationship with Mary Magdalene whose chart reflects many more humanitarian traits.

Undoubtedly, the many stories of miracles sprinkled throughout the Gospels are reflective of Jesus' spiritual power to heal.[6] With Jupiter conjunct Saturn in Pisces in opposition to Mars conjunct Pluto in Virgo, his hands were the instruments used for healing, and his words were intended not merely to inspire but to deliver poignant truth in a way that forced the listener to contemplate his words and gain spiritual insights of their own. As a powerful communicator, he would have instilled great faith in those whom he touched, as his own faith was unshakable.[7]

Jesus would not have had an ideal childhood. His mother would have been a source of pain and psychological turmoil for his developing ego. With his moon in Capricorn, he would have perceived his mother as controlling, overbearing, stern, demanding and very critical. She likely pushed him too hard towards his studies wishing to mold and educate him rather then to nurture his heart with tenderness, love and support. Though respectable, her demeanor would have been reserved and her spiritual attitudes conservative and traditional. Therefore, she would be prone to withhold praise, love and appreciation for a son who she would have deemed far too imaginative and sensitive. It would seem reasonable to conclude that Jesus' mother was not the humble, serene, majestic and idyllic image of the Virgin Mary that we have been persuaded to believe she was by Orthodox Christianity. In an effort to embrace a wiser and more integrated feminine archetype, the feminine within Jesus' own subconscious, he would have had to individuate from the hold of a wounded mother and embrace a more positive feminine example.

This difficulty with his own mother undoubtedly affected the way he viewed women as an adult. Haunted by the shadow of his mother, who defeated his heart, he may have not been willing to value a strong woman. Until he embraced the positive reflection of

---

[6] Jupiter conjunct Saturn in Pisces in opposition to Mars conjunct Pluto in Virgo suggest he was a profound healer and spiritual teacher, whose words could transform the consciousness of others.
[7] With Uranus conjunct Mercury in Pisces he would have had a radical spiritual message to impart.

feminine sensitivity in his soul mate, Mary Magdalene, he probably preferred to forge his own way.

Speaking to the extraordinary difficulty in Jesus' life is a quadruple conjunction in Pisces opposing Mars conjunct Pluto, presenting an inordinate number of fateful lessons to confront on the path of his destiny. A primary lesson of Jesus' fate was, of course, betrayal. And as we know, Jesus was betrayed by the very men he favored, initiated and trusted as his disciples. Not that he didn't expect it – he intuitively perceived even the details. Attesting to his clairvoyance, he predicted that Judas would betray him at the Passover dinner. An aspect in his chart, Mars conjunct Pluto (the transformer planet) in Virgo, is often interpreted as symbolic for death and resurrection. A severe lesson of fate such as betrayal, would have forced a complete turn around in his attitude, a death of allegiances to the disciples he served. As an archetype, Pluto slays the masculine ego and initiates through death and dismemberment, a psychological crucifixion in which part of the personality is sacrificed to allow a greater, more spiritual aspect to emerge. Pluto lends to the energies of Mars in this important conjunction, supporting the death of the masculine ego and the resurrection, a rebirth of consciousness. He would have been forced to sacrifice his ego, in this case an impulsive Aries ego, in an effort to embrace the feminine, the goddess, who offered him the reflection of a mother's love, faithfulness, nurturing and devotion. Therefore, this aspect, as a catalyst for the evolution of his consciousness, would force growth through many fateful lessons of betrayal by those closest to him, men in particular. And for a divine purpose, so it seems, pushing him more deeply into the divine arms of Mary Magdalene so that he might cherish her and appreciate womanhood in general.

The quadruple conjunctions in Pisces in opposition to Mars conjunct Pluto, represents an important play of aspecting energies that presented stressful lessons that would have forced Jesus onto an entirely new path. This planetary aspect could very well have created a tragic fate, such as his persecution and crucifixion. The result could have been a literal death, but in Jesus' case, as I will point out in the next chapter, it resulted instead in a spiritual rebirth – a new and more powerful definition of himself—the resurrection. He would have to forgive those who betrayed him and begin anew. Jesus' spiritual path, hard as it was, led him to new levels of psychological and spiritual maturity, reconciling the split in his soul so that he could integrate the masculine and feminine in balance and embrace womanhood as his salvation. It also put him into the arms of a woman who could heal him, Mary Magdalene. Her planets lined up perfectly to shine the light on his wound and to support and encourage what really mattered to him— serving humanity. At the end of this chapter, I will demonstrate further how her planetary aspects supported his growth, when I discuss the synastry of their two charts.

In summary, Jesus' natal chart, as a blueprint of innate personality potentials, creates a composite picture of a man whose destiny it was to serve as a spiritual teacher and political leader. It undeniably defined him as a 'king of hearts', one whose spiritual strength and unshakable faith would have set a strong example and one whose altruistic ideals of compassion and love for community stood out as godly. Standing alone, it's a profoundly strong chart, but alongside that of his Divine Complement, Mary Magdalene, his chart is further punctuated and redefined.

Magdalena – Gherghe Tattarescu

DREAM OF MARY MAGDALENE

Dreams can awaken us to the otherworldly dimensions where our consciousness rides on waves of love and touches the light. We call these dream experiences spiritual dreams because they enlighten and deeply transform us. They put us in conscious contact with the heavenly realms and demonstrate we are loved and always guided by angels and ascended masters, serving our higher consciousness. The following dream of Mary Magdalene arrived as I was about to write this chapter:

Mary Magdalene came out of a milky-blue haze to stand before me, like a divine apparition but fully human in form. She was a youthful image of purity, innocence and beauty. Her long gown and head-veil were made of the finest white linen, the traditional dress of Jewish women in the first century. I realized she was showing me how she looked as a young adolescent girl during her incarnation with Jesus. Her skin was light olive and her eyes and longhair were dark brown. What stood out most were her thick dark eyebrows, a feature not often depicted in portraits of her. The dream presented merely a glimpse of her face, but was enough to find a comparable portrait, a painting by Gherghe Tattarescu titled — Magdalena.

Mary Magdalene
Natal Chart
Jan 31 0003 BC
9:00 AM — LMT — 2:21:12
Nazareth, ISRL
32° N42° 035° E 18°
Geocentric Tropical
Koch True Node

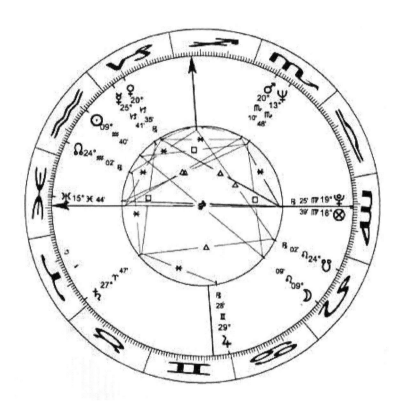

CHAPTER FOUR
The Aquarian Hasmonean Princess

The feminine face of God dwells within us all as the archetype of Sophia, the goddess of wisdom.

The sparse and less-than-complimentary description of Mary Magdalene in the four Gospels offers few details about who she was, her qualities and attributes or as to her relationship to Jesus. The only defining references are that she was the one from who seven demons were cast out (Luke 8:2 and Mark 16:9) giving rise to imaginative images of a crazed woman pitied for her sins and saved only by the merciful heart of Jesus Christ. The casting out of demons was interpreted literally, suggesting that she was possessed by demonic forces and therefore mad before the exorcism. Because of this description, Mary has been degraded, scorned and painted a prostitute and a harlot, much in the same way that Eve has been degraded in interpretations of Genesis as the temptress who cast herself and Adam out of the Garden by eating the fruit of the Tree of Good and Evil. Of late, Mary Magdalene's image has been dusted off and raised to the status of disciple, saint and even "apostile to the apostles" partly because she was the frequent companion of Jesus and the first to witness the resurrection in the Passion scenes.

Many depictions of Mary Magdalene in the art of the16th and 17th centuries, such as Titian Vecellio's *Penitent Mary Magdalene*, are that of a weepy-eyed sorrowful woman sitting in her grotto, mulling over an ancient text or scripture with a human skull at her side. These depictions are reminiscent of the goddess Hecate in the Greek myths, the death goddess and witchy woman associated with spells of magic. She is also like Persephone, separated from the light of the world and cast down into a dungeon of despair as Hades' consort awaiting spring renewal so that she might ascend out of the underworld and become again the virgin of spring. This portrait of Mary is that of a repentant sinner who is to suffer centuries of indignity so that other women may not fall to the temptations of their sexuality. She is only saintly when she sequesters herself in a cave without light and contemplates her sins for the remainder of her life, as the Christianized legends of Mary's exile in the South of France tell us.

Only one penitent portrait from that period, painted by Georges La Tour, seems to illuminate a truer more beautiful and wise Mary. She sits in a chair with blanket covering her legs gazing into a beckoning flame situated on a table in front of a mirror. The reflection of the candle creates two flames and casts a shadow on the wall creating an illusive void in the background. In it, Mary seems to have found herself through the illumination of the divine light that she and her beloved Jesus created together as twin flames and Divine Complements. The portrait reminds us of Mary's wisdom, mystical vision, her reverence, and of her own quest to know herself. As you will see from Mary's natal chart and the interpretations of the aspecting planets influencing her soul and personality Mary was not mad nor did she need saving. She was brilliant, community minded and as much a spiritual sage as Jesus was.

Mary Magdalene's character and traits would have been defined by the qualities of her strongest planetary influences in the signs where they resided. She was born at 9 a.m. Jan. 31, 3 BC, in the Galilee, her sun in the sign of Aquarius, the water bearer. This expansive sign made her a humanitarian; someone revolutionary in her thinking and perhaps even someone characterized an idealist. Her thoughts and motives would have been concerned with the evolution of mankind and how she might serve human progress best. She was probably dominated by concerns for those around her, family and friends as well as the greater community of Judea and even humanity as a whole. Her Aquarian vision most likely offered her the big picture at an early age. As a member of the royal class, she would have been perceived by some as society's princess, having a front-row seat among high priests and leaders of her Hasmonean family who had a great deal of political clout at the time. As Mary explained, Jews who carried an envious grudge against the Hasmoneans scorned her because of her wealth and position. Mary would have been sensitized by the political and religious climate of the times and would probably have been an outspoken progressive, perhaps perceived as rebellious at times. Her authority would have stemmed more from her station in life than from her personal achievements until her focus shifted toward the one she eventually married and she stepped into their greater mission together. She would have been seen as diplomatic, practical and articulate. She would tend to circumvent the agendas of those in power by planning and plotting her own agendas behind the scene. With Jupiter in Gemini, she was probably viewed as energetic and determined, possessing a great deal of initiative. She was probably also very talkative. She would tend to keep busy, dutifully mastering her life and societal obligations.

Mary would have awakened to the psychic side of life at a fairly early age, experiencing otherworldly visions that shifted her consciousness toward her spiritual calling.[8] With her Sun in Aquarius squaring Neptune in Scorpio in combination with Uranus in opposition to Pluto, it's likely that she would have awakened spiritually through some earth shattering experience, one that would have sensitized her to the plight of others. From my conversations with Mary, I suspect that the sudden death of her mother, probably by the hand of Herod Antipas, was the catalyst. An emotional time for Mary, she would have turned towards God through prayer and sought solace through her spiritual practice. The thrashing influence of Uranus in opposition to Pluto would have opened a portal into the spiritual realms, an initiation and awakening resulting in the complete transformation of her consciousness. As a result, she awakened early to her authentic spiritual abilities as a seer and healer. With Neptune culminating in the 8th house and in soft aspect (trine) to Uranus in Pisces, she undoubtedly was supported by the planets to grow towards greater and greater spiritual mastery of her clairvoyant abilities over time. It was her destiny to master her spiritual power for healing and service in a unique ministry. She was probably propelled toward her destiny as a spiritual teacher, visionary and healer the majority of her life, possessing a stronger commitment than most to serve the greater good of humanity (North node in Aquarius). She would gain a great deal of personal reward and self-respect serving her community and spiritual brethren alongside Jesus. In fact, her destiny with Jesus is highlighted in her natal chart with Uranus rising and Pluto setting, suggesting she would be mated with a charismatic leader.

---

[8] Uranus in Pisces conjunct the ascendant trining Mars conjunct Neptune in Scorpio suggests she had a spiritual calling.

Mary would most likely have taken to heart the importance of her spiritual mission and her role alongside Jesus to serve the community they would establish together. With Mars in Scorpio conjunct Neptune she would have possessed unshakable faith derived from a direct connection to God through her enlightened heart.[9] She was well-equipped to step into a destiny as a spiritual revolutionary, challenging the doctrines of religious ideologies of Judaic tradition and offering her healing talents and spiritual knowledge to her family and brethren. With Mars in Scorpio, the ruler of sexuality, conjunct Neptune, the planet associated with transcendent spiritual experiences, Mary would have viewed her sexuality as a vehicle for spiritual transformation. Viewing sexuality as Godly, she would have welcomed her beloved to her bed and appreciated the more sexual intimate moments of their relationship as spiritually uplifting.

Mary was probably a woman of means with a large inheritance from her family.[10] Mary entered her life with a great deal taken care of so that she could focus on more important things such as the development of her spiritual self and her education. With her inheritance, she would later have supported Jesus' mission. We might see her as having been the material and practical provider in the relationship, offering all the financial support Jesus needed to fulfill his political goals. She was undoubtedly generous and most likely a philanthropist, given the humanitarian aspects of her chart.

The Aquarian personality is a spiritual seeker, one who favors the enlightened path. Mary's more spiritual natal aspects would have driven her to study theology, mysticism and philosophy, seeking answers through a variety of sources and fulfillment through the rituals of her spiritual practice.[11] She would have derived her beliefs from her own spiritual experiences rather than from the dictates of fundamentalist Judaic teachings. She would have easily embraced the altruistic ideology of her husband, Jesus, and envisioned their mission as a profound and divinely chosen

---

[9] Adding to the power of this conjunction is Uranus in Pisces trining Neptune and Mars in Scorpio.

[10] Her Sun in the 11th house suggests her father was likely royal, holding a high position in the community. The moon in Leo implies she learned her queenly ways from her mother.

[11] Mars in Scorpio conjunct Neptune trine Uranus in Pisces could have pushed her towards scholarly research in religion, mysticism and philosophy.

path. She would have enthusiastically supported the new paradigm arising from Jesus' ministry.

With Mars in Scorpio, Mary would possess a determined spirit, persevering in even the most difficult situations, pulling up energy from huge reserves to consistently meet the obligations to her community. She would tend to relate to others genuinely and affectionately and those close to her would have considered her a delight to be around (Venus sextile Mars). Her style of thinking would have combined vision and creativity with clarity. She could visualize concepts, apply them practically and put them forward articulately to influence others. With Pluto in Virgo trine Venus and Mercury in Capricorn, she undoubtedly was intelligent as well as articulate, able to excel at creative writing and public speaking.[12] I will elaborate further on this aspect in the next chapter when I present a piece of her destiny with Jesus, one that would have afforded them both the talents and opportunity to put their teachings into writing.

With her ascendant in Pisces, she probably had a highly developed spiritual eye and therefore would have developed her intuitive and telepathic abilities to forecast the future and serve others. If she had truly actualized her potentials as a spiritual healer – and it seems likely that she did – she would have been able to channel her spiritual and psychic power through her hands and demonstrate keen abilities at diagnosing maladies of the body. She would have been a powerful healer in the eyes of her partner and those around her.

With a moon in Leo, which is ruled by the Sun to reflect Mary's fiery passionate and warm-hearted side, she would have been appreciated for her sensual nature, radiance and outer beauty. Venus, the Roman counterpart to the goddess Aphrodite, the goddess of love and beauty, would have become Mary's dominant identification. As a woman, she would be most identified with her moon, the traits that offered expression to her feminine side. Sensuality, beauty, sexuality and love were all attributes of this love

---

[12] The further implication of this aspect when we consider that Uranus is in opposition to Pluto (a generational opposition) is that Mary, alongside her husband (7th house), was a spokesperson for the consciousness movement of that Age. Mercury conjunct Venus above the horizon would add additional energy to support the pursuit of writing.

goddess. She would have positioned herself at the center of her beloved's life, as his Queen of Hearts, and insisted that she was appreciated there always.

She was probably a classic beauty and small in stature, as were the majority of the women in that region at that time. In fact, the day I began writing this segment, I serendipitously ran into an overwhelmingly large number of tiny women with dark hair walking through the plaza during moments when my thoughts were occupied with Mary Magdalene's qualities and characteristics. Often a small woman with a female child in her arms would appear magically from around the corner. I thought it uncanny how many small women arrived to greet me that morning and recognized that the synchronicity had offered me a divine description of Mary's physical qualities as well as her maternal nature With a Leo moon, Mary would also have a strong appreciation of beauty in others, especially for the children she had.

With Venus 20 degrees Capricorn, Mary most likely adored older men and naturally would have admired her husband for his more fatherly characteristics. Psychologically, she may have projected her father onto Jesus, seeing him as a man fulfilling her desires for paternal nurturing. She would probably seek to serve him as best as she could to in turn gain his admiration. She admired men in general, especially those with spiritual position, educated men strong in intellect, those defined as patriarchs. She would have sought to learn from them and win respect and recognition. Considering the times and the legacy of inequality of women, Mary would have had to strengthen her character, integrating her masculine qualities in order to face the often-lethal blows of disrespect degrading the status of women. To help her achieve a balance of masculine and feminine qualities, her moon in Leo, a kind-hearted yet self-serving sign, was placed directly opposite her sun in Aquarius, reflecting the drive and desire to serve the greater good of society. A sun and moon opposition would help her to value the powerful men in her life as the reflection of her own inner masculine. She would have to strive to make her more masculine qualities conscious, drawing them out of the shadows of cultural conditioning about the role of a woman. She would have grown psychologically from the constant reflection that Jesus was with his more self-less and compassionate character. She would have seen her arranged marriage to Jesus as a way to earn respect and serve her own spiritual mission. The psychological pounding of Saturn square Mercury in Capricorn would have created a number of obstacles, though. Saturn's push to limit any boldness with rules and to suppress her ideas with ridicule would make any woman feel a little degraded. In consideration of this aspect, Mary probably faced a great deal of psychological turmoil throughout her life, and as she tried to step out more and more, she was probably met with criticism. Her response would have been either to see the beauty in the lesson as a strengthening exercise or to put up walls. It's likely that, for a time, she felt fearful and even jealous of men who seemed to have all the respect and freedoms she so much desired. This aspect most likely caused a tremendous blow to her ego and she probably shut down her heart. The shadow cast on her feminine soul would have taken its toll, and she would have had to work on opening her heart in order to spiritually develop. The saving grace was that Jesus' Venus in Aries formed a conjunction to her Saturn in Aries, feeding her the love she needed to conquer her inner demons and heal the wounds of disrespect.[13] He would have encouraged her strength and helped her to grow spiritually to notice the beauty in this lesson. The strength of love that Jesus demonstrated was just what she needed to develop in herself.

A woman with a Leo moon would probably handle her duties as a wife with devotion and practical care. She would focus her efforts on the health and well-being of her family – nurturing her children and husband by preparing nourishing meals, for example. In her traditional role as wife and mother, she would have been comfortable serving family and those around her. She was also likely to be the kind of woman who cared a great deal about the woes of the world, seeking to serve her community with the same kind of care and attention as she gave her family. She had a nurturing heart and great humanity.

With Mercury in Capricorn, her thinking would have been grounded more in reality than in fantasy as her practical side took the helm in solving day-to-day problems. The influence of Mercury in Capricorn would have given her a solid framework for delivering her spiritual message with authority and firmness. She would have tended to be logical, pragmatic, disciplined and grounded,

---

[13] The conjunction between Jesus' Venus and Mary's Saturn would be considered wide.

especially in the material aspects of her life. To balance her practical
side, Uranus conjunct her ascendant in Pisces would have awarded
her a great deal of psychic/spiritual power to use as a healer. She
would have been masterful in the ritual practices of her faith and
most certainly recognized as a spiritual wise woman, a mystic and
therefore a perfect complement for Jesus. Others would have
described her as magnetic, friendly and genuine. It was easy for
Mary to relate to everyone regardless of their social status.

Mary would be comfortable abandoning old allegiances as well
as family ties to accept another mission in a far-off land, for
instance.[14] With a Sun and Moon opposition she probably had
children, a boy and a girl to reflect back the balance of masculine
and feminine qualities in her own psyche. This information would
seem to support the legend that she fled to Gaul in exile with child.

---

[14] Mars sextile Pluto and Venus trine Pluto represents comfort with uprooting and
travel, and supports the legacy of her travels to Gaul.

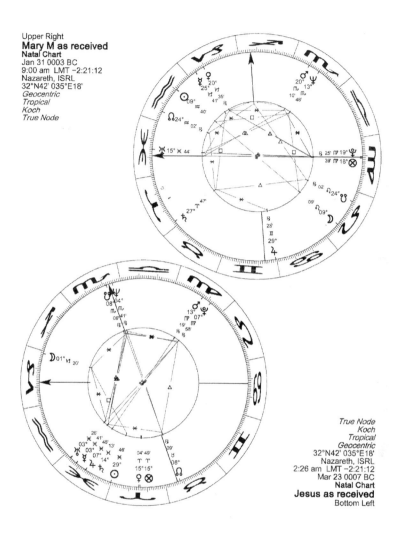

Upper Right
Mary M as received
Natal Chart
Jan 31 0003 BC
9:00 am LMT −2:21:12
Nazareth, ISRL
32°N42' 035°E18'
Geocentric
Tropical
Koch
True Node

True Node
Koch
Tropical
Geocentric
32°N42' 035°E18'
Nazareth, ISRL
2:26 am LMT −2:21:12
Mar 23 0007 BC
Natal Chart
Jesus as received
Bottom Left

CHAPTER FIVE
Divine and Complementary Partners

The divine destiny of twin complements is mapped by the stars and planets, which weave a cosmological tapestry of unique energies at the time of their birth. They walk a starlit path fulfilling great missions, a destiny they mutually designed with the help of God.

Examining the synastry, as a compatibility forecast of Jesus and Mary's charts, we're offered a profound example of the complementary qualities and personality traits that would have naturally blended to make both their relationship and their mission work. Their divine destiny was a remarkably well-laid-out plan, setting up the right planetary energy potentials for each to become enlightened spiritually and to co-create a profound mission to enlighten others.

In astrology, the term synastry refers to the art and science of examining and comparing the natal charts of two individuals in partnership. It is an illuminating study of how individuals interact with one another, stimulate growth in each other's personality and how they view and tend to feel about each other as they go about relating in relationship.

Each individual is born with a personal birth chart (natal chart), a cosmological map of the heavens at the moment of incarnation. The birth chart can be seen as an imprint of the archetypal energies of the planets, Sun, Moon, asteroids, nodes, and constellations (signs) on the psyche of an individual. Each and every individual has all 10 planets and luminaries positioned by sign, house, and aspect making for a unique template of characteristics and energy potentials. When we interact with another person, the individual energies of the planets, Sun, and Moon, become dynamic and catalyzing agents for both individuals.

Synastry further demonstrates how each person affects the other because of their planets' influences on each other. The amplification of the energies is especially powerful when planets form aspects (angles of various degrees), such as when planets are in *conjunction* (within 10 degrees of each other), in *opposition* (180 degrees apart with a 10 degree variant), *trine* (120 degrees apart with a10 degree variant), *sextile* (60 degrees with a 6 degree variant), or *square* (90 degrees with a 8 degree variant).

In synastry, conjunctions between partners' planets represent a point of powerful catalyzing interaction. The planets combine forces and become agents or ingredients for an alchemical union, helping to transform each individual's consciousness and personality. Depending on the planets involved, there can be a strong feeling of familiarity and recognition or there can be discomfort because of the impact of the collision of forces on their subconscious. Conversely, an opposition represents polarity, two planets opposing each other. An opposition can create tension as well as strong attraction, demonstrating that much of the work of relationship is to force growth and integration of complementary qualities. Too often an opposition can bring out insecurities and competiveness until a couple strives for balance and common ground. Sextiles and trines are flowing aspects that suggest a harmonious interaction between two planets. In general, they produce a supportive planetary influence on each others' psyche and personality. Trines generally indicate energies that combine well, while sextiles are usually points of compatibility that the couple can appreciate and value. Squares are the most difficult aspects and often point to energies that need work in order to integrate them easily into a couple's interaction. Producing tension, they force growth and can present an array of difficulties depending on the planets involved. Lack of understanding and frustration can be the result until both individuals surrender to the love between them

The interpretation of Jesus and Mary Magdalene's synastry chart reveals that they were Divine Complements with a great deal in common. The planetary archetypes that ruled their personalities were very complementary, matching up perfectly to reflect back the individual qualities and characteristics that could strengthen and fortify any personality weaknesses or temper any tendencies toward an overzealous ego. They would have learned from each other and psychologically matured through both the positive aspects and the more tension-producing aspects of their horoscope. We might consider them to have been more than compatible by today's standards, perfectly matched, in fact, to support each other's spiritual and psychological process and to synergistically fulfill their humanitarian aims.

The strength and similarities between the two charts suggests an equality of purpose. Mary's humanitarian and revolutionary personality was beautifully matched to Jesus qualities as an enlightened master. They seemed to possess more similarities than differences, and perhaps the reason for this cosmological design was so that they would recognize a commonality of purpose as the focus of their relationship. The most outstanding complementary aspects seem to have been their highly developed psychic sides. With her Piscean and Neptunian intuitive traits, Mary was probably very clairvoyant and therefore able to read her husband's emotions easily, pinpointing their source with accuracy. She would most likely have felt the intensity of his hidden emotions even if he denied them to himself and others.[15] Their psychic abilities were equally matched, creating a psychic synergy that made them appear to be highly in tune with each other, to a higher degree than most soul mates. They would probably have been able to read each other's thoughts and finish each other's sentences with regularity. We might imagine them in dialogue receiving psychic impressions or even revelations from God and formulating their own unique interpretations of the information, discovering that they had received different elements of the same vision. The resulting psychic dialogue between them would have awarded each of them profound spiritual clarity. Perhaps the function and purpose of this influence of energies on their intelligence would have been to help them refine and perfect their psychic abilities so that each could develop spiritual mastery for the mission ahead as well as bond them in commonality.

As I mentioned earlier, we know that Jesus demonstrated a profound ability to see into the future, enough to be able to pinpoint and prophesy events, such as when he predicted that Judas would betray him and that Peter would deny him three times. These are profound examples of psychic ability and spiritual mastery. With the planetary energies influencing Mary's psychic side, she may well have been able to add even more definition and certainty to Jesus' foresight. This play of the planetary energies exemplifies the synergistic telepathic communication that commonly develops between twin souls, to the point where they can play ideas off each

---

[15] The influence of Neptune in Scorpio trine Uranus near her Ascendant in Pisces would have made Mary very psychic and empathic.

other's insights and telepathically communicate at a distance. The heart-centered synergy between them was magnified, catalyzed by planetary influences to create enough magic and creative power between them to manifest what they envisioned. They would have matured side-by-side, developing spiritual integrity through acknowledgment of their equality. With their reflections, each gave the other the opportunity to integrate qualities to evolve psychologically and spiritually. And their synergy gave them the momentum to fulfill each task of their spiritual mission in the creative field of their lives' divine design.

Jesus' Pisces/Aries sun would have complemented Mary's ascendant in Pisces coaxing out her intuitive side as well as helping her to integrate masculine strength. As a woman, Mary's natural tendency would be to project her strengths onto Jesus, admiring him for what she had not yet realized within herself. Sparking her passion at times like a lightning bolt, he would have urged and challenged her to stand up with strength and fortitude, voicing her ideas and opinions even when others tried to shame and suppress her. He undoubtedly was the sun shining on her soul, lighting the way and helping her to define and develop her strengths as a spiritual teacher.

With her Mercury sextile to Jesus' Capricorn ascendant, Mary would have admired Jesus' qualities and his general approach to life. She would have enjoyed the long and deeply meaning conversations about what mattered to him most—spiritual matters and how they might influence the social climate of their community in the coming years.

Mary could be best described as a romantic, driven by strong sexual desires.[16] And with her Mars in Scorpio sextile to Jesus' ascendant in Capricorn she was the type of woman who would insist on more intimacy, considering Jesus far too aloof, distant and consumed with his relationships outside the home. She might, in fact, force the issue on occasion if she felt ignored or discounted, insisting that her needs were what mattered most. This aspect also suggests that they both had a strong appreciation for the classical arts and architecture.

---

[16] Venus trine Pluto is a sensual, romantic, and passionate aspect of Mary's natal chart.

With Mary's ascendant sextile to Jesus' ascendant theirs was a very compatible and comfortable relationship. Those around them would consider them two very idealist and progressive individuals and, therefore, a natural match. Mary's mystique blended well with Jesus grounded spiritual certainty offering the reflection of a balanced and complementary spiritual couple.

Jesus and Mary were mirrors and teachers for each other. Jesus with five planets in Pisces reflected to Mary her own highly developed mystical eye so that she might step boldly forward with her psychic impressions and wisdom in serving others.[17] He would have tempered her tendency to overreact with gentle persuasion and a fatherly pragmatic approach, reflecting her own Capricorn traits.[18] His example of loyalty and commitment to the mission would have supported Mary's sense of social responsibility, her Aquarian heart. Conversely, Mary's courageousness and determination to see it through the difficulties reflected to Jesus a grounded example of faith. And her warm-hearted sensual nature coaxed out the lover archetype in his subconscious, helping him to bond deeply to a woman and appreciate womanhood for all it gives to nurture the human spirit. They both would have admired each other's strength of character, considering the similarities comfortable in making their friendship compatible and rewarding. When they clashed, it was likely Mary who fought to bring Jesus back to her heart because despite his love for her his tendency would be to withdraw from the emotional battlefield.

Jesus truly would have appreciated a strong woman, not someone who would let him push her around, who was complacent or acted only out of servitude. He would have wanted her to step up courageously as an equal among the other disciples because in his eyes she was already above them. His encouragement would have helped her to heal the legacy of shame that followed the women of her heritage, one that dishonored the spiritual worth of women and expected them to serve men as if they were their masters. Like the kiss that awakens Sleeping Beauty, Jesus' love and encouragement served Mary's consciousness, forcing her to rise out

---

[17] An important aspect that relates to Mary's psychic side is Mars trine her Pisces ascendant, a powerful aspect for putting forward one's visions and revelations.

[18] In Capricorn Mary had both Mercury, the planet of communication, and Venus, suggesting that she was grounded in the material aspects of life.

of personal degradation and strengthening her character enough to see herself as equal to men.

With Mary's Venus conjunct Jesus' Capricorn ascendant, her passionate love, value as a woman and beauty would have helped him to appreciate women and womanhood, to see them as beautiful expressions of the Goddess, the feminine aspect of God. He was apt to have fallen in love at first sight.[19] Mesmerized by her radiant beauty, any criticism of her tenacious nature would have been tempered by his admiration. Embracing the feminine as equal was the most important spiritual task for Jesus' masculine-driven Aries character. Without Mary, he wouldn't have been able to grow beyond the conditioning of a culture that had little appreciation for the status of women. As the goddess of love, her Venus ignited his heart and encouraged what really mattered to him, his spiritual mission. She was like the enchantress with a lantern, lighting the way while he steered their unified vision forward. Although his mission began as a spiritual and political movement to unite Judea and reign as King, it later steered toward a more united marital path with a mutual destiny that I'll discuss later in another chapter. With this shift, Jesus would have appreciated what equality in partnership on a marital path could bring, and he would have been forced to respect Mary's role as a spiritual figure.

With two planets in the sign of Capricorn (Mercury and Venus), Mary's logical, cautious side reinforced Jesus' Capricorn traits, stressing to him the need for patience and restraint in fulfilling his public aims. Jesus' fiery Aries temperament, like Adonis' untempered desire to hunt, might have led him to light one too many fires in the community, therefore jeopardizing his ultimate mission to turn the divided community of Jews toward God and their hearts toward one another. She would naturally plead with him to use restraint and to be civil when he communicated with the elders, especially those who would oppose his proclaiming to be the voice of God. Her love would have helped him to further define and design the mission, and with her Venus on his ascendant, she would have wished to help him achieve what mattered most to him while at the same time seeking to take the seriousness out of his heart during times when he was severely tested. Mary, with her

---

[19] The synastry aspect most associated with 'falling in love at first sight' is Jesus with his Venus in Aries trine Mary's Moon in Leo.

Venus in Capricorn, giving her a strong earthy set of traits, would have helped Jesus to draw out and appreciate his own Capricorn moon, which he may have rejected, because it was shadowed by his relationship with his mother. She would have nurtured him through any emotion depression, turning his doubts and regrets into optimism, and supported his ambitions with encouragement. She undoubtedly helped him to ground his vision and refine his spiritual ideas, and to appreciate the value of the Capricorn sensate function, which brings a world of ideas into a plan with attainable steps.

Jesus would have remained a faithful husband and lover, with Capricorn influencing his attitudes about sex. Saturn as a planetary ruler of Capricorn would insist on respect for the sacred covenant of marriage. The statement "Who God has joined together let no man put asunder" is an example of a creed of Saturnian's logic. He would possess an abiding love for Mary, seeing her as a desirable mate and lover — his Goddess of Love.[20]

Jesus would have valued her material support and sound values and she his passion and spiritual clarity. Their relationship would have been filled with depth, wisdom and the strength of commitment. Mary would have collaborated to help Jesus with his goals encouraging his love for humanity and his love for God. The relationship highlighted the importance of responsibility and loyalty to each other as well as to their mission. Presenting a unified front would have been important to both of them.

Mary's Sun and Moon both squared Jesus' Neptune, tension producing aspects that might be viewed as challenging for this couple by many astrologers, but indicative of their complementary differences. They were meant to learn how to value each other's differing points of view and blend their strengths and styles in approaching life. Jesus with his enlightened Neptunian spiritual mind surely believed that one must question everything, sifting out what he would deem 'the illusions of the world' in favor of a transcendent perspective — the Kingdom. He wished to rise above it all and bring Mary with him. Mary, on the other hand with her Sun in Aquarius and Moon in Leo, might prefer to focus on finding solutions to what she perceived as the very real problems that their

---

[20] With Venus in Aries trine Mary's moon in Leo and his Mars in Virgo sextile her Mars in Scorpio, Jesus would have been passionate and enamored with Mary,

community of friends faced, lending a helping hand rather than just contemplating her navel. She might fall to disillusionment and lack confidence when coming up against Jesus' enlightened perspective. With an Aquarian sun, she could have interpreted his point of view as irresponsible and irrational, but in most instances, Mary would have allowed Jesus his indulgence in escapism, especially if she was seduced by the promise of otherworldly perfection and in thinking Jesus was a spiritually perfected man. This square likely pushed Mary to accept greater mastery as a spiritual teacher, helping her to appreciate her own Neptunian qualities as offering an enlightened approach to serving her community. For Jesus, the tension produced by the square was meant to teach him the value in Mary's genuine and warm-hearted style of nurturing others and that he should place Mary's needs at the center of his concerns, cherishing her for all that she gave. Mary was always to steer him towards the community he was meant to serve. The growth demanded for their relationship was to remind Mary she could learn from Jesus' lead and question everything he said and did. By doing so she would gain more respect from him for teaching him about a woman's enlightened approach. Emotional maturity and psychological insight development would help them to appreciate their differing styles as equally valid and therefore strengthen the relationship through respect and admiration.

Jesus and Mary were both altruistic people who tended to put humanity above their personal concerns.[21] They undoubtedly were aligned in their sympathy for the downtrodden, the sick, the innocent and the persecuted and therefore would seldom argue about what was important in their lives – others were. This likeness would have helped them to value each other for the more divinely human characteristics they shared, those altruistic ideals and demonstrations of selfless commitment that punctuated their social concerns. Therefore, they would have admired, respected and valued each other's humanistic qualities and spiritual devotion. With Mary's abilities as a visionary complementing Jesus' spiritual certainty, they must have shared a tremendous amount of goodwill, optimism and enthusiasm, especially in the beginning of their ministry. Each would have drawn support from the other's

---

[21]The complementary aspects that remark on their altruism, are Jesus' Capricorn rising and Saturn in Pisces, and Mary's Sun in Aquarius.

confidence and positive outlook. However, a line had to be drawn with regard to what they could achieve in their mission. Jesus would have a tendency to overestimate what they could do, a grandiose sense of what was possible. Unrealistic goals probably put them in harm's way, and given the aspects of synastry, it makes sense that escape from persecution would have been their chosen course of action.

Jesus' propensity for self-neglect and depression, due to early childhood wounds would have triggered Mary's psychic sensitivity and empathetic responses. She would have strongly identified with his fears and concerns, feeling the emotional weight of his problems. Nurturing her husband through faithful and relentless service to his heart would have been a natural response. The warmth of her Leo moon and keen intuitive abilities (Pisces Ascendant) gave her confidence that she could gain entry into his secret life and his deepest feelings. This deep connection to his heart would have brought him comfort and stability.

We might imagine that Jesus tended to be the one to initiate the changes in their lives, forcing Mary to step up to the challenges ahead with strength, determination and commitment, traits innate to her personality. Mary would have fearlessly embraced the unpredictability of their lives and looked forward to traveling to new places taking in the experiences as food. The revolutionary ideals of her beloved husband would have satisfied her rebellious Aquarian heart and she would have seen the challenges more as opportunities to make a difference in the lives of others than a source of aggravation. Their home was likely to be a gathering place for their brethren and extended family, and as others gathered around Jesus during his early ministry, Mary probably served all of them tirelessly. Her reward was a new sense of spiritual mastery, an expanded worldview and a greater definition as a woman.

There appears to be little question that Jesus and Mary were not only complementary partners but very compatible, because of the shared qualities I've mentioned in this chapter. As enlightened Divine Complements who became cognizant of the Stellar Promise, they would have understood the need to embrace the perfection of the reflection they'd been given in each other in order to help them grow toward mutual respect and acknowledge each other's equality and worth to humanity.

Another important yet challenging synergy revealed in their charts may have radically altered Jesus' concept of his wife's role in his life and helped him to appreciate her for catalyzing his spiritual evolution: Mary's Uranus in Pisces in opposition to Jesus' Pluto in Virgo. This polarity and opposition would have created a great synergistic push of spiritual and psychic power on Jesus' hidden emotions forcing a severance of old ties, associations and habits. Unexpected, unexplainable and uncontrollable events, such as the betrayal by those closest to him, his spiritual brothers, the disciples, pushed Jesus and Mary closer together. Here his loyalty to God meant appreciation of Mary as the clearest example of God in a woman. Any wounds inflicted by his mother, such as emotional neglect during formative years, would have been unearthed and shed through an event that mimic the personal annihilation he felt as a child. His persecution by the community he sought to enlighten, save and unite shattered all hopes for his political mission in Judea. Jesus was about to loose everything including possibly his life as he escorted into the arena of the crucifixion. This would have forced him to appreciate the faithfulness in the women around him in those last moments of consciousness on the cross.

The events of the closing chapter in Jerusalem were creatively synergized through the mutual design of this catalyzing opposition. Undoubtedly, it was divinely timed and perfect in changing the direction of Jesus and Mary's lives. From that point, what happened was not a literal death, as we've been conditioned to believe, nor a mythological sacrificed-king scenario ending the opportunity for reconciliation of twin God and Goddess, Adam and Eve. What occurred instead was a resurrection of the Stellar Promise, a commitment to their relationship and to the mission they had incarnated to perform. I will elaborate on this point in the next chapter, but Jesus did not die on the cross, and it was Mary's commitment that saved him.

From the astrological details of their natal charts and synastry, we've formulated an imaginative yet accurate composite picture of the personalities of Jesus and Mary, the archetypes that drove their character and a few details of their life course. Born to be together and serve together, they were meant to bring about a radical departure from the ideologies of Judaic doctrine and a revolution of a sort enlightening humanity to the mysteries of the Kingdom within. But first and foremost they incarnated to serve each other and God.

CHAPTER SIX
The Exile of the Guardians of the Grail

What has been hidden will be revealed.

From a legend out of the little fishing village Les Saintes-Marie-de-la-Mer, we know that Mary Magdalene, Mary (the wife of Cleopas), Martha, Salome, Lazarus and others composing Jesus' inner circle fled to Gaul sometime after the crucifixion, arriving in a tiny boat on the shores of Provence near Marseilles. It was a voyage into exile. Exploring a history rich with iconography and sanctified sites in her name, we become aware that Mary Magdalene, like the Virgin Mother, was venerated as the Black Madonna, whose cults were credited with spreading Gnostic Christianity throughout Western Europe.

Convincing arguments presented by several authors, including Lincoln, Leigh, and Baigent in *Holy Blood, Holy Grail* and Lawrence Gardner in *Bloodline of the Holy Grail*, have suggested that Jesus survived crucifixion and perhaps was among the family members who arrived in Gaul to join a community of Jews in exile in the South of France. They offer a convincing assertion that Jesus was still alive when taken off the cross and that the Resurrection was an enactment, a well-orchestrated scheme staged to help him escape. None of these writers go on to offer a convincing postscript as to what happened to Jesus and one could ponder the question endlessly because of the absence of a recorded history. I found this theory completely plausible and began my own quest for answers, first following my hunch that wherever Mary was, Jesus was not far behind. Answers arrived on the breath of spirit, touched my heart and opened my eyes to the truth as well as to the deceptions and sins of the Gospels and the Church. Most of the answers came through my dreams and a series of synchronistic symbolic events that helped me to eventually unravel crucial details.

What was confirmed was that Jesus did survive the crucifixion with the help of his inner circle, which by now had dwindled in size to include: Mary Magdalene, Martha, Lazarus, John, Salome, Thomas and Philip. The crucifixion took place in September 31 AD, not during the Passover in March of 33 AD as the Gospel writers say. Why the events of the Last Supper, betrayal and the crucifixion were so tightly woven together around the time of Passover was to proclaim Jesus the sacrificial Lamb of God. The date was chosen to tie the crucifixion and resurrection to an already established Jewish religious holiday in an effort to break from Jewish tradition and to win converts. According to the Gospel of John (18:28), Jesus died on the afternoon of the Passover when the Pascal lamb was slaughtered in preparation of the feast. This enables John to make the theological point that Jesus, the true "Lamb of God," dies at the exact hour that the lambs for the Passover meals will be sacrificed in the Temple. Paul (1 Cor. 5:7) also makes reference to Jesus as the sacrificial lamb: *"Get rid of the old yeast, so that you may be a new unleavened batch — as you really are. For Christ, our Passover lamb, has been sacrificed."*

Survival from crucifixion was not unheard of. From the writings of Josephus, a first-century Jewish historian and apologist, we are given an eyewitness account of three condemned men who where taken off the cross mercifully, one of whom survived. Jospehus wrote,

> "… And when I was sent by Titus Caesar with Cerealins, and a thousand horsemen, to a certain village called Thecoa, in order to know whether it were a place fit for a camp, as I came back, I saw many captives crucified, and remembered three of them as my former acquaintance. I was very sorry at this in my mind, and went with tears in my eyes to Titus, and told him of them; so he immediately commanded them to be taken down, and to have the greatest care taken of them, in order to their recovery; yet two of them died under the physician's hands, while the third recovered."

The majority of events told in the narratives of the Passion scenes in all four Gospels never happened. The accurate portion is that Jesus was betrayed, prosecuted, crucified and left hanging on the cross for several hours. Jesus was not pierced, or was any cup held up to catch his blood or was a tomb prepared or filled. These were all mythologized elements to bring the story to life.

The narrative accounts of Jesus' life, death, and resurrection in the four canonical Gospels, Mark, Matthew, Luke and John, were constructions of an early church, allegories aimed at convincing the pagan communities, Jews, and gentiles alike that Jesus was the authentic Son of God. For instance, John wrote,

"These things happened so that the scripture would be fulfilled: 'Not one of his bones will be broken,"and, as another scripture says, "They will look on the one they have pierced."- Gospel of John 19:36-37

This passage makes clear the intention of the writer is to convince his community that the fulfillment of the prophesy of Isaiah had occurred with the crucifixion, death and resurrection of Jesus. The Gospel of John, which wasn't composed until about 150 AD, is so full of direct citations and thematic references to Isaiah that it should be obvious that the gospel writer had a copy of the Old Testament on the table next to him so that he could pull out enough supporting material to embellish his narratives and make a convincing argument.

A few days into researching the body of information about the Crucifixion, I had a dream that was so vivid and real that the image haunted me for the entire year. I saw Jesus hanging on the cross writhing in pain and anger. He continued his brutal struggle on the cross against the backdrop of a dim amber sunset for what seemed like an eternity. The scene portrayed neither a humble submission to death nor surrender to the otherworldly light of God in martyrdom. There was little question that Jesus was a condemned man seeking liberation from punishment, tortured by pain and fighting to free his body from the cross. He was human and his suffering resembled every bit of human suffering one would expect under the circumstance. It was clear that he hadn't martyred himself; the majority of those who had vowed faithfulness had betrayed him.

What I bore witness to was a snapshot of actual crucifixion, and it proved in my mind that the story of the crucifixion as told in the Passion scene of the four Gospels, though embellished, had been about a very real event, a terrifying and humiliating act of fate, yet one that would also ensure new life for him and his beloved Mary Magdalene. How? Through the faithfulness and devotion Mary Magdalene and a family of friends who had the resources to turn the hand of fate with an outpouring of love and material wealth and through the mercy or greediness of a Roman centurion who was rewarded with the grace of Mary's inheritance and worth. In other words, Mary bribed a Roman soldier. All had succumbed and surrendered to divine plan, a creative miracle synergized by the love and the unity of twin souls whose destiny it was to continue to serve the consciousness of humanity side by side.

To support the facts derived from my mystical dream experience, I return again to Jesus and Mary's underlying mythology, the Adonis-Aphrodite myth, to demonstrate how the real events of the crucifixion and the resurrection mimicked even more of the plot and symbolic elements of the myth. As with the divinely born Adonis and his consort Aphrodite, Jesus and Mary's destiny was marked by the strength of love and an abiding commitment. Their myth was a creative blueprint pointing to their inborn God/Goddess potentials and was the underpinning plot of their relationship.

Many of the same symbolic elements of the Adonis myth mysteriously appear as part the legacy of Jesus' life narrative. Much like Adonis, whose Aries personality is driven by a need for conquest, Jesus stepped in too far, was perceived as a threat, prosecuted and crucified. Like Aphrodite, Mary was cast in the role of a harlot, a goddess of love ridiculed for her sexuality. Synchronistic symbolic elements, such as the blood red anemones said to still spring up at the site of the crucifixion and also on Mount Beautitudes, where Jesus ministered to the multitudes, are also part of the myth. Aphrodite blessed and committed Adonis' blood to the wind, and a field of blood-red anemones sprang up in his memorial. The symbol of the wild boar, like the one that mortally wounded Adonis, interestingly enough was used as an emblem on the shields of early Roman soldiers, a symbol now associated with brutality and greed. In fact, the general mythological theme of a sacrificed hero who dies and is resurrected with the help of his consort is easily recognized as the same theme portrayed in the crucifixion and resurrection scenes in the narratives of the Gospels. Why? Because it represented a mythological blueprint, a public dream of the creative field, materializing and playing out in Jesus' and Mary Magdalene's lives.

One might wonder whether Jesus and Mary were cognizant of the elements of their mythic legacy and used the synchronistic mythological clues as milestones pointing them to the fulfillment of their destiny together. It's likely that they were. Through developing their consciousness to complete the tasks of spiritual attainment and resurrecting the inborn potentials of their God/Goddess nature, they would have risen to their spiritual purpose. Through redemptive acts of love toward humanity, a mission to serve as spiritual teachers, they would fulfill their destiny.

In the final scenes of the Passion, as they really occurred, we're again thrown into the mythic fabric of Adonis and Aphrodite, at the place where Aphrodite becomes rescuer of her beloved Adonis from the underworld. Aphrodite, armed herself with a sword (her spiritual power), set her intention to circumvent her beloved's fate as he faced the shadow of death and the annihilation of the promise of the continuation of their sacred union. Mary was likewise bent on saving Jesus, to renew the hope for their life together. She was undoubtedly willing to give up anything to secure his release at the crucifixion that afternoon. Like Aphrodite, she was armed with a sword of courage and determination. In the myth, Aphrodite enters the gates of Hades ready to avenge Adonis' death and confront her rival, Persephone, the Death Goddess. Persephone here is symbolic of Jesus' wounded feminine side, forced into the underworld with Hades, punished, imprisoned, confronting imminent death and permanent separation from his complement. She also can be viewed as an aspect of Mary Magdalene's personality, the part that could have easily submitted out of fear, accepting the death of her husband as beyond her control. Aphrodite bargains; she agrees to be stripped of all earthly possessions to rescue Adonis from the underworld. In the end, she even relinquishes her sword. With this noble and enlightened move, she's granted the mercy of Zeus, who is symbolic of God, the Father (patriarch). Zeus intervenes to end the dispute between Persephone and Aphrodite and grants Adonis a new life with his beloved consort for three-quarters of the year. In the same way, Mary's love and determination forced the hand of fate and summoned up God's power within her to create the right circumstance to free her beloved Jesus from the cross. Mary passed a supreme spiritual test of love, securing her beloved Jesus' freedom, and they walked out of the symbolic underworld together. Mary sacrificed her inheritance in the end to save her beloved's life, and it was most likely through prayer and pleading with God that a creative miracle occurred, one that would involve her family and evoke sympathy from an opportunistic Roman soldier willing to play along with a plan that would benefit him greatly.

What is synchronistic is that not long after the persecution, crucifixion and supposed entombment of Jesus, a temple to the goddess Aphrodite was erected on the very spot of the crucifixion, a meaningful symbolic triumph for Mary Magdalene who in her role as the divine feminine, Aphrodite, relinquished everything to secure Jesus' freedom that fateful day. She truly deserved honor. However, in 326 AD by order of St. Constantine the Temple to Aphrodite was torn down, citing it, "the building to the impure demon called Aphrodite, a dark shrine of lifeless offerings." In its place The Church of the Holy Sepulcher was erected as a fitting memorial for a King, the Son of God who would be raised up to further the agenda of the Church that viewed itself as the Sacred Bride of Christ.

As my dream of Jesus disclosed with the symbolic elements of the Egyptian obelisk in the center of the English channel and the 1st century map of Western Europe, after the crucifixion and rescue in 31 AD, Jesus, Mary and their inner circle fled into exile. First traveling to Egypt, they remained for a period of about five years among a community of Jews, Syrians and Egyptians. Jesus had extended family living in the Nile Delta at the time who undoubtedly offered them refuge. Jewish settlements were well established in Egypt at the time, scattered from Alexandria and throughout the Nile River Delta. In fact, Jews accounted for one eighth of Egypt's population. As early as the third century BCE, waves of Jewish immigrants were given a safe haven in Egypt by the Ptolemaic kings and grew to become an integral part of the culture. Many Jews functioned as tradesmen, farmers, mercenaries and governmental officials. In Alexandria, they were assigned two of the five districts of the city and were able to govern themselves enjoying a great deal more political freedom than elsewhere.

In the Land of Onias of the Nile Delta in the city of Leontopolis near Heliopolis, Josephus, the historian, tells us that a Jewish temple was built, only on a smaller scale to the Temple of Jerusalem. Onias IV, the legitimate high priest of the Temple of Jerusalem sought refuge in Egypt sometime after the murder of his father Onias III by Antiochus Epiphanes. He was granted territory in the Nile Delta and sought Ptolemy's favor in support of building a temple to Jehovah. His motivation seemed certain. It was to fulfill the prophecy of Isaiah (18-22), that promised a day when Egyptians would "swear by the LORD of hosts." And that in that day, "there will be an altar to the LORD in the midst of the land of Egypt." The Temple was erected in about 170 BCE and stood until 73 AD when it was destroyed just three years after the Temple of Jerusalem suffered the same fate. What is most interesting is that the next line in Isaiah's prophecy remarks of a second coming. It reads, "for they will cry to the LORD because of the oppressors, and He will send them a Savior and a Mighty One, and He will deliver them.

Fulfilling the prophecy of Isaiah, it was within the Nile Delta not far from the Temple that Jesus and Mary Magdalene resided with extended family and within a tightly knit community of Jews. Jesus continued to gather small groups of disciples and conducted a ministry that was less politically motivated. As a Hasmonean, whose family was descendents of the vine of Aaron, Mary Magdalene would have enjoyed a privileged status in the community and among the kohen (priests) of the Temple who were of the same lineage. Mary gave birth to her first child in Egypt in 33 AD, a daughter Sarah.

True to the legends of Mary's arrival in Gaul, the exile party ventured on from Egypt by boat following the well-established Phoenician trade route through the Mediterranean Sea, sailing close to shore and stopping at many coastal ports along their route. They emerged on the shores near what is now Bandol, a small coastal port between Marseilles and Toulon, Provence, known for vineyards that produce some of the best aromatic rose´ wines of France. The Phoenicians were the first to establish vineyards in the area, and in 125 BC, the Romans found the vineyards flourishing when they established themselves in Tauroentum near Bandol, an ancient city mentioned in the writings of Caesar. In the coastal areas and in the Rhone Valley, communities of Jews lived in exile. It was within one of these communities that Mary and her party began their mission. Legends place Mary, Martha and Lazarus in the heart of the Rhone Valley, where a number of relics and churches dedicated to them now stand. The ninth-century church of Holy Maries in the Camargue, the church of St. Maximin that enshrines a body considered to be that of Mary Magdalene, the cave of Ste. Baume where it's said Mary resided in hermitage for some 40 years, the cathedral at Arles commemorating St. Throphinmus, the Church of St. Martha at Tarascon and the fourth century Abbey of St. Victor at Marseilles, a memorial to St. Lazarus, are all relics erected to honor these first Christian saints who, according to legend, landed on the shore of Provence between 35 to 37 AD.

Another man was mentioned arriving with the family, someone familiar from the Passion scenes and whose history and relationship to Jesus' family is muddled with discrepancies. That man was Joseph of Arimathea.

In his 1601 *Annales Ecclesiastici*, Cesare Baronius, the Vatican librarian, recorded that Joseph of Arirnathea first came to Marseilles in AD 35. From there, he and his company crossed to Britain. This history was also cited by GiIdas Badonicus in his *De Excidio Britanniae*, with earlier references by Eusebius of Caesaria (AD 260-340) and Hilary of Poitiers (AD 300-367). The years AD 35-37 are thus among the earliest recorded dates for Nazarene evangelism.

An old *canteque*, a song of Provencal tradition whose age is unknown, provides an account of the arrival of the exile party, listing those who made the journey from Judea to the shores near Marseilles. One verse is as follows:

Entrez, Sara, dans la nacelle
Lazare, Martheet, Maximim,
Cleon, Trophime, Saturninus
Les trios Maries et Marcelle
Eutrope et Martial, Sidonie avec Joseph
Vous perirez dans le nef.

According to this song and similar legends, the three Marys and Martha are said to have been accompanied by the following men: Lazarus, Torphimus, Maximin, Cleon, Eutropius, Sidonius, Martial, Saturninus and Joseph of Arimathea.

Not long after I began my research of the legendary legacy of Mary Magdalene's exile into Gaul, I had a remarkable dream in which I was deep in conversation with Jesus and Mary and woke up mouthing the name Joseph of Arimathea. I had been told in the dream that Jesus lived in exile alongside Mary using another identity: Joseph of Arimathea. Wishing to elude further persecution, a new identity secured his, Mary's, his children's and brethren's future safety. I was astonished by this dream that, rather than satisfying my questions, forced me to pose even more questions in order to rework the puzzle of conflicting Gospel facts and writings that seemed to form a conclusive, authoritative description of who Joseph of Arimathea was. Some of my questions have remained unanswered, but more than enough details were disclosed to offer a good amount of material for my continued research.

A series of questionable identities and conflicting histories can be examined, some of them apocryphal legend, about Joseph of Arimathea's activities and whereabouts after the Crucifixion. From the Gospels, we know that Joseph of Arimathea enters the scene right after the crucifixion to ask Pilate for the body of Christ and to offer his sepulcher for entombment. All four of the Gospels relay almost the exact story, something that rarely occurs with the varying accounts of other important events in the New Testament. I suspect that Joseph of Arimathea's appearance in the Passion scene was added to Mark's Gospel for reasons having little to do with fact. And the other Gospel writers who were dependent on Mark (the earliest Gospel) merely recounted Mark's testimony with some slight variation.

John Crossan, author and noted scholar of the *Jesus Seminars*, suggests Mark's gospel testimony of the Crucifixion, Empty Tomb and Resurrection, as well as the recounting in the other four Gospels, are at best historicized literary fiction. He makes the case that the biblical Joseph of Arimathea's role as a Sanhedrin is farfetched and that Mark presents an implausible scenario in light of the fact that he is not mentioned until the critical moment Jesus is in need of a tomb. He is then miraculously able to meet with Pilate, get Jesus down from the cross and put him in his tomb all in the matter of a couple of hours. Impossible. Joseph is not mentioned at any time afterwards in the New Testament, not even by the earliest Christian writer, Paul.

A thesis presented by Dennis R. MacDonald, a professor of New Testament and Christian Origins at the Claremont School of Theology suggests the author of Mark's Gospel was not writing history, but rather he borrowed from the works of the ancient Greek poet Homer (the *Odyssey* and the *Iliad*), engaging in a literary practice called *mimesis*; that is, the process of borrowing an element from one work and refashioning it for another. The author of Mark "wrote a prose epic" in which Jesus was modeled after the heroes of Homer, namely Odysseus and Hector. The most obvious Homeric hero to model Jesus against was Odysseus. As MacDonald points out, both heroes (Odysseus and Jesus) were carpenters, traveled with companions confronting a series of hardships on the journey, both returned home only to confront those who would attempt to kill them and both heroes returned from Hades alive.

MacDonald also draws parallels between Iliad 24 and Mark 15:42 – 16:2 to demonstrate that Mark borrowed elements and modeled the narrative of Joseph of Arimathea's role in claiming Jesus' body on Priam (King of Troy), who goes to rescue the body of his son, Hector, from his murderer Achilles in the *Iliad*. The parallels in the two stories are remarkably similar. Both Priam and Joseph claim the bodies from the oppressor, both accomplish the task at night, both bodies are anointed and dressed, in each story three women either lament or arrived to anoint the body and both bodies are placed in a tomb or ossuary. Mark only transforms the ending to relay the discovery of the empty tomb and to hint at the Resurrection.

According to the prophecies of Isaiah, after his persecution, the messiah would find his grave among "the wicked and the rich." Could the account of Joseph of Arimathea's noble role, wealth, position as a Sanhedrin (a Jewish senator) and even his presence after the Crucifixion have been fabricated to embellish the Passion scene in support of a personification of Jesus as the authentic king of the Jews?

There is little evidence to suggest the town Arimathea existed in Judea at the time Christ as we were told it did by Luke. Some scholars have associated Arimathea with Ramatha, a town about 4 or 5 miles north-west of Jerusalem, probably because it was in close proximity to the Passion scenes and because phonetically it sounds similar. Instead, Arimathea was a title that Jesus assumed. In biblical Hebrew/Aramaic, Arimathea (*aryeh met [le-]Yah*means), means: "The lion dead to the lord." This title suggests a transformation in identity, something on the order of, "The king is dead, long live the Christ." The symbol of the lion was emblematic of the tribe of Judah, the kingly line from which Jesus descended through his father Joseph. After the crucifixion, Jesus relinquished a political mission and any hope of securing his dynastic inheritance to make way for a more divine mission as Christ and faithful husband to Mary Magdalene. This title, therefore, was a proclamation of his divinity over his dynastic (bloodline) destiny, giving way to a more realistic and even more meaningful purpose. Jesus assumed his father's name, Joseph, to maintain the connection to his roots and paternal legacy.

As to why Joseph of Arimathea was written into the Gospel accounts, we can presume that the architects of Christianity needed a character to fulfill the prophesy of Isaiah, a noted and recognizable name from those who were propagating the seeds of Christianity near and far. We must remember that the Gospels were written some 60 to 120 years after the Passion of Christ and by then there would have been word of a noted disciple called Joseph of Arimathea who had traveled throughout Western Europe ministering Jesus' teachings. They likely thought to tie Joseph to the Passion scenes out of necessity. Therefore, they crafted a story that included Joseph, painted him as a Sanhedrin, a wealthy counselor and a secret disciple of Jesus, and said that he donated his tomb in a garden fit for a king so that Jesus could rest in peace there for three days and rise again, fulfilling the prophesy of Isaiah (53:9), "He was assigned a grave with wicked and rich, in his death. "

There's reason to believe that the Christian fathers, in compiling the narrative history of Jesus, may have discredited or deliberately excluded evidence suggesting that Jesus lived beyond his 33rd year. In about 180 AD, St. Irenaeus, Bishop of Lyons, one of the most noted ante-Nicene theologians, wrote "Against Heresies," an attack on the Gnostics. In it he declared, on the authority of the Apostle John, that Jesus lived to old age. This testimony was attributed to those who were with John in Asia. Irenaeus included this:

"They, however, that they may establish their false opinion regarding that which is written, 'to proclaim the acceptable year of the Lord,' maintain that He preached for one year only, and then suffer in the twelfth month. In speaking thus, they are forgetful of their own disadvantage, destroying His whole work, and robbing Him of that age which is both more necessary and more honourable than any other; the more advanced age, I mean, during which also as a teacher He excelled all others. For how could He have had His disciples, if He did not teach? And how could He have taught, unless He had reached the age of a Master? For when He came to be baptized, he had not yet completed His thirtieth year, but was beginning to be about thirty years of age (for thus Luke, who has mentioned His years, has expressed it: 'Now Jesus was, as it were, beginning to be thirty years old,' when He came to receive baptism); and (according to these men,) he preached only one year reckoning from His baptized. On completing his thirtieth year he suffered, being in fact still a young man, and who had by no means attained to advanced age. Now, that the first stage of early life embraces thirty years, and that this extends onward to the fortieth and fiftieth year a man begins to decline towards old age, which Our Lord possessed while He still fulfilled the office of a Teacher, even as the Gospel and all the elders testify; those who were conversant in Asia with John, the disciple of the Lord, (affirming) that John conveyed to them that information. And he remained among them up to the time of Trajan. Some of them, moreover, saw not only John, but the other apostles also, and heard the very same account from them, and bear testimony as to the (validity of) the statement. Whom then should we rather believe? Whether such men as these, or Ptolemaeus, who never saw the apostles, and who never even in his dreams attained to the slightest trace of an apostle?"

This passage, that somehow escaped being struck from the record, amounts to a confession and suggests not only that Jesus probably lived to a ripe old age but also that he continued to minister elsewhere.

Some of the post-crucifixion storyline and testimony about Joseph of Arimathea lacks credibility and relays an impossible history. The *Acts of Pilate* in the Gospel of Nicodemus, a 2nd century apocryphal gospel, says Joseph of Arimathea was imprisoned by Jews shortly after the Crucifixion and pardoned about 40 years later, at which time he began a long ministry spreading Jesus' teachings to Spain, Gaul and Britain. This same history was recounted in the medieval grail legend by Robert de Boron and became popular literature in the Middle Ages. If Joseph was truly the Virgin Mary's uncle and Jesus' great-uncle, as he was identified by the 9th Century, he would have been over 100 years old by the time he landed in Britain to begin a 20-year ministry. In regard to this non-sensible history, Lawrence Gardner, in *The Bloodline of the Holy Grail*, laid out another well-researched hypothesis. He suggested the real identity of Joseph of Arimathea was James the Just, Jesus' brother. This theory assumes that the account of James' martyrdom in 62 AD, chronicled by Josephus, the Jewish historian, was either inaccurate or a fictitious history. Gardner's hypothesis proved to be untrue, however, his insight and research about the impossibility of Joseph's history in early apocryphal writings was correct.

In much the same way that Jesus was fictitiously identified as a carpenter, Joseph became associated with the tin mining trade by occupation. According to legend, he secured a fleet of ships that delivered tin from Cornwall, England to Phoenicia. On one such trip to Britannia, he escorted his nephew, Jesus, who was a young boy at the time. Some scholars suggest it was this legend that William Blake put to verse in his poem, *Jerusalem*.

From a pieced-together history of Glastonbury Abbey, some of which was derived from Arthurian lore while other details seem to have been pulled out of a deep sea of legendary facts about the area, we can conclude that Joseph of Arimathea landed in Gaul in 36-37 AD with Mary Magdalene, Lazarus, Martha, Salome and others and that many of them if not all traveled to Glastonbury almost 30 years later, in 63 AD. Legend tells us St. Philip commissioned Joseph of Arimathea out of Gaul to Britain to spread the word of the incarnation of Jesus Christ. He arrived with a group of 12, and a sympathetic pagan king named Arvigorus gave him a parcel of land, "twelve hides," on what was described as a small island (Glastonbury). He and his brethren built a small wattle church on that land in the style of a tabernacle and dedicated it in the year 64 AD. Britain's first aboveground church was born. Later called the *Vetusta Eccesia* (the Old Church) it was cited in royal charters of King Ina in 704 and King Cnut in 1032. The site of the wattle church was preserved, later demarcated with a small chapel, Lady's Chapel, dedicated to St. Mary, and represented a hallowed space in the Old Glastonbury Abbey complex built in the 11th century.

Another important element of the legend proves interesting. It says Joseph of Arimathea traveled with a son, Josephes. William of Malmesbury's writings on the antiquity of Glastonbury, a primary source of testimony on the legacy of Glastonbury, offer the following verse by a metrical writer:

Avallon is entered by a band of Twelve.
Joseph, Armathea's flower, is chief of them.
And with his father cometh Josephes,
So to these Twelve Glastonia's rights are given.

In the annals of the history of Wales, chroniclers referred to Joseph of Arimathea as *Ilid*. "There came with Bran the Blessed from Rome to Britain Arwystli Hen (Aristobulus the Aged), Ilid Cyndaf man of Israel (Joseph of Arimathea) and Mawan (Josephes son of Joseph)." Joseph is also referred to as *Ilid* in the Bardic ode, *Cwydd to Saint Mary Magdalene*.

Given that Joseph of Arimathea was really Jesus, Josephes was, therefore, Jesus and Mary's son, the second child conceived of their union. Their first child, Sarah, is still celebrated in festivals held in Les-Saintes-Maries-de-la-Mer, in the South of France. A statue there depicts her as a dark-skinned Egyptian girl, and legend describes her as a servant to the family. According to my divine communications with Mary, Sarah was born January 12, 33 AD in Egypt. Sadly, Sarah died in childbirth along with her infant, a fact that nullifies the theory that the blood royal was probably carried forward from Sarah's descendants. Instead, it would have sprung from the vine of Josephes, Jesus and Mary's only son.

Documented at Glastonbury Abbey, beginning with a poem titled *The Lyfe of Joseph of Arimathia* and dated 1502, is the association between the healing energies of the site of the abbey and the sacred hawthorn or holy thorn on Weary-All Hill. Both were sites of pilgrimage for a number of saints, including St. Patrick and St. David, and stories have emerged of miraculous healings resulting from the intercession of St. Joseph of Arimathea. To this day, bands of travelers visit Glastonbury in quest of miracles of healing and initiation into the mysteries held within this hallowed land.

While the legend from the south of France tells us that the Sangrael was brought to Western Europe through Mary Magdalene, it's also true that Joseph of Arimathea (Jesus) brought his vine, the Sangrael, to Gaul and then to Britain, not as Jesus' great-uncle but as Jesus himself. Jesus and Mary arrived together, dwelled together and would usually have traveled together in devoted service to their mission. Their son, Josephes, accompanied them on their journeys.

Although there's little to prove that Mary Magdalene was ever in Glastonbury, it seems reasonable to conclude that she and her son Josephes were among the 12 said to have accompanied Joseph of Arimathea to the isle of Avalon (Glastonbury). The sites commemorating Mary Magdalene and her sister Martha and brother, Lazarus, are instead spread along the Rhone Valley in Provence not far from where they would have landed. Now considered the earliest missionaries of Christianity, their legends are full of embellishments and many distortions. By legend, Mary died in the South of France in 63 AD, a date that coincides with Joseph of Arimathea's arrival in Glastonbury. Her body is said to lie in rest in the Basilica of Saint-Maxmin-la-Sainte Baume, where according to the lore she lived the majority of her life in hermitage in a cave. What's more likely is that the cave linked to Mary was one used by a group of Cathars who lived in exile in Gaul. They were known to have built their churches in caves. It's likely this cave gravesite was a Cathar site and of a later date. The idea of Mary Magdalene, "society's princess," living in a cave for 40 years is odd and even absurd, akin to the archetypal goddess Persephone, the Dark Goddess, being dragged into the underworld with Hades and held captive in a legacy of shame, grief and suppression. This fabricated history reminds us of a continued theme of sinner status despite noble blood, a portrayal consistent with what's found in the Gospels. The key elements of Mary's forty-year hermitage were probably borrowed from the legend of the fifth century St. Mary the Egyptian, who was also a prostitute, turned hermit, and whose hermitage lasted some forty-seven years. For Mary, there seems to have been little liberation from the shadow cast on Eve, even in the legends from the South of France, where she dwelled with a close-knit group of family and brethren and alongside her husband, Jesus. Who's in that grave in St. Baume? It's not Mary, who survived several years after the final ascension of Jesus, who rose again in 82 AD. Through my divine communications with Jesus and Mary, I was shown that Mary had accompanied Jesus to Glastonbury and onward to Ireland.

The only piece of legendary evidence connecting Mary Magdalene to Glastonbury is Lady's Chapel, on the site of the original wattle church dedicated to St. Mary. By legend, it was Jesus himself who made that dedication. A supporting legend says that St. David arrived with seven bishops planning to dedicate the chapel to the Blessed Virgin Mary but that he had a dream the night before warning him that Jesus had dedicated it long before. This might lead a more mystical mind to wonder which Mary, his wife or mother, Jesus was honoring when he dedicated it. Jesus (Joseph of Arimathea) blessed and dedicated his church to his beloved Mary Magdalene while they were in residence there. As with many of the churches spread throughout Western Europe originally dedicated to Mary Magdalene, it also now is identified with the Blessed Virgin Mary. A beautiful stone inscription still lies in the chapel wall commemorating the spot where the original church stood. It reads simply "Jesus Maria." Contrary to what Orthodoxy wishes us to believe, in my mind, the inscription "Jesus Maria" best describes the two who were joined as one, brother and sister, bridegroom and bride, Jesus and Mary Magdalene.

In the romantic Holy Grail legends, of which there are numerous versions, we can wander through a trail of clues that offer a rich history of notable characters, all connected through bloodline. Names like Joseph, Josephes, Lot, Joseus, Josuias, Gilead (Galahad), Alain, Petrus, Brons or Hebron, Bruns Brundalis, Urien, Jonas, Pelles and Ban are all Hebrew names or indicate a Hebrew association.   In Le Morte D'Arthur, Thomas Malory's narrative work on Arthurian legend, containing the quest for the Sangrael, digressions on King David, King Solomon, and Judas Maccabee are intermingled among the names of the Arthurian Knights without much explanation. As I mentioned earlier, Mary Magdalene's lineage, as a Hasmonean, was the House of Aaron, whose descendants were the Maccabees, and Jesus descended from the House of Judah. Their marriage merged two important dynastic lines.   The key point in all the legends is that Arthur, Gawain, Lancelot and Galahad were all said to have been direct descendants of Joseph of Arimathea, the guardian of the Grail. Joseph brought with him the Sangrael –Christ's blood— the blood royal, not through his role as merely its guardian or because he was another relative of Jesus, but because he was Jesus Christ. The blood royal was carried in his own veins.

Facts pulled out of the romantic language of allegorical tales such as Arthurian lore and from the poetry of bards who conveyed mystical secrets through oral tradition can help us piece together the legacy of Jesus and Mary Magdalene and how their bloodline was passed on through the generations, beginning with their son, Josephes. Although allegorical, we can't dismiss them as merely fictitious romantic renderings of the imagination, because their characters were historical figures in the early Christianization of Britain, names that can be traced to a heritage and blood-royal lineage of the most important kings of Judea, such as David, Solomon and Judas Maccabee.   These legends can also be recognized for the spiritual value of their quests for the Grail, the mystical secrets and magical healing power associated with Christ transmitted to the most worthy initiate and knight.

From both the historical legend of Glastonbury and Arthurian lore, it's clear that Joseph of Arimathea is the central figure who transmits the power and purpose of Christ and bestows on the worthy knight the mysteries of the Holy Grail. Whether it is in the form of a stone, the plate used at the last supper, the cup or chalice that caught the blood of Jesus, the hawthorn staff, the white shield with red cross, or the sword in the red marble stone, it holds supernatural power, protection and great mastery for the holder. And it has a connection to Joseph of Arimathea. In all the legends, Joseph is the one consistent bearer and guardian of these symbolic sacred objects, and though it seems his entitlement came through the role he played after the Crucifixion, there are elements in the legends that point to his having been the vine from which the branches of the royal blood sprang and the one who determined initiates' worthiness to receive this secret legacy. The identity of Joseph of Arimathea as merely one of Jesus' disciples or that of a missionary and saint or even as a comforter and rescuer who escorted the royal family to Gaul doesn't seem to explain or support the central importance he's given in these legends. He's portrayed as the holder of the keys to the Kingdom, the Holy Grail, as well as the vine whose descendents are the most royal and noblest knights of King Arthur's Court.

The Red Cross Shield
The Red Cross Shield figures prominently in several of the literary quests for the Holy Grail. The following excerpt from Thomas Mallory's popularized version of Arthurian lore is one of many describing the sacred shield with red cross passed on from Joseph of Arimathea to Sir Galahad.

"The next day Sir Galahad took the shield, and within a while he came to the hermitage, where he met the white knight, and each saluted the other courteously. 'Sir,' said Sir Galahad, "can you tell me the marvel of the shield?" "Sir," said the white knight, "that shield belonged of old to the gentle knight, Joseph of Arimathea; and when he came to die he said, 'Never shall man bear this shield about his neck but he shall repent it, unto the time that Sir Galahad the good knight bear it, the last of my lineage, the which shall do many marvelous deeds.' And then the white knight vanished away."

The snowy white shield with a blood-red cross has a mysterious protective power. Prophesied to go to the last noble character of Joseph of Arimathea's (Jesus') lineage, to Sir Galahad, it denotes the

Shield of Joseph of Arimathea

Templar Flag

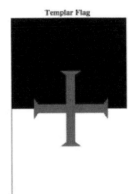

Knights Templar Cross

award of spiritual power to he who is most worthy. This entitlement appears to be twofold, due to both bloodline lineage and the fact that it's his destiny to enter the quest as an initiate and be proved worthy of receiving its mysteries and heraldry. The shield therefore represents Jesus' authentic Shield of Arms, denoting lineage and the passing on of the spiritual power and legacy of Christ. Another legend says Joseph of Arimathea gave the shield to Arviragus, Prince of Cornwall, later king of Southern England, after he was converted through baptism. The same red cross shield was associated with St. George, depicted in the iconography of his slaying the dragon and later adopted by the Knights Templar who wore white mantels emblazoned with a large red cross.

To bring light to the meaning and mystical power behind Jesus' shield of arms, we must be able to interpret the symbols it incorporates. The symbolic elements of the shield point us to spiritual secrets imprinted in our collective memory, elements of a symbolic language that has been distorted by Orthodox Christianity and misinterpreted for centuries. As applied in the mystery schools of Hermetic and Cabalistic teachings before it became emblematic of Jesus' suffering and sacrifice, the cross signified the union of heaven and earth, spirit and matter, male and female. The vertical line, representing the masculine spirit, intersects the horizontal feminine principle, the material. The horizontal bar was alternatively interpreted as the pair of opposites, male and female, right and left, merging with vertical bar, representing the union of the above with the below, heaven and earth. The symbolism of the cross points us back to the mystical marriage of the bride and bridegroom. It holds spiritual power and intrinsic meaning for one who initiates into the mystery of the Bridal Chamber of the Stellar Heart.

One version of this tale in the quest for the Holy Grail tells us that the cross was marked on the shield with the blood of Joseph of Arimathea, another version says that his son, Josephes, marked the cross before he died. In both versions, it was kept hanging on a wall guarded by the holy hermit Nacien until it could be claimed by the most noble knight. This blood cross signified a covenant, a promise that Jesus made to his disciples.

We need to look back to the Last Supper scene in the New Testament to understand what the blood symbolized in Jesus' mind and put other interpretations of the blood of Christ aside. Mark 14: 24-25 reads:

> "This is my blood of the covenant, which is poured out for many. Truly, I say to you, I shall not drink again of the fruit of the vine until that day when I drink it new in the kingdom of God."

Although this passage has been interpreted as an oath made in martyrdom and sacrifice, pending Crucifixion and suffering to take away the sins of humanity, its truer meaning was an oath to serve humanity till the end of times – until salvation had come for all. At the Last Supper meal he was at the table with his disciples knowing full well was going to be betrayed by most of them. The ritual pouring of the wine, symbolizing his blood, was not intended to pass on anything more to these men who were not trustworthy. He was not giving his blood for any of them. He was merely restating an oath he had already made. The "blood poured out to many" translates as the spiritual force of the love and the abiding promise Jesus made to serve humanity throughout all the ages. He had already given his all and he was promising to give more.

I arrived at this understanding after a great deal of frustration one evening in contemplating the blood on the shield. I knew its intended meaning would be illuminated eventually through some form of divine communication. That night I had a dream in which I sat across from Jesus enjoying a meal at an outdoor restaurant on a familiar street in Los Angeles, Larchmont Avenue. Our table was on the sidewalk in front of the restaurant, well within the public's view and among the masses. We enjoyed our meal together in deep conversation about the "last days". I interpreted our meal together as the fulfillment of my promise, an intimate Passover supper in a neighborhood that I associated with my own role as a spiritual teacher and counselor. For years, I taught workshops on dreams and shamanism in the Los Angeles area. After a weekend class, I would enjoy shopping and a nice meal on Larchmont as a reward. Jesus and I were there again as we had been many times before, he as my guide from the dimensions of spirit supporting me in my promises and heartfelt mission. He was reminding me that the outpouring of love I shared with my students was the fulfillment of my promise, a promise that was not unlike his.

The shield of the most worthy was emblematic of Jesus' vine, which he made clear was not so much the vine of his ancestry or claims of Messianic inheritance but the vine God planted in him. "I am the vine God planted." (John 15:1). In conclusion, the red cross shield passed to Sir Galahad in the Arthurian legends and adopted by the Knights Templar of the 12th century undoubtedly was the true shield of arms of Jesus Christ, emblematic of his blood-oath and symbolic of the protective power of Christ's intercession. It was Jesus himself, as Joseph of Arimathea, who passed it on to those he recognized as worthy initiates and spiritual brethren, and with it his more secret teachings.

The Hawthorn Staff

Another symbolic power object associated with Joseph of Arimathea is the hawthorn staff, which, according to Glastonbury legend, took root when Joseph plunged it into the ground while seeking rest on Weary-all Hill. This variety of hawthorn blooms twice a year, at Christmas and in May, and is not indigenous to Britain. It's a variety native to the Mediterranean regions, offering evidence for the majority of believers that it was brought to Britain and propagated by Joseph of Arimathea himself. As a metaphor for the propagation of the vine of Joseph of Arimathea (Jesus) at Glastonbury through his son, Josephes, the flowering staff is symbol of dynastic succession. Like that of his father, Joseph, whose flowering staff was a sign of his chosen status to be betrothed to Mary (the Virgin) so that the prophecy of Isaiah could be fulfilled through his son, ("There shall come forth a Rod from the stem of Jesse, and a Branch shall grow out of his roots'"), Joseph's (Jesus') rod/staff would branch out, continuing the bloodline in a new land. This similarity between the hawthorn staff and the flowering staff of Joseph –- with its promise to fulfill the messianic inheritance, can be seen as yet another clue to the hidden identity of Joseph of Arimathea as Jesus Christ. It also supports the idea that Glastonbury was the famed Avalon of Arthurian lore and that perhaps Arthur himself was a direct descendant of Jesus. Lore puts King Arthur's final resting place at Glastonbury Abbey, along with Joseph of Arimathea suggesting a divine connection between the two. Glastonbury records record Joseph's death as July 27th, AD 82. There seems to be little proof that either King Arthur or Joseph of Arimathea was buried there. Because of the passionate mission that Jesus and Mary were committed to, they traveled further on. I was pointed to Ireland, near Dublin, where they lived out their remaining years together.

In the works of James Ussher, Archbishop of Armagh, Church of Ireland (1580-1665), known for his extensive research as a theologian, there's reference (vol. vi) to a legend that says that under the wisdom and advice of Joseph of Arimathea, learned from the teaching of King Solomon, Ireland was freed of the venomous reptiles (paganism). From this legend we might gather that Joseph of Arimathea (Jesus) and Mary traveled on to Ireland and perhaps set up another community much as they had in Glastonbury. The most revealing and interesting fact in the legend is that Joseph was said to be familiar with the teachings of King Solomon, the "keys of Solomon." Solomon, the son of King David, was considered a divinely born king, known for his supernatural powers, a magician in every sense of the word. He was an initiate of the ancient mysteries and was said to have knowledge superior to that of the Egyptians. According to Talmudic legends, Solomon understood the mysteries of Qabbalah, alchemy and necromancy and was able to exorcise demons and communicate with spirits from the invisible dimensions. Best-known for his infamous initiation temple, Solomon's temple, his legends are interwoven with Freemasonry, the Knights Templar and the Grail. What can be drawn from the description of Joseph of Arimathea is that he, too, had supernatural powers and mystical knowledge and probably initiated others into secret mysteries as he traveled through the countryside of Ireland. This description seems to support that Joseph was indeed Jesus Christ.

Scotland also has a tradition with fascinating legends purporting Jesus visited its shores. The most intriguing are those centering on the Scottish Hebrides and a tiny sacred island called Iona. The oral tradition there tell us Jesus and Mary Magdalene once visited the tiny island and another version adds their son was born there. Christine Hartley's recounting of still another legend in her book, *The Western Mystery Tradition* (1968), offers an alternative burial site to St. Baume for the remains of Mary Magdalene—a cave in Iona. Only twenty miles away at Kilmore Church, Dervaig, on the Scottish Isle of Mull, a stained glass window depicts Jesus and a very pregnant Mary Magdalene. Commissioned in 1906 the stained glass window echoes the same legends and depicts Jesus and Mary Magdalene as a unified couple—Divine Complements.

Certainly, the most intriguing legend associated with Iona is a prophecy mentioned by William Sharp, writing as Fiona Macleod in 1910. He elaborates on a Second Coming of Christ to the island of Iona. But this time Christ is prophesized to appear as a woman, Christa, who not only returns to Iona's shores but who also will bring the promise of everlasting peace to the world. He wrote:

> "When I think of Iona I think often, too, of a prophecy once connected with Iona....the old prophecy that Christ shall come again upon Iona, and of that later and obscure prophecy which foretells, now as the Bride of Christ, now as the Daughter of God, now as the Divine Spirit embodied through mortal birth in a Woman, as once through mortal birth in a man, the coming of a new Presence and Power: and dream that this may be upon Iona, so that the little Gaelic island may become as the little Syrian Bethlehem.... A young Hebridean priest once told me how, 'as our forefathers and elders believed and still believe, that Holy Spirit shall come again which once was mortally born among us as the Son of God, but, then, shall be the Daughter of God. The Divine Spirit shall come again as a Woman. Then for the first time the world will know peace'."

Although this legend does not mention Joseph of Arimathea per say, it does mention Jesus as returning once more, presupposing he had already visited the Isle. This prophecy may have arisen to reconcile a dark piece of Iona's history, the sins of one St. Columba, a missionary who established a church and monastery on the island in the 6th century. A religiously pious man, he banished all women, cows, frogs and snakes from the island, deeming them Satan's instruments of temptation and sin. What better retribution for sins against women than a prophecy whereby Jesus returns as a woman, the Daughter of God.

The Sword in the Stone

Joseph of Arimathea was also known as Joseph de Marmore, a name thought to identify him with Marmoica, Egypt, where it's alleged that he lived before moving to the fictitious location of Arimathea. Again, Marmoica was not necessarily the exact location where Jesus and Mary resided for the five years prior to their voyage to Gaul. But the fact remains that Joseph of Arimathea was being connected to Egypt. The meaning of the word *Marmore* is "marble" and was more likely a title given to Joseph than a name relating to citizenship. The Latin, *Marmor,* is also one of several names for Mars, the Roman god who was celebrated as guardian of the boundaries, fields, livestock and home and who later became the Roman God of War. To the Greeks, he was Aries, ruled by the planet Mars, who in the astrology of Jesus was his sun sign as we remember. Could the title Marmore have been one honoring the sign under which Joseph (Jesus) was born? Joseph of Arimathea certainly had been imbued with the honor as guardian of sorts in his role as carrier of the Grail; like the God Marmor he was also viewed as protector.

We can look again to Arthurian lore and to the symbolic element of the sword in the stone of the Grail legend to find yet another clue to Joseph of Arimathea's identity as the initiator of the Grail mysteries. King Arthur is summoned by a squire to witness a miracle of sorts on a riverbank. Floating beneath the surface of the water is a jeweled sword stuck in a piece of "red marble." The following passage is from Le Morte D'Arthur:

> "So all the knights went with him, and when they came to the river they found there a stone fleeting, as it were of red marble, and therein stuck a fair rich sword, and in the pommel thereof were precious stones wrought with subtle letters of gold. Then the barons read the letters which said in this wise: Never shall man take me hence, but only he by whose side I ought to hang, and he shall be the best knight of the world."

As with all the symbolic objects in the Grail legends, the chosen knight must be deemed worthy to assume the grace and responsibility of the object's power. Here it is the sword, a symbol of spiritual illumination, power and higher truth held in what we might consider the cornerstone of wisdom, red marble. Remembering that Joseph of Arimathea's title was Marmore (marble), the symbol of the sword becomes connected to Joseph in that it is embedded within him. And as King David's sword, it mentions Joseph's genealogy and his dynastic inheritance. The sword in the stone has, of course, other connotations as a metaphor for a spiritual secret, one that must be quested for. Taking this avenue of interpretation, we realize the more esoteric symbolism of the sword in the stone as the manifestation of spirit (the sword) into matter (the marble). Like the symbol of the red cross, the sword in the stone represents a key to realizing the Christ within, the manifestation of spirit into matter accomplished through the sacred marriage within the Bridal Chamber of the Stellar Heart. The sword also represents masculine intelligence and the illuminated mind, the stone feminine wisdom and the womb of the material, holding the spiritual force of light. As Christ's sword, its power cuts through the illusion of the material world as separated from Source, and its power and purpose is not to slay the material world but to illuminate and serve it. The marble of Joseph's title denoted his integrity and the pillar he was to his spiritual community.

The Holy Grail

Of all the symbols of the quest for spiritual illumination, the Holy Grail is the most prized. It holds a secret power so magnificent that it can raise the dead, heal all wounds and turn a wasteland into a paradise of perpetual bounty. In the majority of the Grail romances it is referred to as Saint Graal, or Sangrael. The word *graal*, its earliest spelling, is Old French meaning a dish and usually represented a shallow dish or plate that presented the various courses of the meal. It has been suggested that it was a borrowed and Christianized symbol from an earlier Celtic tale, analogous to the magic cauldron of Celtic lore. The Christianized symbol of the Grail is that of the dish used by Jesus at the Last Supper, or as described in Robert Boron's version of the Grail quest, the cup used to catch the blood of Christ that Joseph of Arimathea brought with him to Gaul and later to Albion (Great Britain). More recently, several conspiracy theorists including Baigent, Leigh, and Lincoln in their book, *Holy Blood Holy Grail*, have presented a whole new theory as to the meaning of the Holy Grail. They suggest it's secret is not in it's mystical properties but in the name "Sangrael" itself. They have pointed out that by dividing "sangrael" this way, "sang" "rael" rather than "san" "grael" its true meaning can be decoded to represent "blood royal". The vessel itself they suggest was, in truth, the body of Mary Magdalene who bore Jesus' child seeding future generations of the Davidic bloodline. There is every reason to believe that the symbol of the Holy Grail held more than one meaning, in fact, layer upon layer of meanings. Not only does the symbol of the Grail hint at a bloodline carried through the womb of Mary Magdalene whose descendants live to this day, but as a vessel of spiritual attainment, magic, creativity, alchemical union and a mystery housed within each and every individual—God's power.

The authors of the Grail quests had each spun their story as an allegorical tale containing many disguised facts with hidden meanings pointing to the tenants of their mystical tradition and the sacred knowledge they held in secret. For most of them the Grail quest was a quest for enlightenment earned through successive tests and trails proving the worthiness of the individual to receive the spiritual illumination of God's little secret and of a legacy passed on to them through Joseph of Arimathea.

In the beginning chapters of *La Queste del Saint Graal,* attributed to a Cistercian monk in the 13th century writing under the name of Walter Map, the Holy Grail is not described in detail other than to say it is a vessel with a miraculous power. It is left to the imagination to conjure up the form it takes when it appears covered with a red velvet cloth before Galahad who had earned a glimpse of its mystery. Although its form is illusive, its supernatural power is evident, uplifting the initiate into a transcendent state and imbuing him with the power to create miracles of a supernatural nature. Although any knight can quest to see the Grail, only one deemed worthy could see it; others are said to be blind. This blindness is reminiscent of Jesus' teachings about the Kingdom of the Father, as with saying 113 of the Gospel of Thomas when Jesus says, *"Rather, the Father's kingdom is spread out upon the earth, and people don't see it."* In many ways, the Grail is analogous to Jesus' Kingdom of God because its power is of a transcendent nature and emerges from a rarely seen heavenly dimension that interfaces this world. Only the enlightened mind has "eyes to see" and "ears to hear" according to Jesus' understanding of God's presence and manifestations on earth.

The quest itself is no simple quest for enlightenment. In this version of the Quest, it is accomplished through redemptive tests, the scope of which is beyond merely accepting God and his Son, following scripture or mere contemplation and prayer. The initiate must seek out guides, be given dreams and visions and perfect himself before he is initiated further into the mystery to fulfill the tasks of his destiny. In *La Queste del Saint Graal,* to see the Grail the initiate must possess five specific virtues: virginity, humility, endured long suffering, justice and charity and he must be cleansed at the heart through Christ's intercession. Furthermore, he must become an open vessel himself. As the vessel and conduit of God's power the initiate serves as a healer and gives to those who require

God's bounty and grace. As with Cabalistic and Gnostic teachings the initiate can only realize the God-self by rising up spiritually and becoming a perfected man.

Like the red cross shield, the Grail's miraculous power initially belonged to Joseph of Arimathea and with it, he, as the perfected and anointed Christ, was able to use its secret alchemy for his purpose. Joseph is the carrier, master and guardian of the Grail, the initiator into the mystery of the secret housed within a most sacred vessel. The vessel, in fact, represents his own perfected self in human form and he sits at the head of the Grail Table because he was recognized as a spiritual master and the founder and the leader of The Church of the Holy Grail—a Gnostic tradition. He was Jesus Christ.

La Queste del Saint Graal, is the most Christianized grail romance according to scholars because of its Cistercian roots. In it are a series of hidden clues that point to the fact that Joseph of Arimathea was, in fact, Jesus Christ. The following passage has embedded within it some fascinating parallels that unmask the true identity of Joseph of Arimathea. In it Joseph's performance is identical to Jesus, when he, like Jesus, demonstrates the power to feed the multitudes. It almost exactly mimics the narrative of Mark 8:6-10 in which Jesus multiplies the loaves of bread to feed a crowd of 4000 men. *La Queste del Saint Graal* reads,

> "One day they had nothing to eat, but an old woman brought them twelve loaves, which Joseph cut in pieces, and the Holy Graal made them sufficient for the 4000 people."

Compare to the Gospel of Mark 8:6-10,

> "He told the crowd to sit down on the ground. When he had taken the seven loaves and given thanks, he broke them and gave them to his disciples to set before the people, and they did so. They had a few small fish as well; he gave thanks for them also and told the disciples to distribute them. The people ate and were satisfied. Afterward the disciples picked up seven basketfuls of broken pieces that were left over. About four thousand men were present. And having sent them away, he got into the boat with his disciples and went to the region of Dalmanutha."

From this comparison, it appears that Jesus and Joseph of Arimathea share the exact same spiritual talent and level of mastery, creating the bounty and sustenance to feed and to bless. Joseph is portrayed as Jesus' equal. Both Jesus and Joseph broke or cut the bread. Both were able to feed the exact number of individuals, 4000 with only 7 or 12 loaves, and both demonstrated the power to use "God's secret" (the Grail).

What is curious is that this passage bears some similarity to Saying 96 of the *Gospel of Thomas*, a gospel not discovered until 1945, suggesting perhaps that some of Jesus' more secret sayings were known to the Cistercian writer. The saying compares the Father's kingdom to a woman who hid a little leaven in her dough and made it into large loaves of bread. It can be interpreted symbolically to represent God's little secret within us all, the Grail, that which multiples as creation and feeds the multitudes.

In the last chapter the quest, the form of the Grail is finally revealed, but not as the cup that caught the blood of Christ as it is identified in Robert Boron's version of the same tale. Instead, it is the dish that Jesus used at the Last Supper meal and we are told Joseph of Arimathea brought it with him to Britain. In this case, the Grail does not represent the blood royal (*Sangrael*) or Jesus' sacrifice, but instead it is his spiritual power and with it he could bring forth God's creative light to feed and nurture. Nowhere does it say in any of the Gospel accounts that the gospel character, Joseph of Arimathea, was present at the meal to have obtained the dish from the table. He is not amongst the twelve apostles. He doesn't appear on scene until after the Crucifixion when he asks Pilate for Jesus' body to prepare for its burial. And as the author very well knew, someone who was present at the table would have brought it with him. And that was Jesus himself.

The history and linage of the Grail Church is given in *La Queste del Saint Graal*, when one of the questing knights, Perceval, is met by a recluse (a lady) who tells him the histories of three chief tables.

> "After Christ's coming were three chief tables: first, that of Christ, at which the apostles often ate, and of which David spoke; second, the table of the Holy Graal, brought here by Joseph of Arimathea, when he came with 4000 poor companions."

According to this piece of the tale, not only did Joseph bring the Grail and the Grail Table, but he also transported the same 4000 poor companions that Jesus had taken into the desert, preached to and fed according to the Gospels of Mark (6:31) and Matthew (14:13). At this point in the grail quest the secret has been let out, but so contrary is this fact to Church canon and Gospel accounts that no one to this day could have pieced it together, except, of course, someone in the know. The passage also brings to light the enormous following that Jesus as Joseph of Arimathea had gathered, carrying with him thousands of souls whom, of course, he didn't literally bring with him to Gaul and Great Britain, but whom he would always carry in his heart. Jesus was ever expanding his flock through his continued ministry and they stretched from Judea, Egypt, Gaul to Albion (Great Britain). He was the shepherd of the true church— the Church of the Holy Grail. And it is likely he had a remarkable reputation as a spiritual leader, honored by those who gathered to hear his teachings.

The history of three chief tables mentions three time periods in the legacy of the Grail Church and a dynastic succession beginning with King David. The table that "David spoke of" referred to the account of the love bond and covenant between King David and Jonathan, the son of Saul. This relationship of kinship propelled David to offer the "kindness of God" to Jonathan's son Mephibosheth, a cripple, seating him at David's own table rather than eradicating Saul's line. The covenant symbolically united two tribes of Israel that of Benjamin and that of Jesse. In the same way, Christ's table as described in the Grail quest was merciful, inclusive and the place where a covenant was formed between the apostles, brothers and brethren. The Grail Table, as the second table, represented the continuation of Jesus' ministry in Gaul. It was the table of initiation where the dissemination of the mystical teachings from master to disciple was accomplished and where the covenant was continued. These rites of initiation and teachings were brought to Gaul by Jesus as Joseph of Arimathea and represented the second chapter of his ministry, hence the second table.

The third table is identified as the Round Table constructed upon the advice of Merlin. We are told in the story, that by its name, the Round Table signified the round world and the round canopy of the planets and elements in the firmament such as stars. The Round Table represented the continuation of Jesus' covenant through the leadership of Gilead (Galahad) and a group of knights who were connected by blood and who had earned the right and authority to be seated there. Though not disclosed, these knights were the founding members of the Knights Templar, as we will see in the next chapter.

Like Jesus, Joseph had disciples and his status glorified amongst them. The following passage reveals some interesting tidbits about the history of the Graal table, Joseph's disciples and his noble seat. It reads,

> "In the Graal table was a seat for Josephe, consecrated by our Lord's own hand. After a time two relatives of Josephe get envious of his leadership, and say they'll no longer be his disciples. One sits in Josephe's seat, and the earth swallows him up; whence the seat was called the Dreaded Seat."

Josephes who by legend is identified as the son of Joseph of Arimathea, and whom we now recognize was Jesus and Mary Magdalene's own son would have been the favored and beloved disciple. He was also the next in line, according to the rules of dynastic succession, to inherit his mother and father's legacy as his birthright. The passage mentions his seat was consecrated by the "Lords own hand", made Holy. For "the Lord" to have consecrated Josephes' seat at the Grail table "with his own hand" he would have had to have been there, alive and breathing at the time. This is not the image of the resurrected Gnostic Jesus, a spirit apparition blessing the seat, but is one of a "living spirit" in a human body, someone who had a hand in creating his own son. The author's secret unfolds, not in any way that is obvious but which makes the storyline incongruent enough with what we were told about Jesus' brief ministry and untimely death to perhaps spark some curiosity and raise some important questions. Although years and dates are not given, the events at the Grail Table are post crucifixion and in another land—Gaul. Joseph (Jesus) would have been in his forties at the time and his son Josephes a young boy.

The second interesting element in this history is the fact that two of Josephes (and Joseph's) relatives became envious of his position, tried to usurp his leadership and as stated, no longer wished to be disciples. My immediate question was which two relatives sought to usurp Josephes' position and could stake claim to that seat of authority? Three seconds after entertaining the question, an email popped into my inbox from a man named "James". The synchronicity was too obvious to dismiss, therefore, I could only assume that at some point during Jesus' ministry a rift between Jesus and James developed and James excused himself or was extricated from the group of disciples. The second relative was Jesus' youngest brother Juda.

In another of Perceval's adventures, a great secret is disclosed— Jesus had a son. The quest reads,

> "And on his way he looked and saw a serpent carrying by the neck a lion's cub in his teeth, and it stopped on the top of the mountain. After the serpent came a lion running and roaring and making such an outcry that it seemed to Perceval it was making lament for the cub which the serpent was carrying off."

As the adventure continues, Perceval heroically slays the dragon. The adult lion carries his cub back to its lair and returns to Perceval that night to lie by his side until dawn in gratitude for saving his cub. That morning two women, one seated on a dragon (Synogoga) and another seated on the lion (Ecclesia), appear for a brief encounter and a wise "good man" comes to explain to Perceval the meaning of this entire adventure. The passage reads,

> "She on the lion signifies the new dispensation, which is founded on the lion, that is on Jesus Christ, which by Him was established, raised up and shown forth to the view of all Christendom, and so that it might become the mirror and true light of all those who set their hearts upon the Trinity. And this lady is seated upon the lion, that is upon Jesus Christ, and she represents faith, hope, belief, and baptism."

What's significantly disclosed within this adventure and the interpretation that follows is that the lion represented Jesus Christ and, therefore, what else could be assumed but that the cub was his own son. After all, the lion carried it back to his lair. This subject of fact is never breeched again in the quest, but there is no doubt in my mind this was no careless mistake on the part of the writer. He was fully aware there was always a bloodline to protect and that Jesus had sired a son, the same son mentioned as belonging to Joseph of Arimathea, Josephes.

La Queste del Saint Graal, written in French, is only one of five volumes of what are often referred to as the *Vulgate Cycle* or the *Lancelot-Grail*, and most scholars consider them to have been written by the same pen. Like the vast majority of the Grail romances, the branches of this lyrical cycle were written about a very real order of knights—the infamous Knights Templar who in the 12th and 13tth centuries had already made their mark on the Christendom as warrior monks with an enormous bankroll to finance a profound spiritual mission. They had formed a Round Table in pursuit of spiritual gold and saw themselves as the inheritors of Joseph of Arimathea's (Jesus') legacy. It is enough to say that members of the Order had a hand in writing the volumes of the Vulgate Cycle and encoded many of the secrets about the origins of their tradition in its story.

Although *La Queste del Saint Graal* is attributed to Walter Map it is unlikely he was the true author. Scholars agree it was written in the 13th century but sometime after Walter Maps death in 1210. And because Walter Map had demonstrated that he was no fan of the Templars, having written uncomplimentary satiric pieces about the order, it would be a farfetched assertion that he would have written such a meaningful and complimentary allegory about the gallantry of these knights. Most scholars believe *The Vulgate Cycle* was written and compiled by Cistercian monks between 1215 and 1235, because Cistercian spirituality pervades the work. The Cistercians were the religious arm of the Knights Templar and both were under the guiding hand of Bernard Clairvaux, the most influential abbot in history and advisor to the Pope.

Whoever the writer was he was someone in the know. If not a member of the inner circle of the Knights Templar then someone closely associated with them, someone who knew the secret legacy of the Order and who would have participated in its initiations. The writer masterfully wove a tapestry of mythological elements mixed with secret facts to form a seemingly innocent allegorical tale that on the surface appeared aligned with the Church's doctrine. So well were his secrets concealed that no one outside of the Order would have suspected the heresy. The question arises whether the writer had any hopes the truth would eventually be unraveled. Not likely.   He probably inserted them into his epic quest for his own amusement laughing in the face of his oppressors, the papacy, in private. Or perhaps unconsciously he had hoped that at some point in time the secret would be unraveled.

For those not in the know, this tale of Christian heraldry and chivalry was little more than entertaining fiction, a sequel to other

Grail romances, such as *Perceval, le Conte du Graal* and the various other versions of quests for the Grail that gained a great deal of popularity in the 12th and 13th centuries. One might wonder however whether there were circles who understood that these allegories held a mystical tradition within them, one connected to the Knights Templar. The Grail romances met with a great deal of opposition from the Church and it is no wonder because, even though they seemed to uphold the Orthodox view at the same time they supported mystical tenets foreign to the Church's traditions.

As a member of an underground branch of Christianity, he did not write this quest in support of the Orthodox Church and its tenets. His was a heresy rooted in the authentic teachings of Jesus Christ, a legacy passed down through successive generations. For this author, the Grail was not analogous with the sacrament of the Eucharist, as most scholars assume because the elements on the surface appear Christianized. Instead, the Grail is a mystery that could not be separated from the Grail table and an altogether different branch of Christianity, the Grail Church, a church that embraced the mystical tenets of Gnosticism, Judaic traditions such as Cabalism, the keys of Solomon and other occult knowledge. The Grail Church disseminated Jesus' true teachings and spiritual rites (initiations), namely the Bridal Chamber initiation. The third table, the Round Table, seated members of the Order of the Knights Templar and the influential elite who supported them, those who could further their spiritual mission. It was their solemn oath to protect the bloodline, their mystical secrets as well as the details of the origins of their Order. The biggest secrets they vowed to protect beyond the bloodline inheritors was that Mary Magdalene, who they venerated as the Mother of their church, was Jesus' wife, companion and Divine Complement. They were well aware they sired children and that Jesus did not die on the cross, but continued his ministry in the third person, as Joseph of Arimathea.

The question arises: Did the Vatican know all along that Joseph of Arimathea was truly Jesus Christ? I would say yes. At the very least they knew he didn't die on the cross, as evidenced by Irenaeus' letter of 180 AD, in which he wrote that under the testimony of John the Apostle, Jesus was very much alive after the crucifixion and continued his ministry elsewhere. Despite this knowledge they moved in support of a counter history, a pseudo myth about the life, death and resurrection of a solar hero name Jesus Christ who brought salvation to all through his suffering, sacrifice and resurrection. In doing so, they secured their authority, positioned themselves politically and united a divided priesthood.

For some, the idea that Joseph of Arimathea was really Jesus Christ will seem preposterous, failing the test of reason for its lack of consistency with the Gospel narratives. But for others, who embrace the possibility, the truth could be illuminated further in perhaps even more miraculous ways than I have experienced. Jesus and Mary stand poised in heavenly dimensions, ready and eager to initiate the worthy spiritual sage into the mystery of the Grail, someone who can truly understand its mystery, and who like Perceval in Chretien de Troyes romance can ask and answer the important question: "Whom does the Grail serve."

Whom *does* it serve? The whole-kingdom. Who serves the Grail? One whose destiny it is to embark on the quest and proves his or her worthiness to receive its meaning and its spiritual power.

CHAPTER SEVEN
The Thomas Code

A destiny written in the stars must be realized on earth.

Looking again into the astrological synastry of Jesus and Mary Magdalene, we're offered a composite picture of not only the characteristics of their personalities but unique individual talents that would have blended nicely as they collaborated to fulfill their mutual destiny.

A set of complementary astrological aspects, revealing hidden talents, offers clues to how Jesus and Mary's divine destiny could have been actualized. As two enlightened and progressive spiritual teachers with a radical message to convey, the written word was a likely vehicle for disseminating their wisdom. As mentioned in another chapter, Mary's talents as a writer are brought into view when we consider the aspects, Pluto in Virgo trine Venus conjunct Mercury in Capricorn that describe an intelligent and articulate woman who would have been driven to write transformative philosophical material. The position of Jupiter at 29 degrees Gemini in Mary's natal chart, would add even more energy to her chart for writing, helping her to express her brilliance. With these talents, she could have easily expressed the ideologies of her husband in eloquent language and added her own lengthy and meaningful dialogue to the body of his spiritual insights. She would have been an eloquent writer with a strong vocabulary, capable of defining and clarifying the language, something necessary when trying to convey spiritual principles of a complex nature. With these planetary influences supporting her desire to convey their ideas, it's unlikely that she wouldn't have had the urge to write. She would have been driven to it and to also encourage Jesus to offer his knowledge and teachings in writing. With his Mercury trine Neptune, Jesus would have been afforded the same talent. He was capable of writing a poignant and meaningful spiritual dialogue. We might imagine that they inspired each other's thoughts and ideas to such an extent that writing would have been a pleasurable and inspiring experience, one they would have been passionate about. It's likely that a good part of Mary's divine destiny was to offer a written dialogue of their teachings, the mysteries of the Kingdom within, as a legacy for humanity. And with her husband's encouragement, she, too, probably stepped into the role of a spiritual teacher in later years, cultivating her own style to convey her ideas and revelations, and transcribing them into a written dialogue that could be disseminated further.   Out of their experiences and love for God, a body of wisdom emerged that could point others to the path of self-realization and tri-unity with God. It was their mandate as self-realized examples to minister together, to offer a written legacy and to gather initiates who could also spread the teachings.

If it was their destiny together to write a gospel of truth, one might naturally wonder where these writings of Mary and Jesus are now. We know that there was a Gospel of Mary among the codices found in Egypt in 1945, amounting to a few pages of papyrus, a sparse representation of what she would have been compelled to write. The Gospel of Mary dates back to the second century, when Gnostic sects such as Manichean writers were spreading their philosophies and ideology in competition with the Paulists. Therefore, it is not possible it was written by Mary. The idea of a dialogue between the risen Jesus Christ and Mary Magdalene before an audience of disciples, as if she were channeling the ascended Jesus, seems a bit contrived, especially in light of the fact that Jesus was still very much alive and with Mary in exile. And its content is too dissimilar to the body of Jesus' authentic teachings, conveying instead a doctrine of wisdom about the soul and its nature that's more characteristic of Manichean doctrine and other Gnostic writings.

Lacking authentic writings of Jesus Christ and Mary Magdalene, we're left with the testimony of four Gospels, Luke, Matthew, Mark and John, the earliest having been written presumably in about 60 AD. Devoid of the kind of mystical truths that could define the inner mysteries of the Bridal Chamber, these gospels support instead a religious ideology that celebrates a resurrected messiah, a Son of God, whose offering was a salvation plan guaranteed by his personal sacrifice and suffering on the cross. Given that a literal death and resurrection were aborted and that a different destiny plan was in place, we're left to wonder what the true legacy they left was, outside of the handful of parables and sayings that Jesus disseminated during a brief ministry in Judea, most of which have been corrupted.

We must first recognize that Jesus' resurrection was a transcendent experience attained through his living body, not through literal death. He received a mysterious initiation in the Bridal Chamber of his Stellar Heart, one that uplifted and transformed his soul and consciousness. Through this initiation within his Stellar Heart, he was reborn to his divinity. He'd achieved the miracle of complete transfiguration and tri-unity with God and was reborn as Christ, a godman. What was also resurrected into clearer definition was the spirit-to-spirit and soul-to-soul communion with Mary Magdalene, his twin complement, as well as the acknowledgment that she had saved his life through her devotion, prayers and even her monetary inheritance. This event must have turned his mind and heart around, leading him to embrace Mary as savior and faithful servant to his spiritual evolution, bringing new meaning to his life and any future mission. The deepest memory of their soul bond had been opened up and with it the greater spiritual mission. He was forced to recognize the feminine face of God in the face of his Divine Complement, and his future mission demanded a greater commitment to her. What would be their future contribution? The answer lies in another gospel, the Gospel of Thomas.

The Gospel of Thomas was unearthed about 300 miles outside Cairo near the Valley of the Kings in 1945 and its papyrus is thought to date to about 350 AD. The papyrus of Coptic texts that makes up the 13 codices in the Nag Hammadi Library, of which the Gospel of Thomas is one, was thought to have been translated from its original Greek to Coptic by Gnostic monks who may have hidden the leather-bound sheets in caves to protect them. The Gospel of Thomas itself, however, was written much earlier, perhaps as early as 43 AD, well within the lifetimes of Jesus and Mary Magdalene. It is therefore the oldest testament of Jesus Christ, preceding Mark, Matthew, Luke and John, yet it's been excluded from the New Testament, probably because its mystical tenets didn't support the emerging doctrine of Orthodox Christianity. Today, it's considered to be Gnostic in origin, probably because it was discovered among other Gnostic writings such as *The Sophia of Jesus Christ* and *The Gospel of Truth* and because its tenets are consistent with a self-realizing path to enlightened consciousness.

However, the sayings and parables of the Gospel of Thomas lack much of the mystical terminology of other Gnostic writers of the 2nd century, terms such as *aeons, demiuge, pleroma* and *archons*, all of which are important to the Gnostic doctrine.

Of the Gospel of Thomas Cyril of Jerusalem, a bishop of the 4th century who was later venerated as a saint wrote, "*Let none read the gospel according to Thomas, for it is the work, not of one of the twelve apostles, but of one of Mani's three wicked disciples.*" Mani was a prophet born in Persia in 215 AD from whose beliefs Manicheanism developed. As a sect of Christianity that incorporated the beliefs of Gnosticism, Mithraism and Judaism, and its prophet Mani, it was deemed a heretical religion, and Mani himself was persecuted and crucified. Associating the Gospel of Thomas with Manicheanism, however, ignores the fact that the Gospel of Thomas preceded Mani by about 150 years.

Of the 114 sayings in the Gospel of Thomas, 21 or more, in one form or another, are found in Mark, adapted into an embellished narrative. There has been a great deal of argument among theologians and scholars as to whether Mark drew from the Gospel of Thomas as the basis of his gospel or whether Thomas drew from Mark. Because Mark contains allegorical narratives that appear to embellish the more primitive, raw nature of the sayings of the Gospel of Thomas, it's more plausible to say Mark drew from Thomas. For instance, compare saying 31 of Thomas:

> "No Prophet is acceptable in his own village; a physician does not heal those who know him."

with Mark 6:1-6 –

> "And he went out from thence, and came into his own country; and his disciples follow him.
>
> And when the Sabbath day was come, he began to teach in the synagogue: and many hearing him were astonished, saying, From whence hath this man these things? And what wisdom is this, which is given unto him, that even such mighty works are wrought by his hands?
>
> Is not this the carpenter, the son of Mary, the brother of James, and Joses, and of Juda, and Simon? And are not his sisters here with us?

And they were offended at him.

But Jesus, said unto them, A prophet is not without honour, but in his own country, and among his own kin, and in his own house. And he could there do no mighty work, save that he laid his hands upon a few sick folk, and healed them. And he marvelled because of their unbelief. And he went round about the villages, teaching."

The Mark passage renders the Thomas saying a long narrative, an embellishment put into the context of a day in the life of Jesus when he meets criticism while ministering to his own community.

Another example of an embellished dialogue is Mark 7:14-23, probably derived from a combination of two sayings in Thomas, 14 and 45, which deal with Jesus' challenge of the religious rules concerning food. Saying 14 of Thomas reads —

"Jesus said to them, 'If you fast, you will give rise to sin for yourselves; and if you pray you will be condemned; and if you give alms, you will do harm to your spirits. When you go into any land and walk about in the districts, if they receive you, eat what they will set before you, and heal the sick among them. For what goes into your mouth will not defile you, but that which issues from your mouth — it is that which will defile you."

Compare to Mark 7: 14-23 —

"Again Jesus called the crowd to him and said, 'Listen to me, everyone, and understand this. Nothing outside a man can make him 'unclean' by going into him. Rather, it is what comes out of a man that makes him 'unclean."

"After he had left the crowd and entered the house, his disciples asked him about this parable. "Are you so dull?" he asked. "Don't you see that nothing that enters a man from the outside can make him 'unclean'? For it doesn't go into his heart but into his stomach, and then out of his body." (In saying this, Jesus declared all foods "clean.") He went on: "What comes out of a man is what makes him 'unclean.' For from within, out of men's hearts, come evil thoughts, sexual immorality, theft, murder, adultery, greed, malice, deceit, lewdness, envy, slander, arrogance and folly. All these evils come from inside and make a man 'unclean'. "

These two comparative examples, out of some twenty or so

others, demonstrate that Mark borrowed from Thomas in constructing his narrative Gospel and that he took great creative liberty in rendering the sayings into a narrative embellishment that in some instances over amplified Jesus' teaching and in other instances changed the meaning entirely. Those who continue to insist and argue that Mark preceded Thomas seem to ignore all logic. Why would the author of Thomas extract one simple sentence from a whole narrative on the subject in Mark, an already widely circulated Gospel, and call it a secret teaching? What Mark accomplished was to take the Thomas saying and add his own lengthy thoughts on the topic as well as to tell a fantastic tale to provide a context. Mark was merely meeting the challenge of the Gospel of Thomas: *"And He said: " Whoever finds the meaning of these words will not taste death."* And in Mark's mind, Jesus meant that what would defile a person was a long list of evil and unclean thoughts.

The source of the Gospel of Thomas has been debated. The first line reads, *"These are the secret words that the living Jesus spoke and Didymus Judas Thomas wrote down."* Herein lies one of the most mysterious aspects of the Gospel, the identity of its author. Both the names Thomas and Didymus mean "twin," and Judas in Hebrew means "praised" or 'praised one." Some Christian scholars and theologians assume that the writer was attributing the gospel to the Thomas who's often called "Doubting Thomas" and mentioned in the Gospel of John in three places but not by the other three Gospel writers. Thomas' identity is never well defined as an apostle. Others have assumed that Thomas' true identity was Jesus' brother James, but it seems unlikely that he would have called himself a twin, given that he was more commonly referred to as the "lesser" brother or, in other words, the younger brother of Jesus.

Was Thomas a pseudo-identity taken by Mary Magdalene? This was my beginning hypothesis. The fact that the word "twin" is twice stated in the name of the writer seemed an oddity to me. Strung together, the name translates into "Twin Praised Twin." The most likely person to be identified as Jesus' twin would have been Mary Magdalene, his sacred sister-bride and twin flame. I considered that she may have wished to disclose the co-authorship of this Gospel in a code of hidden meanings, making the author as much a mystery as the sayings and parables themselves. As stated in the first line, she would have laboriously written down her beloved's words to offer as a gospel of truth, the authentic teachings of the inner mysteries that Jesus had delivered to his disciples, of whom she was considered the most important one. The second thought I had was that perhaps Jesus himself was the author, not seeking to disclose his identity but to praise Mary by acknowledging her as his beloved twin, a proclamation in the vein of "long live the King."

A second perplexing fact is that the three names have origins in three different languages and that the first name, Didymus, and the last, Thomas, aren't names at all but nouns; the Greek *Didymus* means "twin," the Aramaic *Thomas* also means "twin," and the Hebrew *Juda* means "praised". The choice of name appears to have been well-thought-out and deliberately inserted and hints at a mysterious hidden meaning, one that would incite further investigation and inquiry, a code that one day might authenticate the author.

Was the author of this gospel Mary Magdalene or perhaps Jesus himself?

My intuitive query turned into a deliberate quest to verify my first and strongest theory that Mary Magdalene was the author of the Gospel of Thomas. I set out on a vision quest in the creative field of a waking dream, knowing that Jesus and Mary would probably give me the answers through verifying signs and synchronistic messages in much the same way they had shown me their birth dates. I went shopping for signs at a marketplace not far from my home. I walked up to the table of a vendor selling unframed oil paintings of Maui landscapes and seascapes and talked with her for a while as I sifted through the canvases admiring the artwork. I immediately noticed the artist's signature on one of the paintings. It read 'Thomas J'. I thought to myself "J" for Jesus, "Oh, my God, it was Jesus who wrote the Gospel of Thomas." The adjoining vendor table was that of a woman, with a French accent. We also chatted for a few moments and she told me that she was from a little coastal town in Provence, the South of France, called Biaritz. Putting two and two together I gathered that Jesus wrote the Gospel of Thomas while in Gaul, which, by the way, would support a consensus of scholarship supporting an earlier date than any of the other gospels for the Gospel of Thomas.

My second hypothesis I thought was therefore correct. Jesus had penned the Gospel of Thomas. What happened next in the field of my waking dream, with Jesus and Mary guiding the way, was nothing short of a flurry of confirming signs assuring me that I had discovered the truth. The most profound sign was a delivery truck for a suntan-oil company that read "Secret Revealed." It was later revealed to me that there truly was a disciple named Thomas who was martyred sometime before Jesus commenced in putting his sayings into a list. In fact, he was the youngest and Jesus' favorite. I must mention also that during the months preceding my research, I'd been pointed toward the Gospel of Thomas numerous times. In fact, years before, I experienced a great number of synchronicities with the name Thomas. For example, Thomas is the name of the astrologer who helped me to construct the natal charts of Jesus and Mary. I've come to realize that the early synchronicities were pointing me to the Gospel of Thomas all along so that I might draw from its wisdom and, more important, identify its author.

The Gospel of Thomas consists of 114 sayings and parables, 21 of which are recognizable variations on the parables or sayings in the canonical Gospels. Described as "secrets" by the author (Jesus), they rely on valid translation and insightful interpretation to decipher the hidden meaning of each saying. The first saying begins a contemplative quest for truth. Jesus says, *"Whoever finds the interpretation of these sayings will not taste death."* —Saying 1 GTh.

The promise here is not of literal immortality of the body but of a transcendent experience of awakening outside what Jesus considers death, spiritual deadness arising from an unawakened heart and mind. The world is described as dead or "a corpse" in several other passages because consciousness must be raised to experience the true Kingdom. In Jesus' view, one's authentic self must be resurrected if one is to witness the magic and meaning of life and be reborn embodying his spirit. Through contemplation of his words, one is initiated into the mystery of the Kingdom that is spread out in full view after the heart is awakened.

The second passage represents the criteria for awakening and the resulting conflict that ushers in the boom: the awakening to the Kingdom. *"Let whoever seeks not cease from his seeking until he finds. When he finds, he will be troubled. When he is troubled, he will marvel and will reign over all."* The conflict arises when confronting one's previous illusionary perceptions of self and the material world, a confrontation necessary to awakening out of ignorance and unconsciousness into enlightenment. The world no longer makes sense or has the same order to it. Much like when Dorothy arrived in the Kingdom of Oz and said, "I don't think we're in Kansas anymore, Toto," the awakened initiate now marvels at the beauty and the greater meaning in it all. *"And will reign over all"* points to the power of the master who realizes that the creation is of his own making, created out of his mind and heart. He or she will have great power over his dominion, the creative field of his life.

Within this gospel are also some ten or more remarkable sayings describing in some way the mystery of the sacred union, "making the two one" and reference to the Bridal Chamber and Jesus as bridegroom. Nowhere in the four canonical Gospels of the New Testament have any of these sayings been included. In Thomas, the mystery of sacred union is given great weight, and it's reasonable to conclude that the mystery of the Bridal Chamber was made paramount in Jesus' teachings. For Jesus, this mystery had been realized and achieved. He'd become the Son of God, a "Son of the Bridal Chamber," not through divine birth but by successfully resolving the split in his soul, reconciling the fall, and returning to a complete realization of the Stellar Promise, his tri-unity with God through the bond with his beloved Mary Magdalene. As a result, he was more than an enlightened teacher – he was Christ, a god man.

In comparing some of the parables in the Gospel of Thomas with parallel ones in the four canonical Gospels (those covering the same topic or using similar metaphors), one is confronted immediately with a stark contrast in meaning.

Compare, for instance, Thomas 8 SV with Matthew 13:47-50 NIV. Thomas 8 SV reads:

> "And Jesus said, 'The person is like a wise fisherman who cast his net into the sea and drew it up from the sea full of little fish. Among them the wise fisherman discovered a fine large fish. He threw all the little fish back into the sea, and easily chose the large fish. Anyone here with two good ears had better listen!"

In other words, the enlightened and wise man chooses only that which will sustain him and his mission and lets go of that which has not yet grown to maturity and fullness. It may also prove to be a great deal more work to clean a net full of small fish than to clean one big one, and one needs no more than what will sustain him— perhaps a lesson against greed. Considering that Jesus was instructing his disciples on how to carry forward his ministry, he probably meant that it would be more advantageous to convert an influential person (big fish) in the community than to gather a large group of converts who had little influence.

In contrast, Matthew 13:47-50 NIV reads:

> "Once again, the kingdom of heaven is like a net that was let down into the lake and caught all kinds of fish. When it was full, the fishermen pulled it up on the shore. Then they sat down and collected the good fish in baskets, but threw the bad away. This is how it will be at the end of the age. The angels will come and separate the wicked from the righteous and throw them into the fiery furnace, where there will be weeping and gnashing of teeth."

In Matthew, we have a moral allegory that compares the net to the Kingdom of Heaven, and the fishermen are the angels sent down by God the Father to separate the good from the bad. Here the meaning supports an altogether different doctrine and religious ideology, pertaining to the last judgment in which God as the fisherman judges humanity. Was this what Jesus intended to convey?

Jesus offers a different view of the Kingdom of the father. *"The Kingdom of the father is like a woman who took a little leaven, hid it in dough and made it into large loaves"*(saying 96, GTh*)*. In this saying, God is both Father and Mother (Goddess), whose yeast represents the mystery elixir of divine magic that multiplies the dough into large loaves. It is enough to sustain everyone. Jesus adds in Thomas 113, *"The kingdom of the father is spread out on the earth and people do not see it."*

The Orthodox Christian view of the Kingdom of God is that of an otherworldly dimension from which we're separated and from where God judges us, while Jesus' view sees the kingdom as interfacing with the material world—God is in everything as expressed in, *"…Split a piece of wood: I am there. Lift a stone, and you will find me there."* (Saying 77: GTh). For Jesus, God is both father and mother, offering spiritual illumination as well as material sustenance. These two views are in opposition to each other, and it's likely that the mystical philosophy of Jesus threatened the aims of the architects of Christianity who sought to impose their own budding ideology onto their community. Therefore, the four Gospels were reconstructions of both Jesus' image and his words to support the aims of the creators of a new religion, one that was already gaining popularity through oral tradition.

As an example of the extent to which translation can alter meaning and, furthermore, how other Gospel writers' rewordings and embellishments of the authentic teachings could corrupt them entirely, another saying appears in both Thomas and Mark relating to the "the stone the builders rejected." Thomas 66 reads, *"Show me the stone the builders rejected, it is the cornerstone."* The most common Orthodox Christian interpretation is that Jesus is the rejected stone, but one must ask why Jesus would ask anyone to point out ("show me") the stone if it was he that he was referring to.

In another translation of the same saying, Patterson and Meyer (1992) replace *cornerstone* with *keystone*, which alters the meaning of the saying significantly because *cornerstone* applies to the foundation of a structure, while the keystone is the last wedge-shaped piece of an arch regarded as binding the whole. Both are meaningful metaphors when applying them to the structure of enlightened consciousness, the realized God-self, and necessary to understanding God's nature. But which is the correct translation?

To complicate the interpretation further, a comparison between Mark and Thomas adds yet another translation to ponder: Mark 1:10 reads,

> "Have you not read this scripture: `The very stone which the builders rejected has become the head of the corner; this was the Lord's doing, and it is marvelous in our eyes'?"

This embellishment may seem innocent, but it changes the meaning as well as the entire message of the saying. In still another translation of Mark, the saying reads, *"Haven't you read this scripture: "The stone the builders rejected has become the capstone."* The capstone completes the structure at the top of a building and, in the building of the temple, may have been carved with decorative symbols. The use of *capstone* here supports an image of Jesus as the crowning glory of God, someone idealized but never realized.

Keystone, cornerstone, head of the corner, capstone – which metaphor is it? The varied translations of this one saying should raise suspicion about the motives of the writers, translators or editors who gave themselves free license to edit meaning, changing the authentic teachings of Christ. Was it perhaps that they were opposed to Jesus' authentic teachings, as they didn't support their own beliefs? An innocent but faulty translation like that of Patterson and Meyer (*keystone* from *cornerstone*) is one thing, but the kind of editing that purposefully changes the meaning to support a whole different doctrine like the two translation examples of Mark amounts to the robbery of the authentic words and teachings of Christ.

Jesus may have been restating Psalm 118 verse 22, and referring to the building of the sacred temple, the temple of Solomon, when he wrote this piece of metaphoric wisdom. The temple represented a structure of concise measurement used for initiation rites aimed at attaining consciousness of the Godhead. Ancient masons carefully constructed the temple according to a sacred form of mystical architecture consisting of exact measurements and cubical proportion. The structure was both an art and a science arising from mystical secrets. The temple represented the structure of God. Each stone supporting the structure was specifically chosen, and many would naturally be rejected and judged as not supporting its design. As a metaphor, the rejected stone did not conform to the structure and conceptualization of the Godhead or was deemed unnecessary in the attainment of spiritual illumination. The stone that was rejected was a metaphor for some aspect of God that had been rejected again and again in the doctrines of Judaism, something that may be within us all and has been ignored. Humanity itself was therefore suffering from its own ignorance, having discarded a significant piece of understanding of the nature of God. Jesus comments on this ignorance when he says, *"Show me the stone the builders rejected, it is the cornerstone."*

I muddled through the different translations and versions of the saying for more than four hours and labored over whether *keystone* or *cornerstone* was the authentic translation for the Gospel of Thomas. After considering several reasonable answers, I decided to let go, knowing the meaning would eventually be illuminated through divine inspiration. I was given two clues, an arrow pointing downward and the name "Sophia," both arriving by way of one meaningful synchronistic event. With these two clues I easily recognized that *cornerstone* was the correct translation. The cornerstone was therefore the Divine Feminine, Sophia (Goddess of Wisdom), who points us downward to retrieve the mystery of God within the material. To the Kabbalist's she is Shekinah at the foundation and bottom of the Tree of Life. She is the container of God's wisdom, the all-knowing feminine who derives her knowledge from the intuitive understanding that God and nature are one. She would most likely be the stone rejected by those seeking illumination of God's intelligence through an ascending path to the Godhead, ignoring God within the bosom of womanhood and within every piece of experience on Earth. Feminine wisdom is the cornerstone of spiritual attainment, the horizontal axis of the cross, the womb of mankind and the goddessness within. For Jesus, Mary was his cornerstone, the earthy Goddess who helped him to ground his spiritual mission. It was Mary's Leo moon and Venus in Capricorn qualities that grounded Jesus' Neptunian and Piscean mind to appreciate the earthbound material experience. She was his Sophia, and he undoubtedly saw her as supporting the foundation of his life and his spirit. She was a cornerstone of his wisdom, and she was whom he appreciated most.

Jesus' image and voice was drastically altered by the four Gospel writers. An example of how seemingly minor redactions of his words altered Jesus' image as well as the teaching style he employed, can be seen in the parallel by Luke to Thomas Saying 26. Thomas reads,

> "You see the splinter in your brother's eye but you do not see the plank in your own eye. When you have taken the plank out of your own eye, then you will be able to see and remove the splinter from your brother's eye."

The saying, which both Luke and Mathew paraphrased and embellished, is reworded as a statement against judging others. For instance. Luke 6: 41-42 reads,

> "Why do you look at the speck of sawdust in your brother's eye and pay no attention to the plank in your own eye? How can you say to your brother, 'Brother, let me take the speck out of your eye,' when you yourself fail to see the plank in your own eye? You hypocrite, first take the plank out of your eye, and then you will see clearly to remove the speck from your brother's eye."

As we see, Luke's redaction of the Thomas saying changes Jesus' voice from a pragmatic teacher who chooses his words carefully to a dogmatic and judgmental master who on occasion enjoys lambasting his disciples. However, this paraphrasing not only significantly alters the tone Jesus uses to deliver his teaching but also may have altered the intention and meaning behind Jesus' words. Rather than a metaphorical condemnation about judging others, perhaps Jesus was merely stressing the need to work on yourself before diving in to help someone else and mentioning that it is often easier to "see" someone else's blocks and imperfections than your own. Furthermore, once you remove your own blocks you can see more clearly the beauty in who is in front of you. Jesus seems to have been forcing his disciples back on the path of developing insight into themselves, a familiar tenet of his teaching:

> "…When you come to know yourselves, then you will become known, and you will realize that it is you who are the sons of the living father. But if you will not know yourselves, you dwell in poverty and it is you who are that poverty." (Saying 3 –GTh).

The key to deciphering the intended meaning of the sayings lies in one's ability to see behind and beyond the words with keen intuitive insight and, if awakened enough, through Jesus' clarifying transmissions. But even with great insight, many of the sayings in the Gospel of Thomas are extremely difficult to decipher and perplexing to most. For instance, Saying 11 of Thomas that reads:

> Jesus said, "This heaven will pass away, and the one above it will pass away. And the dead are not alive, and the living will not die. In the days when you used to ingest dead, you made them alive. When you are in the light, what will you do? On the day that you were one, you made two. And when you are two, what will you do?"

The Thomas saying is a riddle that is difficult to comprehend without knowledge of the Bridal Chamber mystery and initiation. Jesus' words suggest there is a level of consciousness (heaven) above the one his disciples had awakened to and this other level too will pass away in favor of the ultimate realization of God as the light. In Jesus' view, when we are a neophyte in our evolution we consume what is dead (ignorance) and make it alive, meaning we believe the fallacies of prevailing beliefs to be the truth until that time when we have risen in consciousness to stand in God's light. We then become one, experiencing our unity with the consciousness of God, and we walk with God as "two".

Even within the Gospel of Thomas there were errors in translation and of omission. And it's likely that overzealous monks deliberately expunged a few sayings from the original Greek version. However, Jesus assured me that 89 percent of what remains of the sayings that make up the Gospel of Thomas is authentic transcription of his original text. With this in mind, and recognizing that most of the parables and sayings that are key to his teachings had been changed in the other Gospels to such an extent that they no longer represent his words, it's clear that we have very little left of Jesus' authentic teachings to reconstruct the path he wanted us to follow. We must understand the man, his personality, the nature of his illuminating experiences, his struggles, his passions and his destiny to understand the full scope of his message in the Gospel of Thomas. To understand his parables and his sayings, his wisdom must touch our hearts. To guess at their meaning without his guiding hand is futile, as I all too well know from my own experience with the metaphor of the cornerstone.

When reading the Gospel of Thomas, we must acknowledge that Jesus' intent in writing it was to disclose and convey a secret doctrine of mysteries that could be deciphered by those few who were touched deeply by the worth of his wisdom. Those who relentlessly sought higher truth and the hidden meaning in his words would become initiates in his teachings. From there they must then seek further answers by journeying within to unearth the keys to the kingdom of the heart and then serve their greatest mission by initiating others.

Through words filled with metaphoric content, we're offered a glimpse of the method Jesus chose to initiate his disciples, through a secret language that encouraged pondering of the deeper meaning of life and that, ultimately, would awaken them to the hidden kingdom of God within the material world. I offer this saying from the Gospel of Thomas as an example of Jesus' method:

> "Recognize what is in front of your face, and what is concealed will be revealed to you. For there is nothing hidden that will not be disclosed." — Saying 6, Gospel of Thomas

His parables appear to be intended to awaken his initiates as much as to inspire them. From the Gospel of Thomas, the following passage (Saying 108) conveys this intention well: *"Whoever drinks from my mouth will be as I am, and I shall be that person, and the hidden things will be revealed to that person."*

With this statement, which requires some unraveling to understand, what should appear obvious is that Jesus wished his initiates to take in his words and open their hearts to receive his consciousness through transmission, a communion of sorts. His words were meant to enlighten and to convey consciousness, a higher level of truth igniting the hearts of the initiates so that they may know that they, too, could accomplish and experience what Jesus had. They could thereby end the separation that had denied them access to the hidden dimensions of spirit. They could be enlightened. Jesus was in the business of consciousness-raising, not merely instilling faith in a supreme being whose promise of salvation was only in the afterlife. Within the Gospel of Thomas are the words of a self-realized Christ evoking the Christ within us all. Saying 24:

> "His disciples said, "Show us the place where you are, for we must seek it."
>
> He said to them, "Whoever has ears to hear let him hear. There is light within a man of light and it illuminates the whole world. When it does not shine, there is darkness."

We must also recognize that, above all, by choosing the code name "Didymus Judas Thomas," Jesus wished to acknowledge and praise his beloved twin, Mary Magdalene. It's clear to me that Jesus, as a twin complement praising his twin, was also revealing the deepest mystery of all: the Stellar Promise, the root connection and promise between twin complements. As a son of the Bridal Chamber, he'd revisited this root, the miracle that God created in the beginning, and touched the signature in his heart where his beloved Mary dwelled inside him. In their hearts, they were in unity with each other and in tri-unity with God. It's likely that Jesus wanted to convey what had been illuminated to him, that without honoring her as his equal complement, his kingdom was only half a kingdom – no kingdom at all.

It is, of course, hard to accept that Jesus and Mary probably wrote numerous authentic Gospels and diaries to leave as a written legacy of their teachings and that they were probably lost, hidden or, worse yet, destroyed. Their combined wisdom might have offered humanity keys to understanding the origins of our spirit, the true nature of human evolution and, most important, the steps of initiation into the Bridal Chamber. With their keys of knowledge, we would have embraced a different image of God, one that's both male and female and one that could be realized through an inner awakening to our unified spirit. As Jesus said, *"He who knows all but fails to know himself lacks everything."* — Thomas 67.

And we would have had an accurate account of their history, where they lived, the children they sired and many details of the course their lives took. Perhaps some writings are preserved and hidden. I like to imagine that diaries or other Coptic texts like the Gospel of Thomas are hidden below the roots of an ancient tree in a grove in Scotland or perhaps in Ireland, where Jesus and Mary lived out their senior years. If not, perhaps it's enough to know that their legacy was written in the stars and that they continue to be connected to our hearts, guiding those who seek spiritual understanding and who will listen for the voices that echo from within   After all, it was Jesus' solemn oath and promise to remain with humanity till the end of times. He and Mary intervene in matters of the heart and help those who are in search of their greater purpose. Jesus reminds us,*"Whoever searches will find. It will be opened to him."* — Thomas Saying 94.

.

CHAPTER EIGHT
The Inheritors of the Grail

History and mythology are always interwoven.

In September of 1997, approximately two weeks after the death of Princess Diana, I had a remarkable dream about a legacy passed from mother to son — Diana to Harry.

In the dream, I was sitting in the back seat of a limousine with young Prince Harry who at the time was only 12 years of age, barely an adolescent. I was a special companion and caregiver to the Prince looking out for his emotional wellbeing since the death of his mother. I pulled out a greeting card from my purse and gifted it too him. Harry smiled in response to a moveable humorous clown that popped up from the card. There was a cheerful greeting written inside. As his caregiver, I was naturally concerned about his emotional state. With the loss of his mother Princess Diana, who had tragically died in a car crash on the fateful night of August 31st the same year, I thought his spirit and soul needed tending, mothering from someone deeply connected to him. Even though our paths in this life had never crossed our souls were old friends. It seemed that our hearts had grown fond of each other from lifetimes before, his soul a very familiar one to my own. I wanted to lift his spirits and spend some time communicating heart-felt love.

In the next scene of the dream, we arrived at Buckingham Palace and made our way through a grand foyer and emerged in a formal dining room. The Queen greeted us with what might be described as a poker face, appearing emotionally detached, stiff and unwelcoming. Harry walked straight up to her and boldly asked for his silver christening cup, a gift from his mother at the time of his baptism. The Queen retrieved it and Harry and I sat at the long table polishing it with a soft cloth. We removed the tarnish from years of neglect.

Even at the time of the dream, I realized this was no ordinary dream. It represented a communion and communication between two souls, a dream that knew no boundaries despite the long distance geographically between the dreamers. Harry and I were as close as if we were truly in the same car or in the same room which in this case was a grand dining hall, with me nurturing his grieving heart and pointing him towards his legacy and a destiny. Dream researchers, like myself, refer to dreams like this one as telepathic dreams, as they involve a sixth sense and represent communications at psychic and spiritual dimensions. Two dreamers come together at an invisible dimension, a dreamscape, touch each other's consciousness for a personal and divine purpose. They commune to heal one another, offer a helping hand of sorts and usually communicate something important. For Harry, my intercession represented a call to his soul to begin his quest for the Holy Grail, perhaps not consciously at first but with time doors would open for him to advance spiritually. He would embark on a unique destiny path of service, one as fulfilling as Diana's was for her. And true to what my intuition told me at the time, Harry would follow in his mother's footsteps at least for a time. In 2004, he became inspired to compassionately serve Aids orphans and other vulnerable children by funding community projects providing needed services in Africa. I remember being delighted after seeing a documentary about his mission in Africa, realizing full well he was becoming his mother's son, touching children compassionately and allowing their desperate need for help to transform him. The charity formed in honor of his mother is called Sentehale, which means "forget me not" in the local language. Through this charity he would keep his mother's memory alive replicating her selfless service and devotion to impoverished and suffering children. Harry has continued on with his charity and in the beginning of 2010 could be seen riding his polo horse in a special match to raise needed funds for his charity. Demonstrating his commitment to his mother's cause, a mishap that caused his horse to go down, resulted with his displaying a fit of anger because he thought he had lost a sizable $100,000 donation, a bet that he could stay on his horse. Fortunately, the generous gentleman made good his promise of the donation, because the horse went down rather than Harry having fallen off.

As with the questing hero Perceval, Harry was called to ask himself, " *To whom the Grail serves"* and to answer the question by stepping into his mission full-heartedly. My dream in some ways was a prophecy commenting on Harry's devotion to his mother's heart, his worthiness and innate spiritual tendencies. Undoubtedly, he is an advanced soul whose light shines brighter than his brother

William's who has been groomed by his grandmother, Queen Elizabeth, to inherit the monarchy. As the worthy initiate Harry is likely to continue to rise above his brother and not acquiesce to the pressure to conform to a model of a monarchy that is viewed as cold hearted. He knows, as did his mother Diana, that he must serve as an open vessel of love giving generously his time, energy as well as money.

The Grail object in this case was a tarnished silver Christening cup representing Harry's Christian roots but more importantly his connection to the feminine vessel that bore him. Diana embodied the goddess, as a life giving spirit who possessed a compassionate style of care giving, sincerity and generosity, but whose image as seen through the eyes of the Windsor's, her husband Charles, the Queen and Prince Philip was less than complementary. Diana was considered an embarrassment for her outspokenness. Her emotional fragility was something the Windsor's could not handle or tolerate. Hard as they tried to keep her in the shadows, she rose and shone before the public who adored her. The tarnished patina of the cup that Harry and I carefully removed represented centuries of shame burdening womanhood and the tarnished image of Diana's own feminine soul. Silver is the metal often associated with the feminine principle where as gold is viewed as masculine. Harry, who was deeply connected to his mother, was to value womanhood above all and the feminine qualities his mother embodied and modeled through her charity work.

Not only did the Grail object symbolize the feminine vessel, but it also represented the Sangrael, the royal blood running through Harry's veins. Not his lineage from the Windsors who were self-proclaimed monarchs, but the true blood royal vine branching from Diana's descendants of the Royal House of Stuart who gave England four kings, James I, Charles I, Charles II, and James II. As a Spencer, her vine connected her to the Merovingians, the Fisher Kings who ruled the Franks in the 5th Century and before that to Jesus and Mary Magdalene. With the recent birth of George Alexander Louis to William and Kate (Duke and Duchess of Cambridge), on July 22, 2013, a new *Desposyni* (Heirs to the Lord) becomes 4th in line to inherit the throne as King of England. But perhaps more meaningful is the fact that he was born on Mary Magdalene's Feast Day, an auspicious day to honor his bloodline lineage to Mary Magdalene through his grandmother, Princess Diana—another Goddess of Love.

Diana's death that fateful night in Pont de l'Alma tunnel shocked the world, so much so that dreamers from two continents submitted dreams for interpretation through my global dreaming project at DreamThread.com. There were sixty dreams in all. From the dreams, it was clear that Diana's soul was connected to many. Some of the dreams were precognitive foretelling a tragic ending to her brilliant life while others revealed something about the sincerity of her heart, her compassionate work and the dynamics within the Windsor family and her relationship with Prince Charles. One dream was haunting. It revealed the horrific moments before her death in the blackness of the tunnel, at Pont de l'Ama in Paris. The dreamer saw Diana riding in the back of the Mercedes as the driver sped up to put distance between them and those following them, perhaps paparazzi; perhaps not. Either way it was a high-speed chase. Ice was being thrown at the window of their vehicle and at first Diana thought it a game and was merely amused. Her amusement turned to terror when she realized this was no game and that someone was out to kill her. The dreamer awoke as the car crashed. From this dream, what is certain is that someone was deliberately trying to overpower the vehicle and was attacking it with something that would cause the driver to crash. The ice against the window symbolized a coldhearted terrorist.

What is most interesting and synchronistic was the location of the crash, Pont de l'Alma. The etymology of the name "Pont de l'Alma" means "bridge of the soul", a meaningful name to mark the place of a beloved princess' transition from this world to the next. What is even more meaningful is the Pont de l'Ama marked the spot of an ancient legacy connected Diana, a line of descendants called the Fisher Kings, the Merovingians. Pont de l'Alma had been the precise spot of an underground chamber and series of tunnels built by the Merovingian Kings of the 5th century, a repository of their wealth perhaps, as well as a place where rituals were performed in celebration of the Goddess Diana, Princess Diana's namesake. According to some sources, the Merovingians who established the City of Paris may have used the underground tunnels as the place to settle disputes over property. By legend, they went to Pont de L'Alma, because they believed a portal existed into the heavenly realm and if they were killed in battle they would ascend directly to the Throne of Heaven and oversee and direct the victor's fate on earth. The spot held significant power as a vortex spun up from an ancient legacy that Diana's soul had incarnated to revisit and claim as her divine inheritance. Perhaps, Diana unconsciously chose Pont de l'Alma as her point of departure so that her sons, William and Harry, might later make the synchronistic connection, discover the Merovingian thread leading to their mother's genealogy and trace the bloodline to Jesus and Mary Magdalene.

That fateful night Pont de l'Alma became a battleground between the forces of the dark and the light and black magic likely had a hand in Diana's death. Kings and Queens were known to dappled in the occult and some used black magic to influence the fate of those who opposed them. In fact, a dream I had at the time I was compiling Diana dreams suggested a curse of sorts was in force aimed at interfering with anyone seeking information about Diana's death. In the dream, I was startled by a woman's voice chanting an incantation or spell in tongues. I could see the image of a hairbrush float into my visual path and I awoke with a startle screaming, "NO!" Locks of a victim's hair acquired from a hairbrush are sometimes used in black magic arts to cast a spell and invoke power against an individual. What was clear from my dream was that I had entered dangerous territory by continuing my research into the life and death of Princess Diana and that I was given a glimpse at the lengths the individuals had gone to close the chapter of Diana's life. The conspiracy theories abound as to who was really behind Diana's death. Some say the monarchy, the Windsors themselves, plotted her demise and succeeded with the help of the British Secret Service who used some kind of device to cause the car to crash. What seems reasonable to conclude is that Diana posed a very real threat to the Windsors not only because of her mass appeal as the people's princess, but because of her influence on her sons who would inherit the monarchy. She was embarrassing the crown by planning to marry Dodi Al Fayed, a Muslim, who would become stepfather to Princes William and Harry. And rumors that she was already pregnant made matters worse. Some theorists suggest that Diana had a secret that she was about to make public and that the monarchy wished to silence her permanently. None of the conspiracy theories of course could be proven and the crash was deemed a tragic accident.

The Davidic bloodline, the branching of the vine of Jesus and Mary Magdalene, ascended through the generations to a line of Franks known as the Merovingian kings, longhaired fisher kings. Laurence Gardner has traced their genealogy through the Arimathea line of descent, confirming a descent from Jesus and Mary Magdalene through their son, Josephes. Evidence of the Merovingian connection, emerged in a vivid dream image in the early-morning hours just as I was about to awaken. The image was that of a book titled *The Merovingian Dynasty*. The book cover portrayed Mary Magdalene dressed in dark garments and looking quite somber if not sullen, discouraged and regretful. It wasn't a book likely to be found in a library but instead a symbolic confirmation that the blood royal had branched into lines of the Merovingian Dynasty of the fifth century.

It's also significant that this group of monarchs called "fisher kings" claimed origins all the way back to the biblical Noah. They adhered to some of the customs of Judaic tradition and pledged allegiance to the memory of King Solomon, whom they attempted to emulate. Following in the footsteps of King Solomon, the Merovingian kings were known for their priestly function as judges with clairvoyant powers. They held knowledge of occult magic and astrology. Noted sorcerers in the manner of the Samaritan Magi, they believed in the power of the honeycomb, a symbol of divine harmony in nature holding the blueprint for the mysteries of life: creativity and manifestation. The bee became emblematic of the cult. In general, they appeared to be schooled and learned in the mysteries of all ages, deriving their beliefs from a variety of mystery schools, including feminine mysteries associated with Artemis (Diana) cult pagan practices. King Merovee, the Franks' ruler in the middle fourth century, for example, was said to have been endowed with supernatural powers derived from his supernatural birth. According to lore, he was conceived twice, once through his father and a second time through insemination by a sea creature that raped his mother while she swam in the sea. This mythological motif of a supernatural insemination may have been a metaphor pointing to the planetary influence of Neptune in his astrology, or it could have pointed to a mystery cult initiation, perhaps the likeness of a sexual rite called hieros gamos. The deity embodying the divine feminine and the object of this passionate lovemaking ritual might have been likened to the goddess Aphrodite, the Hellenistic goddess of love who was born out of violent interaction between Uranus and Chronos and emerged from the sea foam with her brother Eros. A further association is with Mary Magdalene herself; the name Mary, derived from Mirium, means "myrrh of the sea" or "star of the sea," a name and association also given to Aphrodite. Margaret Starbird, author of *Woman with the Alabaster Jar* points out that "Merovee" could be phonetically broken down to "Mer Vin," the vine of Mary Magdalene, perhaps intended to point out his descent from the vine of Mary Magdalene. Could there have been a Mary Magdalene's cult?

Mary's association as a love goddess like Aphrodite may have grown in the same way that the Gnostics believed Mary was the incarnation of the goddess Sophia. Symbolic relics of this dynasty such as the fleur-de-lis, emblematic of Clovis, who was best-known for his conversion to Roman Christianity, are associated with a Mary Magdalene cult. The Merovingian had probably initiated a cult in worship of the Magdalene, one that incorporated rites and ritual through which its members sought to derive mystical powers. Judging from the expression on Mary Magdalene's face on the book in my dream, it probably wasn't a cult honoring Mary Magdalene's authentic image or her spiritual purpose and integrity. The Merovingian were known polygamists who on the one hand revered the goddess, seeking her mysteries and paying her homage, and on the other hand seemed to consider it their entitlement to further degrade the women in their lives. It's also likely that they practiced black magic rather than divine magic. It seems their goddess worship, or, specifically Mary Magdalene worship, was merely a method of initiation to gain more power, wealth to support their opulent lifestyle and further a sense of entitlement through the vine of Mary.

Needless to say, the bloodline continued on through a succession of Merovingian kings whose reign spanned over 300 years and whose territories included most of Germany, France and Belgium. By the sixth century, this very prosperous and even opulent dynasty had ended, but the blood royal continued to flow up to include at least two members of the original nine founders of the Templars and further on into the royal houses of the Stuarts, branching all the way up to the present day with the grandchildren of the present monarchy of Great Britain, William and Harry.

In the fifth century the royal line of the Franks intermarried with the Merovingian dynasty, which ultimately linked with the genealogical trees of the Habsburgs, the House of Lorraine, Plantard, Luxembourg, Pontzat, Montesquieu, Sinclair, Stuarts, and many other of the royal families of Europe.

There is every reason to believe that the original members of the Knights Templar of the 12th Century, the monastic order of knights whose influence on the Christendom was second to none, were keepers of the secret legacy of Jesus and Mary Magdalene and connected by bloodline through the House of Burgandy and the Capetian Kings who were descendants of the Merovingians.

Somewhere between the years of AD 1118 and 1120, King Baldwin of Jerusalem granted a small group of knights' quarters at the Royal Palace on the Temple Mount, the Al Aqsa Mosque. It was chronicled that King Baldwin of Jerusalem sent two messengers to Bernard of Clairvaux, the influential abbot and advisor to the Pope, explaining that there were two brothers of the Temple, Andrew and Gundemar, who wanted confirmation from the pope for their order. As their mission, they vowed to protect pilgrims traveling to the Holy land. They also requested a Rule to live by. Baldwin begged Bernard to use his influence with the Pope and the "princes of Christendom" to aid them. This request undoubtedly came as no surprise to Bernard, because Andrew (Andre de Montbard) was his younger uncle. Bernard was well aware of the mission these two brothers had embarked on because he was central to its planning.

There is some evidence that the Knights Templar could have been organized before 1118, in fact, close to the end of the First Crusade. A charter of Anselm, dated to around 1145 suggests the Templars were confirmed by Pope Urban shortly after the First Crusade which would have meant they would have been confirmed before 1099 as Pope Urban died in that year. It reads,

> "A certain new religious institution began in Jerusalem, the city of God. Laymen have congregated there, religious men, and they cut themselves off from the superfluity and costly clothes, prepared to defend the glorious Sepulchre of the Lord against the incursions of the Saracen. Pope Urban first confirmed these men's way of life and intention at a council of many bishops whom he had called together to the council, laying down that whoever placed himself in the society hoping for eternal life, and persevered in it faithfully should have remission of all sins. He confirmed that they are not to be of

less merit than either monks or canons call themselves the Knights
of the Temple. Having left their own property they live a common
life, and fight under a vow of obedience to one 'master."

The conflicting history about when the Knights Templar were
formed has caused a great deal of speculation that Godfrey
Bouillon, the first ruler of the Kingdom of Jerusalem and leader of
the First Crusade, may have been steering the formation of the
Knights Templar near the end of the First Crusade.

Another piece of evidence marking the beginning of the
Templars long before Tyre's date of 1118 is the fact that Hughes, the
Count of Champagne, made numerous mysterious visits to the
Holy Land accompanied by Hughes de Payen. The first such visit
was in 1104 from which he did not return until 1108. The founding
members of the Templars were in close alliance with Hughes I of
Champagne and, in fact, were blood relatives of this nobleman of
extraordinary wealth and influence. Hugh ruled over Champagne,
which included the city of Troyes and Hughes de Payen would
have been his vassal. After the count's second visit to the Holy
Land in 1114, Ivo, Bishop of Chartres, wrote to Hugh Count of
Champagne criticizing him for abandoning his wife and vowing
himself to the "knighthood of Christ". He accused him of taking up
a futile mission rather than attending to his responsibilities to
family and country. What can be concluded from the date of this
chastising letter is that the Knights Templar were already well
established by 1114. Hugh I Count of Champagne officially became
a Knight Templar in 1125, returning again to the Holy Land to join a
most mysterious mission alongside Hughes de Payen and the other
eight knights on Temple Mount.

For the first nine years that the Templars were at Temple Mount
they were led by Hughes de Payen and consisted of only nine
members leading many to wonder how a group of only nine
knights could possibly have succeeded in protecting the many
pilgrims traveling through districts filled with ruthless bandits who
reportedly slaughtered as many as 100 pilgrims at a time. They
were obviously motivated by something else.

Their headquarters at Temple Mount held the key to their secret
mission, because it rested atop the ruins of Solomon's Temple.
What secrets and treasures they found there has been a topic of
much investigation, discussion, speculation and conspiracy
theories. A labyrinth of underground tunnels thought to have been

dug just after the Crusades was discovered by a British excavation team in 1867 and a later investigation found pieces of a lance, a spur, a sword and a Templar cross. These artifacts were given in 1912 to the grandfather of Robert Brydon, a Scottish Templar historian. Historians now argue that the Templar's earliest motivations may have been to gain access to the site of Solomon's Temple and as an archeological team to locate and excavate the most prized relics of the Davidic legacy. Legends abound speculating the Templars possessed a host of treasures including; The Ark of the Covenant, a piece of the crucifixion cross, Mary Magdalene's skull, the Grail cup used at the last supper, secret documents and other relics. But there is little physical evidence that they possessed any of these treasures.

Whatever the Knights Templar had acquired in their excavations seemed to give them the "Midas touch", because on their return from Jerusalem they acquired numerous donations of property throughout Provence, Languedoc, the Ile de France, Normandy, Spain, Portugal, England and Scotland. With a tidy bankroll from large donations they were able to finance a string of cathedrals such as Chartres, Amiens, and the infamous Temple Church in London. They may have financed as many as 300 churches and cathedrals.

But the true treasure they sought was of an altogether different nature, one buried deep within the collective soul of humanity, a legacy of mystical and esoteric wisdom that could be studied, digested and integrated, ones that would become the secret tenets of the Order. Not only is there evidence the Templars were learned scholars of the occult mysteries including hermeticism, alchemy, sacred geometry and other occult knowledge, but they ascribed to a heretical branch of early Christianity, Gnosticism. Like the Gnostics, the Templars were in search of "gnosis", the ultimate truth and the wisdom of all ages. Each initiate's quest would have been to touch the divine through series of initiations and to perfect himself spiritually. Therefore, the Templar mission was not as much to protect pilgrims, but to be pilgrims themselves returning to the roots of their own heritage in Jerusalem. They were adepts, spiritual seekers, following the deepest call to preserve a heritage rich in mystical tenets, a heritage which they believed belonged to them.

The two most important Templars were Andre de Montbard and Hughes de Payen. The importance of Andre de Montbard to the

Knights Templar is not well documented, other than to state that he was uncle to Bernard Clairvaux and that he served as Grand Master beginning in 1153 after serving as Seneschal for fifteen years.

Andre de Montbard's pedigree was royal. He was directly related to the Count of Champagne, the Duke of Burgundy and through his mother, Humberge, he was descended from the Merovingian comtes de Tonnerre, who had been dukes during the Merovingian dynasty. Tonnerre meaning "Thunder" had been a title the family had taken to bear as descendents of the Judaic high priesthood. Some historians believe they were related to Jonathan Annas who served as high priest of Jerusalem during the first century. This was not necessarily the case. The family may have wanted to retain the fact that they were actually descendants of Jesus and Mary Magdalene in which case "Thunder" was a title connecting the family to Jesus. In Mark 3:17, Jesus designates the title, "Sons of Thunder" to James and John who sought to sit at Jesus' right and left hands. Andre's family saw themselves in the same light, sitting at the side of Jesus in faithfulness and service to the great secret.

Andre's father, Bernard de Montbard, was related to Thibault IV who was instrumental in calling the church council together at Troyes in Champagne to legitimize the Knights Templar mission in Jerusalem and approve a set of rules for the Knights Templar to live by. The drafter of those rules was Bernard de Clairvaux, the Cistercian abbot who was advisor to the Pope and as mentioned happened to be Andre's nephew. A point of fact is that Bernard was actually older that his uncle, Andre. Hughes de Payen, the first Grand Master of the Order and whose mother was Helie de Montbard was Andre's cousin. What is clear is that the formation of the Knights Templar was a family affair of those connected through bloodline. With Andre, Bernard and Hughes all related, we see a family's mission to preserve and protect the bloodline inheritance of the Davidic line. They would go to great lengths to not only protect the Holy Land but to position themselves within the church to set about creating an empire.

Along with Hughes de Payen, Andre represented the Order of Knights at the Council of Troyes in 1128 where the Order was legitimized. He participated in the Second Crusade from 1148 to 1150 and was Seneschal of the order by the end of it. In about 1150, he wrote a letter to Everard de Barre, the Grand Master, who had returned with King Louis VII to France. In the letter, he reported that things were not going well in the Holy Land. Andre tells Everard, "we are constrained on all sides by lack of knights and sergeants and money, and we implore your paternity to return to us quickly." Everard did return to Jerusalem, but seemed unsuited to the task as Grand Master because he was the first ever to retire from the Order. He was replaced by Bernard of Tremelay, while Andre de Montbard continued as Seneschal. Andre became Grand Master in 1154 after Bernard was killed. In 1154 under King Henry II of England, Andre de Montbard superintended the Masons and commenced in building Temple Church in High Holborn on land that was donated to Hughes de Payen. The Knights Templar moved their London temple to a new site between Fleet Street and the Thames in 1161 after Andre's death.

Half a century after Andre's death in 1156, the Grail romance *La Queste Del Saint Graal* surfaces to add its Christianized version of the quest for the Holy Grail to the list of romances published in the era. As mention in a previous chapter, most scholars agree the attribution given to Walter Map was an unlikely one, because Map had died some years before the quest was written. Who then authored it? It is widely accepted that *Le Queste del Saint Graal* was written by a scribe in the Cistercian Order whose Christian values chime throughout the allegorical tale making this quest for the Holy Grail stand apart from the others.

The quest introduced a questing hero named Galahad, a strapping young knight, who was deemed the "the chosen one" to receive the secrets and mysteries of the Grail and "confidences of the Lord." Though considered allegorical fiction, there is every reason to believe that this particular quest was written to mythologize the history of the Knights Templar and in particular one notable figure within the organization— Andre de Montbard. In a dream, I was told that the fictional character and protagonist of the quest, Galahad, was in actuality Andre de Montbard, a descendant of Jesus and Mary Magdalene. The name Galahad is the Christianized name for "Gilead", a Hebrew name meaning "hill of testimony" for its association with the mountainous region of Gilead just east of the Jordan River. Both Galahad and Andre mean "strong" or "manly". The author of the quest cleverly told the story of Andre's quest for enlightenment and his bloodline connection to Joseph of Arimathea (Christ) without divulging his identity or membership in the Templar Order. The motive for secrecy was undoubtedly to protect Andre's descendants whose blood was nothing less than royal. The quest was, in fact, a heresy written partly for the Order's amusement at a time when the Church vehemently squashed all creative licenses. Secondly, it recorded the Templar legacy as an interesting allegory for those already in the know. Those in the know, understood what was hidden within the pages: the genealogy of the Knights Templar, the fact that Joseph of Arimathea was Jesus Christ, had a son named Josephes and that the secret teachings of Christ had survived.

Although, Andre never rose to sainthood in the way his nephew, Bernard Clairvaux, did, he seems to have been held in the highest esteem by the Cistericians who praised him in the quest as the most gallant, virtuous and, therefore, worthy knight. In fact, his Christ-like qualities set him apart from all the other knights questing for the Grail and above those of the brotherhood of White Friars (Cistercians) who were also woven into the story as mentors and advisors. He was described as possessing all the virtues deemed necessary to be given the secrets of the Grail and to inherit the Perilous Seat at the Round Table. His worthiness came partly through inheritance as a direct descendant of Joseph of Arimathea and partly through his willingness to serve. Galahad says, " *I have come because I was bound to do so."*

The fact that Galahad was viewed as a Christ-like savior and the last of Joseph of Arimathea's lineage is a important detail to consider, one that becomes clearer when the story tells us of the approaching "end of times". With this in mind, it appears that Andre was viewed more than merely Christ-like. To the Cistercians, he was the Second Coming of Christ. In the same way that Jesus was prophesized as the coming Messiah so too was Galahad the prophesized knight who would be "sent by God to terminate the great marvels of the land and to achieve the adventures of the Grail."

The question arises: Where did this notion that the end of times were upon them originate? The answer is: Bernard Clairvaux.

At the age of 23, Bernard Clairvaux joined the Cistercian order, but not alone. He arrived with 25 to 30 or more family members, a very large group of brothers, cousins and other relatives and rode into the abbey of Citeaux in Dijon. In fact, two of Andre de Montbard's brothers were among those who accompanied Bernard to the abbey. This abbey was the first Cistercian monastery and had been set up somewhat earlier by a small group of dissident monks who chose to strictly abide by Benedictine rules. At the time of St Bernard's arrival, the abbey was under the guiding hand of Stephen Harding, an Englishman. The natural question arises: Why would so many members of one family who were middle nobility enter a monastic life, a hermitage, leaving behind their worldly possessions, friends, alliances and such at the urgings of a 23-year-old? What might have convinced them to choose such a radical conversion in mass? What were they hiding and what were they hiding or protecting themselves from? Were they preparing their souls for an apocalyptic forecast based on the revelations of Bernard who the family considered a mystic and their spiritual advisor? Considering that the majority were descendants of the Davidic line, it is conceivable that they were under some kind of threat seeking refuge in the monastery at Citeaux to protect themselves and the bloodline. This seems a plausible explanation for what might ordinarily be considered cultish behavior or an extraordinary religious zeal. But it is even more plausible that Bernard had convinced everyone close to him that the "end of times" was upon them and that they must take the Cistercian vows to insure the salvation of their souls.

Three years later, Bernard was to establish a new house for the Cistercian order to which he would be named abbot. He acquired a parcel of land in Vallée d'Absinthe, donated by his cousin Hugh, Count to Champagne, and with a band of 12 monks established the Abbey. Bernard named the land "Claire Vallée" or "Clairvaux" on June 25, 1115, and the names of Bernard and Clairvaux would soon become inseparable. But Clairvaux was only a small piece of Bernard's vision. His vision was far grander than to govern a small band of monks within one monastery. It seems as though he thought it his duty and mission to fashion a New Jerusalem in the already expanding Christendom. The number of Cistercian houses rose from a handful to over three hundred under Bernard's influence and the Templars were well on their way to establishing themselves as political ambassadors and financiers with a great deal of clout. In fact, the Knights Templar and Cistercian Order were not two separate organizations at all. They were two arms of the same organization under the guiding hand of Bernard Clairvaux. Whatever this influence was that Bernard had, it was powerfully applied to create a religious empire that stretched throughout France, England, Germany, and Italy as well as in the Holy Land. The Templars were responsible for half of the success Bernard achieved.

From the degree of religious zeal for their mission and their unprecedented success in establishing themselves throughout the Christendom as financial wizards, protectors, ambassadors, if not imperialists, it seems as if the Knights Templar held some special power and authority beyond that given to them by the Mother Church through a set of rules. A great deal of divine providence, in the form of large donations, certainly came their way, far beyond the ordinary especially after their return to France in 1127. What was it that put them in such good favor? The Ark of the Covenant.

Without a doubt, their early mission in Jerusalem was in fact to locate and excavate the Ark of the Covenant as many theorists such as Lawrence Gardner (2007) and Louis Charpentier (1983) have lain out. In fact, the Vulgate cycle romances allegorically present the Grail as so similar to the Ark of the Covenant that there is every reason to believe they were one and the same. Both were imbued with spiritual and magical powers, enough to save armies of Israelites and enough to feed the multitudes.

In one sequel of the Vulgate, the Grail is stored in an ark that was constructed for the purpose of holding it and the common people were prohibited access. This storyline is reminiscent of the Ark of the Covenant contructed by Moses to hold the stone tablet of the Ten Commandments, the rod of Jesse and the vessel of manna. It was also kept from the masses, placed in the Holy of Holies where only the high priest had access. Therefore, the *La Queste de Saint Graal* has always held the clue that the Templars were in possession of the Ark of the Covenant and that they concealed that fact from the masses. A miniature illumination from a 13th century copy of *La Queste de Saint Graal* depicts the Grail flanked by two cherubim mirroring the positions of two cherubim on the lid of the Ark of the Covenant. The illustration hints that the mystery of the Grail was linked to the Ark of the Covenant.

Another fossil of evidence that suggests the Templars had succeeded in bringing the Ark back to France is an image of The Ark of the Covenant resting in a wheeled cart carved into a pillar on the north porch of Chartres Cathedral. The porch is known as the Portal of the Initiates. The image echoes a European legend that tells that Hughes de Payen was commissioned to find The Ark of the Covenant and bring it to Europe. The same legend says it was buried beneath the crypt of Chartres Cathedral.

For the founding members of the Templars the quest for Solomon's treasures was not born out of a desire for wealth in the form of material gold. Instead, they sought honor in the Kingdom of God, the afterlife, as well as enlightenment in their present life — spiritual gold. Like the Crusaders their mission was for Christ and all Christians. Undoubtedly, the Templar's early mission was driven by a profound spiritual calling catalyzed by the vision of Andre de Montbard and Bernard Clairvaux who were both mystics. In their minds, the time of the Great Tribulation was approaching. It is conceivable that they saw it their duty and mission to retrieve the Ark of the Covenant so that the prophesies of Ezekiel (Ezek 40-48) and Daniel (9:16-27) might be fulfilled with the building of the new temple that they would commence to build. While Ezekiel prophesized the complete reconstruction of the city of Jerusalem which was to include a new Temple being built and the Ark returned to its altar in the Holy of Holies, thus restoring the Jewish tradition, the Book of Revelations (3:12 and 21:2) envisioned an otherworldly city of greater proportion descending onto a whole new earth. The revealing of the New Jerusalem was preceded by the Second Coming of Christ. Perhaps, it was this vision of the Book of Revelation that the Templars were hoping for. As heirs of Kingship of the New Dispensation (Christianity) the Templars undoubtedly considered the Ark of the Covenant to now belong to Christ and they saw themselves as the preparers for the Kingdom of God. In April 1128, Hughes de Payen and Andre de Montbard visited the court of King Henry I of England who gave the Templars large parcels of property. They set up a preceptory at London. On the same trip, they met with Scotland's King David I and set up another preceptory at Balantrodoch. Before returning to Jerusalem in 1129 with some 300 new recruits, they were given papal sanction by Pope Honorius II declaring the Templars to be an army of God. It was also in 1128 that Bernard Clairvaux formally praised the Templars in De Laude Novae Militiae – In Praise of the New Knighthood. The following year, at the Council of Troyes, the Templars were granted their Rules of Order written by Bernard Clairvaux.

Within these rules, Bernard Clairvaux explicitly stated that the Knights Templar were to swear allegiance and obedience to the house of Bethany, the castle of Mary and Martha. This fact has led many researchers to believe that it was not the Virgin Mother that was so revered and venerated by Bernard, but Mary Magdalene. The rise in popularity of the cult of the Black Madonna in the 12th century, as evidenced by the number of cathedrals dedicated to Our Lady St. Mary Magdalene, may very well have arisen out of Bernard's mariology. Many believe the Templars themselves participated in Goddess worship. Bernard seemed to have been a bit fixated on the Goddess, the Divine Feminine, and on the eroticism in the Song of Songs about which he wrote some ninety sermons interpreting and expounding on the longings and yearnings between the bride and bridegroom. Of Mary, Bernard wrote:

"If the winds of temptation arise; If you are driven upon the rocks of tribulation look to the star, call on Mary; If you are tossed upon the waves of pride, of ambition, of envy, of rivalry, look to the star, call on Mary. Should anger, or avarice, or fleshly desire violently assail the frail vessel of your soul, look at the star, call upon Mary."

Here Bernard was referring to the ancient title, Star of the Sea, *Stella Maris,* a title designated for both the Virgin and Mary Magdalene. Because the Templars were sworn to uphold the house of Bethany, it is reasonable to conclude Bernard was praising Mary Magdalene not the Virgin in his sermons.

Although, the Templars took monastic vows including vows of chastity, the chroniclers of history recorded marriages. It is claimed that Hughes de Payen married Catherine St. Clair, the niece of Baron Henri St Clair of Roslin, who may have fought alongside Hughes in the first Crusade. The Sinclairs are "hereditary grand masters of Scottish Masonry" and thought to have descended from the Merovingian families whose bloodline was linked to the throne of Jerusalem. Other records show instead that he was married in 1113 to one Elizabeth de Chappes. It is probable that all nine Templars were married and sired children, as not do so would have ended the bloodline descent. Although no marriage is recorded for Andre de Montbard, he too naturally would have married.

When Andre de Montbard became Grand Master in 1153 he had already served the Order for thirty-eight years. His quest for the

Holy Grail ended with his death in October of 1156. Some say he died in Jerusalem and others say he had retired to Clairvaux in 1156 and died there.

The question arises: As Master of the Round Table, was Andre de Montbard and his descendants privy to a body of secret teachings of Christ? *La Queste del Saint Graal,* which was written to mythologize Knights Templar's quest, tells us yes. The following description of the quest for the Holy Grail suggests there were confidences and teachings of Jesus Christ that would have been held sacred and in secret. According to the quest, Galahad (Andre), was the one to whom these secrets were revealed, illuminated and most realized. It reads,

> "This Quest is not a quest for earthly things, but is to be the search for the deep secrets and confidences of Our Lord and for the great mysteries which the High Master will show openly to that fortunate knight whom he has elected among all the other knights of earth to be his servant. To him he will reveal the great marvel of the Holy Grail and will show him what mortal heart could not conceive nor the tongue of earthly man utter."

This passage tells us that the nature of the Grail is not an earthly thing, such as a relic imbued with spiritual power because of its association with the resurrection of Christ as it is in Robert de Boron's version of the Grail quest. There it is the cup used at the Last Supper and brought to Britain by Joseph of Arimathea. Nor is it the bloodline alone. Bloodline inheritance from Joseph of Arimathea's lineage represents only a small piece of the story. In this version, we are told the Grail represents the confidences of the Lord, the secret teachings and mysteries of the Master. This fact offers some evidence to support the premise that the Templars were in possession of a "great secret" or perhaps numerous secrets passed down through the generations and held for centuries in confidence. A few pieces of that secret legacy were woven into *La Queste del Saint Graal* while others remain unknown and in the hands of those unknown.

It is striking how similar the last line in the description of the quest is to Saying 17 of the Gospel of Thomas. The Gospel of Thomas reads,

Jesus said, "I will give you what no eye has seen, what no ear has heard, what no hand has touched, what has not arisen in the human heart."

Could this parallel suggest the Cistercians and the Templars were in possession of a copy of the Gospel of Thomas, some portion of it or other writings of Jesus? Although there is little evidence that a copy of the Gospel of Thomas was circulating at the time, it is possible the Templars were privy to some of Jesus' authentic sayings. Of course, it could be argued that the source of the last line was actually derived from Corinthians 2:9 which reads,

"But as it is written, Eye hath not seen, nor ear heard, neither have entered into the heart of man, the things which God hath prepared for them that love him."

In February 1117, Bernard Clairvaux journeyed to Seborga in Northern Italy to a Cistercian house he had established in 1113. According to the local legend the house had been established to protect a "Great Secret". Under the direction of the Prince Regent, Edouard, were two monks, Gondemar and Rossal who may have been family members of Bernard. Bernard released them from their vows to join the brotherhood of the Knights Templar in 1118. Documents associated with Serborga suggest that prior to departing for Jerusalem in the company of other knights, Hughes de Payen visited the Cistercian house in Seborga and it was there that Bernard nominated him Grand Master of the "Poor Militia of Christ". Seborga was maintained as a sovereign Cistercian State until 1729.

What this particular "great secret" was is left to the imagination, but what is certain is that the Cistercians held numerous secrets, some of which I have laid out. There was certainly more to the histories of the Knights Templar, Bernard Clairvaux and the Cistercians than meets the eye.

The long held secret that the Templars and Cistercians had in their possession the Ark of the Covenant leaves us to wonder where it is now. The carving of the Ark in a cart on the façade of the north porch of Chartres Cathedral may hold a clue. A relief inscription on the pillar reads, "The Ark of the Covenant was yielded from here". "To yield" means to "give up" or "to let go of". To have been yielded from there also suggests that at one time it had been hidden at Chartres Cathedral. When it was relinquished and to whom and where it is now has remained a mystery. We can conclude that the Ark was relinquished sometime before 1215 when the north porch of the cathedral had been completed and the carving of the pillar made. It is also reasonable to conclude that it was surrendered to the authority of the Church, which would meant it was given to the Pope. My otherworldly angelic sources tell me the Vatican has had the Ark of the Covenant in its possession since the 13th century.

The Cistercian monks of the Middle Ages were credited with producing a number of religious illuminated manuscripts as well as various paintings. A Psalter miniaturist painting titled, *Crucifixion and Deposition*, from the 13th century illuminated manuscript of Blanche of Castile (queen of France) may hold a heretical secret according to some amateur conspiracy theorists.

Pictured at the end of this chapter, this Psalter miniaturist painting is composed of four roundels depicting the crucifixion and deposition (Jesus' removal from the cross) with Ecclesia holding a chalice and cross staff (representing the Church) and Synagoga (the Synagogue) as she was often depicted with a severed head and broken flag. Ecclesia symbolized the victorious and confident church having defeated the Synagogue and Jewish religion, the old dispensation. Representations of Ecclesia and Synagoga are often found in medieval Christian manuscript art and became conventional decoration on the facades of many medieval churches, especially in France, England, and Germany during the 12th and 13th centuries.

What may or may not be immediately noticeable is that the depiction of Jesus being brought down from the cross in the bottom roundel looks very human and alive. His arm extension is not that of a dead man or it would have been limp. The elbow rests against the figure bringing him off the cross and his hand extends to rest on Mary's shoulder. At the same time, Mary 's head tilts so that her face lovingly caresses Jesus' hand. It is not known which Mary, Jesus' mother or Mary Magdalene, is depicted to the left in both roundels, upper and lower. The change in dress of the figures from top to bottom could have been created to denote a change in time or a change in person. Either way, the pictorial representation of the deposition hints at the secret of Jesus' survival of the crucifixion. The secret facts were kept by some within the Cistercian order and hinted at within some of their art.

Blanche de Castile who was Queen and consort to King Louis the VIII of France was a patron of the Cistercians and in fact had strong ties to the order. Like a number of her female relatives, including her sisters and nieces, she took the veil of the Cistercians. Throughout her reign as Queen consort, Blanche demonstrated her preference for the Cistercians over other religious orders. She helped build two Cistercian houses and traveled with her children on numerous occasions to visit several Cistercian houses. After her retirement Blanche founded three Cistercian nunneries, Biaches, Maubuisson and Le Lys. What is relevant is that the illumination in Blanche's Psalter, depicting an alive looking Jesus being brought down from the cross, was rendered during the same decade that a Cistercian writer hid his secret clues in *La Queste del Saint Graal.* This fact leads us to wonder if Blanche Castile and her family including her husband Louis VIII were amongst those in the know of Jospeh of Arimathea's secret identity.

The illumination, *Crucifixion and Deposition,* is not the only Cistercian piece of art that hints at heretical secret. At the Royal Monastery of the Holy Cross, in Aiguamurcia, in the province of Tarragona in Northern Spain are a number of interesting Cistercian works of art. The Cistercian house was founded by Bernard Clairvaux and is amongst numerous others established for the growing order during his tenure. Amongst the art pieces is an iconic painting on wood depicting the crucifixion. Sitting on the ground beneath Jesus on the cross is a very pregnant Mary Magdalene wiping away tears with a handkerchief. Positioned next to her a skull, an element often present in her iconography during the Middle Ages. Without a doubt Mary's belly is protruded and her breasts enlarged denoting she was with child. She clings to the cross in a lamenting pose. This iconic piece, painted in 1603, is another piece of evidence that members of the Cistercian order along with the Templars held a profound secret: Jesus was married to Mary Magdalene and they had children.

The Templar's success and presence in the Christendom continued for some two hundred years. But with the failure of the Second Crusade and their defeat at the last stronghold in Acre in 1291 their popularity dwindled. Their final dissolution occurred by papal order and with it accusations of heresy, secrecy, financial corruption and Satanic practices launched against them by Philip IV of France. On Friday, October 13, 1307, King Philip IV of France ordered scores of Templers along with their Grand Master, Jacques de Molay, arrested as enemies of the Christian faith and their assets seized. The Templars recanted the confessions made under torture and maintained their innocence to the bitter end. Jacques de Molay was burned at the stake on March 18, 1314. The religious arm of the organization, the Cistercian order, continued to flourish until the Protestant Reformation of the 16th century.

If we were to believe that documents and relics were in the hands of Templars, then their heirs could very well possess them. Perhaps there are documents that prove the continuation of the legacy of Jesus and Mary Magdalene's teachings. If so, why is it that they have not been released to the world? What conspiracy would be behind such a deliberate silence? If they have existed, hidden away somewhere for centuries, it seems reasonable to conclude that they will never be released.

Psalter of Blanche of Castile- circa 1235

Iconic Cistercian Painting Royal Monastery
of the Holy Cross, Aiguamurcia

THE TEMPLARS ROUND TABLE

The Quest for the Holy Grail - Appearance of the Holy Grail to the Knights of the Round Table - Roman 13ᵗʰ century. Manuscript copied, Ahun by Evrard workshop Espingues, 1470 - BnF, Manuscripts, French 116 fol. 610V

This 13ᵗʰ century miniature illumination contained within a copy of *La Queste del Saint Graal* brings to life the appearance of the Holy Grail and the role of Gilead (Galahad) as head of the Round Table. Significantly, it also ties the Ark of the Covenant to the Holy Grail because of a likeness of representation.

The scene depicts the Grail emerging out of the well of the Round table in front of King Arthur and the knights of the quest. The knights, some of whom appear to be royalty, distinguished by their crowns and fur-trimmed robes, marvel as they bear witness to this profound miracle. In *La Queste del Saint Graal*, the appearance of the Holy Grail is preceded by a clap of thunder and an illuminating light. A scent of spices and other beautiful aromas fill the air and the Holy Grail, covered with a white cloth, is carried in by someone who cannot be seen. The scene takes place on the Pentecost and mimics the descent of the Holy Spirit on the disciples on that day in Jerusalem (Acts 2:1-21). The *Queste* reads, *"And straightway they were as if illumined with the grace of the Holy Spirit."* But rather than being able to speak in tongues as was the case for the disciples, the knights are rendered speechless unable to utter a word. What occurs next is that the Grail's power manifests food enough for all the knights of the Round Table, more than they could possibly eat. Herein lies the magical power of the Grail to create and to sustain.

While the narratives of the *Queste* do not describe the physical characteristics of the Grail in detail, the illuminator took liberty to fashion the Holy Grail to resemble two sacred objects. Firstly, it resembles the Mass ciborium and therefore ties the Grail to the celebration of the Eucharist and the body of Christ. And secondly, the winged cherubim flanking the sides of the ciborium are reminiscent of those that flank the lid of the Ark of the Covenant. The Book of Exodus tells us that God spoke to Moses from between the two cherubim. This association of the Grail with the Ark of the Covenant, is also made in a later quest of the Vulgate Cycle in which the Grail was actually placed in an ark. This ark was constructed specifically to hold the Holy Grail, just as Moses constructed the Ark of the Covenant to hold the 10 Commandment tablet, the rod of Jesse and the receptacle for the *manna*. In some ways, the Grail can be likened to the receptacle (bowl) of *manna* held inside the Ark of the Covenant, because of its ability to magically provide food and sustenance.

Sixteen knights circle the table chaired by Gilead (Galahad) sitting under a canopy of honor in the Perilous Seat. Identified by the names written in gold behind their seats, the others are: Perceval, Arthur, Helias, Tristan Kay, Bademagu, Ydier, Caradoc, Rion, Etor, Lionel, Gawain, Bors and Lancelot.

For the Cistercian writer of the *Queste*, these name identifications were in fact aliases for the founding members of the Knights Templar about whom the *Queste de Saint Graal* was written. The fact that many have crowns on their heads supports the theory that the founding members of the Templar organization were blood royals who had proclaimed themselves heirs of Kingship connected to the throne of King David of Jerusalem. Furthermore, the Round Table represented their gathering and meeting place where they would have laid out their plans and the place where they performed the rituals and initiations of their secret tradition. The Templars considered themselves founders of the New Dispensation in the tradition of Jesus' covenant, but not necessarily synonymous with the New Dispensation of the Mother Church of Rome. They were afforded a certain degree of sovereignty and according to their rules were their own state.

Could this illumination be hinting that the Templars were in possession of the Ark of the Covenant? Certainly, it seems to be.

Magdalene Madonna w/Child and John the Baptist – Da Vinci
Fiona McLaren

CHAPTER NINE
Da Vinci's Last Testament

There are three classes of people: those who see, those who see when they are shown, those who do not see. –Leonardo Da Vinci

Since 2003 when Dan Brown's Da Vinci Code hit bookstores, amateur theorists and art historians alike have considered whether Leonardo Da Vinci's *The Last Supper* contains hidden imagery. Although the debate has waned to some degree of late, theorists continue to glean out symbolic elements from the composition pointing to a variety of heretical themes, some hidden through Leonardo's use of optics and sacred geometry, while the majority lie within the composition as symbolic clues. The primary element in the composition that has caused the most controversy is the figure sitting next to Jesus at the Pascal table. The majority of conspiracy theorists are in agreement: Mary Magdalene was the central figure, not an effeminate looking Apostle John as thought for centuries. They have pointed out that her clothing present a mirror reflection of Christ's robes and, therefore, in Da Vinci's mind, Mary Magdalene was Jesus' significant other — his feminine complement.

There is little doubt that Da Vinci was a master a creating illusions in his paintings. I can't help but think that the quotation I presented beneath the title of this chapter reveals the opinion and philosophy of a spiritually awakened mind, not unlike that of the shaman who sees a symbolic and elemental world beyond the veil of the ordinary view. But as Da Vinci suggests, many are blind and cannot see what is in front of their faces and no matter how hard one tries to convince them, they fail to grasp the truth. And so it is that many have rebuked the idea that Leonardo painted anything other than a traditional painting of the Last Supper with John sitting next to Jesus as the "beloved disciple".

To express his superior genius, Leonardo replicated the hidden dimensions of life in some of his paintings through his use of optics, sacred geometry, divine proportion and meaningful symbolic elements that to the un-awakened mind seem nothing more than ordinary depictions of real subjects. But his symbols had greater and deeper meaning that in some instances pointed to heretical secrets that he and a group of Renaissance artists shared, ones that become even more evident in a painting that was unveiled in August of 2012.

With the discovery and unveiling of what could very well be Leonardo Da Vinci's final masterpiece, there was only a whisper of excitement when one would expect a thunderous roar. Outside of a week's worth of syndicated articles in August 2012, the discovery did not elicit many commentaries. The lack of enthusiasm was probably due to a weak first impression and because the painting has not yet been authenticated and scientifically dated. However, the expert evaluations done by Harry Robertson at Sotheby's, Sebastian Times of Antique Roadshow, and Professor Carlo Pedretti at the University of California form a consensus that if not painted by Da Vinci himself, at the very least, it is a 16th century work of the Da Vinci school. The painting of a Madonna and Child hung in Fiona McLaren's family residences in Scotland for nearly half a century after it was gifted to McLaren's father in the 1960's. It was passed on to McLaren by her mother some time after her father's death and was nearly relegated to a rubbish pile because it was thought to have little or no value. Now, when authenticated as a Da Vinci, it is anticipated to fetch over 100 million at auction.

Few have attempted to analyze the painting or offer many insights and interpretations, except for those given by Fiona McLaren, author and owner of the painting. In her book, *Da Vinci's Last Commission*, she makes a gallant effort to authenticate the painting by drawing a few parallels to other Da Vinci works.

I must confess, in the first hours of examining the composition, it looked like any another generic Madonna and Child with John the Baptist, a common composition of the High Renaissance. However, after re-examining the painting with fresh eyes I was astonished by what and how much was cleverly concealed. The façade faded away to reveal what the "Master" Da Vinci encoded and envisioned: a heretical masterpiece composed of arcane symbols, optical illusions, purposeful omissions and layered meanings to put forth his last testament. There is no doubt in my mind, none whatsoever, that this painting was put to canvas by the man history has hailed the "Renaissance Man"—Leonardo Da Vinci. And there is no doubt in my mind that the Madonna in the painting is really Mary Magdalene, an opinion shared by McLaren.

Despite the fact that the experts I contacted such as Pedretti, Martin J. Kemp and Ross King have their doubts the painting was produced by Da Vinci's own hand and no matter what the scientific authentication process reveals, I am confidant the master Leonardo conceived and put it to canvas, enough so that I have proceeded to interpret it, confident I will be proved right at some point in the future.

I want to mention, I approached the task of interpreting the painting not as an art historian but as a dream and symbols expert who has a keen eye for hidden elements (good figure ground skills) and an understanding of the metaphoric language of the soul, symbology, mythology and the history of Christianity. All of the hidden elements, whether optical illusions or arcane symbols, are not figments of an over active imagination. Nor do they require mirrors or magnification to see. Similarly, others have seen some of the very same clues I discuss within these pages, however, the majority were either not clearly identified or left un-interpreted because they were not fully understood. As with dreams, a masterpiece must be seen not only for its individual symbolic elements but also for what the entire composition communicates.

Literary theorist, Northrop Frye wrote,

"Art is a dream for awakened minds, a work of imagination withdrawn from ordinary life, dominated by the same forces that dominate the dream, and yet giving us a perspective and dimension on reality that we don't get from any other approach."

This painting brings to light the secret symbolic world of the artist and unveils a legacy of heretical facts that Leonardo held as truths. Like a dream it is composed of many layers of meanings and contains both universal and personal symbols. It had to be painstakingly analyzed and interpreted with unbiased intuition to glean out the intended message of the artist dreamer. It was a puzzle that I had to piece together.

Art like dreams are often misinterpreted. A case in point was Sigmund Freud's interpretation of Da Vinci's *The Virgin and Child with St. Ann*. Freud "imagined" a vulture in the Virgin's garment when the painting was viewed sideways. He associated the vulture with Leonardo's earliest childhood memory of a bird flapping its tail at his mouth. From this, Freud postulated Leonardo manifested a "passive homosexual" childhood fantasy caused by the memory of sucking on his mother's nipple (the vulture tail flapping at his mouth). Much to Freud's dismay however, the word "vulture" was a mistranslation by the German translator and, in fact, the bird in Leonardo's memory was a kite.

Hopefully, I have made no mistakes as grave as Freud's. My approach in the following analysis and interpretation was to let the painting speak for itself and for my intuition guide me in deciphering the clues.

The Facade

For the moment, let us consider the painting just as it appears on the surface — a Madonna and Christ Child with John the Baptist. Certainly, the Madonna's mantle, a rich ultramarine blue over a red under-dress is her standard attire and dates back to the Byzantine period. Ultramarine was used for the Madonna's mantle in paintings because it was the most expensive pigment, considered more valuable than gold. The worth of the pigment and its color was considered appropriate for the Madonna's divine status as the Virgin Mother. It signified motherhood and her humanity. The color also denoted royalty, an attribute transferred over from the Byzantine empress. The red is said to represent her virginity according to Catholic sources, but for many it denotes her passionate love. Her attire in the painting is well within the parameters set by the Church in the 17th century that the Virgin was only to be depicted in her traditional blue mantle. We have only to search art catalogues for an hour or so to find fifty or more paintings of the Madonna in her Marian colors.

And certainly the symbol of the carnation she holds tightly pressed between thumb and forefinger also has associations with the Virgin Mary. In fact, Leonardo used the symbol previously in his painting *Madonna with Carnation*. A Christian legend tells us the first carnation started blooming on earth when the Virgin Mary wept for Jesus as he carried his cross. From this legend, the carnation came to represent a mother's undying love.

But can we conclude from her attire and the carnation alone that the subject of the painting is without a doubt the Madonna and the Christ Child? Those who have analyzed Da Vinci's masterpieces are convinced that with Leonardo "all is not as it seems." The owner of the painting and I agree — the subject is Mary Magdalene — but for only a couple of the same reasons.

A Christ Without Halo

The Christ child sitting on the Madonna's lap is without a halo, a curious omission. Instead, the infant has a fleur-de-lis, a trefoil or tri-leaf symbol or emblem projecting from the crown of his head. We notice, however, that the Madonna is adorned with her halo, as is John the Baptist, signifying their divine status. Had Da Vinci lost faith in Christ, stripping him of his halo and portraying him as a mere mortal? Was he hinting he was not the Son of God? Or did this incongruence mean something else entirely?   Yes, it was something else. He was hinting at a secret, in much the same way that he hid clues in the Last Supper that Mary Magdalene was the "beloved disciple," not the Apostle John. What the missing halo signifies is that we are not looking at the baby Jesus at all.

The infant's pointing gesture is another clue that the Christ Child in the painting is not Christ. The most common gestural pose for this theme is with the Christ child holding two fingers (index and middle) up signifying Christ's blessing on John the Baptist. One example of the blessing gesture is in *Virgin and Child with the Young Saint John the Baptist,* Correggio (Antonio Allegri, circa, 1489-1534) and in Da Vinci's own charcoal cartoon titled, *The Virgin and Child with St Anne and St. John the Baptist* which presents the same theme as *Virgin on the Rocks.* Although a subtle gestural change, it is significant in mentioning another identity, status and role for the child.

The Madonna's Facial Features: A Comparison

The face of the Madonna in our painting is quite demure, humble and compassionately maternal. In repose, she glances down at the child she holds with great respect and maternal love. Whether Da Vinci used a model or merely conceived her through his imagination is a question we will never be able to answer. But the face is not an unfamiliar one for those acquainted with his sketches. A sketch known as *Study for the Head of Mary Magdalene* (1465-1519 ca.), conserved at the Gabinetto dei Disegni e Stampe, of the Uffizi Gallery in Florence, holds many similarities to the Madonna in the painting. So much so that we certainly could argue they are one and the same woman. The angled pose with head slightly bowed, the heart shaped face, pronounced broad forehead, delicate nose, eyelids and such are strikingly similar, in most cases identical. In fact, Da Vinci more than likely used his sketch as the foundation in

Study For Head of Mary Magdalene- Da Vinci

constructing the face of the Madonna in the painting. Perhaps, he sketched her earlier in his career or just before commencing with his painting.

Not to say there are not slight and subtle differences such as the width and darkness of the brow, hair style, thickness of her lashes and a slight size variation in her lips. But for the most part, the faces resemble each other. The differences, perhaps, changes made at the last minute to his liking.

One could invariably argue that the Madonnas in Da Vinci's *The Madonna Litta* and *Madonna of the Carnation* also resemble the Madonna in our painting as well as the Magdalene in the sketch. In fact, there are some slight similarities in the facial features and hairstyle, especially in the depiction of the Virgin in the *Madonna of the Carnation,* whose hair is presented with small braids at the crown and delicate curls in the style of the sketch. However, the sketch was identified as the Magdalene not as the Virgin. The Madonna in our painting bears far more similarities to the sketch of Mary Magdalene than either of the other paintings I mention. Beneath the façade of Mary the Madonna (Virgin Mother) is Da

Vinci's Mary the Magdalene, the beautiful maternal image he envisioned earlier when drafting the sketch.

A Madonna With Fleur-de-lis Tattoo

A prominent symbol of the painting, the stylized fleur-de-lis that appears tattooed near the Madonna's clavicle just off the shoulder, immediately causes one to ponder its significance and poses a problem. With a change of perspective, it could be viewed projecting from the back of the infant's head as the insignia of a royal house of France. If a tattoo, it would be considered blasphemous. In the Christian world of the 16th century, tattoos were not a fashion statement, reserved only for prisoners and generally frowned upon because of their association with pagan practices. In fact, there is evidence to suggest they were prohibited. In the eyes of the Church, they would have been considered the mark of a sinner as set forth in Leviticus 19:28, "Ye shall not make any cuttings in your flesh for the dead, nor print any marks upon you." Certainly, it would have been considered unbecoming for the Virgin Mary to be adorned with a tattoo, if not blasphemy. The inclusion of a tattoo on the Madonna would have been considered a brazen act of heresy and not likely to slip by unnoticed in a commissioned painting. This suggests the painting was never intended for public viewing, lest the artist be hauled in front of Church inquisitors.

As for the symbol, the fleur-de-lis means, "flower of the lily" and is a well-established and recognizable emblem of France. Its origins at the very least are Merovingian, the French dynasty known as the longhaired Fisher Kings, whose royal blood was professed to trace all the way back to the biblical Noah and whose rule lasted over 300 years. The propaganda of the Church suggests that King Clovis (481 – 511 AD), who united all of Gaul under Merovingian rule, was the first to adopt the symbol at the time of his conversion to Christianity. Versions of the supernatural conversion vary from a vial of oil sent from heaven and delivered by a dove to anoint and sanctify Clovis at his coronation to a variation that says a lily appeared at Clovis' baptismal ceremony as a gift of blessing from an apparition of the Blessed Virgin Mary. What is probably truer is that the fleur-de-lis was not given as a blessing of the Virgin Mother but one given by the Magdalene, especially in light of the fact she was Christ's anointer. The church has had its way of revising authentic legends to support their own Mariology doctrine.

What is mysterious and true is that there has been a shroud of secrecy surrounding the symbol of the fleur-de-lis, hinting at a bloodline connection of matrilineal descent from Mary Magdalene. Therefore, the fleur-de-lis was emblematic for the dynastic bloodline propagated through the vine of Mary Magdalene as well as a symbol of her cult. The bloodline produced a genetic pool of blood royals that included the Capetian kings and the descendants of Louis VII who was the first to adopt the symbol of the fleur-de-lis on his heraldry shield as a coat of arms. It represented the vine of Mary Magdalene, much in the same way that the lion came to represent Jesus' dynastic inheritance from the vine of Judah.

As mentioned earlier, Margaret Starbird, author of *Woman with the Alabaster Jar,* points out that "Merovingian" could be phonetically broken down to "Mer Vin", the "vine of Mary", perhaps intended to point out Merovee's descent from the vine of Mary Magdalene. Whether or not there was any phonetic connection intended, it is true the Fisher Kings stood out for their worship of the feminine, the cult of Diana, which was later transferred over to another goddess—Mary Magdalene as the cult of Mary Magdalene.

In Leonardo's mind, the child on the Madonna's lap is Mary Magdalene's own biological child. He discloses the secret with the omission of the halo and by replacing it with a fleur-de-lis. Mary Magdalene was another "madonna" to whom he was devoted and whom he believed deserved veneration over the Virgin Mother. This long held heretical secret was one that he and a brotherhood of others were bound to protect, but at the end of his life perhaps he had less fear and decided to throw out all caution to the wind. The fleur-de-lis springing forth from the baby's crown signifies his royal inheritance from his mother who also bears the insignia as the Hasmonean Princess who would become "Queen of the Heavens."

A coronation is an interesting theme conveyed symbolically in the composition. If we move away from the Christian legend connected to the carnation and towards its more esoteric and historic meaning, we can unravel the clue of the carnation. The carnation was originally named *dianthus* by a colleague of Plato, the Greek botanist Theopharastus (372-288 BC). The name *Dianthus* is from the Greek, dios ("god") and *anthos* ("flower"), and translates as "flower of God" or more precisely, "God's flower." Some scholars believe that the name "carnation" comes from "coronation" or "corone" because it was used in Greek ceremonial crowns as a garland of flowers. Others believe the name was derived from the Greek *carnis* (flesh), which refers to the original color of the flower, or *incarnacyon* (incarnation), which refers to the incarnation of God, "God made flesh." All three meanings bring new definition to the symbolic representation of the carnation. For Da Vinci, Mary Magdalene, was the coroneted Queen of the Heavens, "God's flower" and even perhaps the feminine face of God in the flesh.

The fact that the Madonna in the painting is really Mary Magdalene is supported by undeniable evidence found on the back of the canvassed wood on which it was painted, according to McLaren. Barely visible in writing, a description reads: "Magdalena." Alongside is a papal bull, a document and seal of decree from Pope Paul V. This strongly suggests the Vatican once possessed the painting and had discovered Da Vinci's heresy.

The John Gesture Debate About the Lamb of God

John the Baptist, who figures prominently in the composition as a child of comparable age to the child on the Madonna's lap, lends to the façade that the painting is a composition of the Virgin Mary and Christ Child with John the Baptist. John is easily identified wearing his woolen tunic, holding his cross staff and standing in close proximity to a lamb, as he is often depicted in art conveying the Gospel narratives in John 1:1-32, summarized in the quote, "Look, the Lamb of God, who takes away the sin of the world!" In the painting, John is seemingly pointing to the lamb while looking in the direction of the child. At the same time, the baby on the Madonna's lap points back to John the Baptist in contradiction, as if to proclaim John the true Messiah (the Lamb of God). This heresy is also depicted in one of the two versions of Da Vinci's *The Virgin of the Rocks* in which the angel Uriel all-knowingly points back to John the Baptist while John reverently bows in prayer before the Christ Child. This allegorical debate within the composition represents a controversial stance about who in the artist's mind is the legitimate bearer of the title, Lamb of God. What is fascinating is that Leonardo painted a second version of *Virgin on the Rocks* in which Uriel no longer points to John the Baptist. Perhaps the change was to safisfy a patron who was not amused by the suggestion in the

Virgin on the Rocks – Da Vinci – circa 1483-1486

St. John the Baptist- Leonardo Da Vinci- 1513-1516

Virgin and Child with St. Elizabeth, John the Baptist
and Michael, unknown artist— 16th century.

first painting. For Da Vinci, at least for a time, it was John the Baptist who he venerated. According to Lynn Picknett and Clive Prince, authors of *The Templar Revelation*, the "John gesture" (pointing finger up) was an arrogant pose of superior knowledge that suggested Leonardo might have adhered to the Gnostic tenets of the Mandaeans. The Mandaeans were a Gnostic sect from the Northern part of Mesopotamia, who migrated there from Judea and whose name is derived from the Aramaic root, "manda", meaning: "knowledge." They claimed to hold the secret laws of God and believed that John the Baptist was the true Messiah. They rejected Jesus Christ as the Son of God, maintaining that he corrupted John's teachings. John's gesture, as rendered in the portrait *John the Baptist*, doesn't seem to be born out of arrogant superiority, but is instead a simple yet meaningful proclamation: "There is only one God." The index finger in the air pointing up coupled with his other hand at his heart, reminds us that the one God in heaven is in our hearts.

This heretical debate over who was the legitimate Lamb of God is even more clearly defined in a 16th century painting from an unknown artist who may have been one of Da Vinci's contemporaries. Titled, *Virgin and Child with Saints Elizabeth John and Michael,* the painting depicts John the Baptist perched next to his mother Elizabeth holding onto a lamb and the Christ child on the Virgin's lap with his hand in the bowl of a balance scale held by Archangel Michael. Interpreted, Michael is determining the measure or worth of Christ's soul, presumably to determine if he is the legitimate Messiah as prophesized in Isaiah 53:1-12.

By reviewing the collection of paintings attributed to Leonardo Da Vinci, we notice the main subject of the vast majority of his paintings was John the Baptist. Some have suggested that his painting *John the Baptist*, like the *Mona Lisa,* possesses transgender or androgynous features. Others, including myself, have gone so far as to conclude that *John the Baptist* was in fact a self-portrait. Da Vinci may have painted himself as John the Baptist because he strongly identified with John as the archetype of the mystic preacher who had not received his due recognition. He painted John the Baptist in a darkened background perhaps to reference the description of St. John in the Bible as 'a light that shineth in the darkness'. Perhaps, Da Vinci himself wished to be hailed: a bright shining light in the world. On the surface, it appears that this last painting re-opens the same subject portrayed in *Virgin on the Rocks* for the same debate. But again, all is not what it seems, as I will explain later.

The Picturesque Setting

The backdrop and setting of Da Vinci's *Madonna and Child with John the Baptist* has been identified by experts as in Aix en Provence, where according to legend Mary Magdalene and Joseph of Arimathea, along with others who fled Judea after the crucifixion, resided and ministered. By legend, Mary died in Aix en Provence, at St. Baume in a mountain cave and was laid to rest at St. Maximin, not all too far from the valley in Da Vinci's representation. A trinity of three mountains, Mount Aurelien, Sainte-Baume and Sainte-Victoire, stand as sentinels for the valleys of Aix, a region of frequent pilgrimages in honor of the Saints who evangelized in the area bringing Christianity to Gaul.

The white limestone mountain in the distance, jeweled with tiny villages at its base, is Mount St. Victoire. Up until the 17th century, St. Victoire was called St. Venture a name probably derived from the earlier name, "Vintour," from the ancient Celtic-Lingures who named it to honor the gods of the wind. A chapel was built at its summit in the 13th century dedicated to "Sainte Venture." Since then the Provençaux call the mountain Sainte-Venture, Sainte-Adventure or Mont Venture. The Cross of Provence stands erect near the summit.

Leonardo probably chose St. Victoire as a backdrop because of its distinct features. It is a recognizable point of reference in Aix en Provence and therefore the viewer could easily make the connection between the location and the legends of Mary Magdalene. Or perhaps, Leonardo had his own more personal reasons for choosing this particular location such as memories born out of his own spiritual pilgrimage to the area.

With two strokes of his brush, Da Vinci brings attention to the apex of the mountain by painting a bird that after closer examination we notice forms an arrow pointing to the mountain summit. It is difficult to make out but there appears to be a tiny golden cross on the peak. Its significance may point to something less noticeable, something I will explain in due course.

John's cross-staff angles, pointing our eyes towards a small chiseled mound of earth and rock that serves as a pedestal for a cedar, yew or cypress tree, a dominant feature in the scenery. What may not be immediately recognized is that the mound, in size and shape, possesses some of same features as Golgotha (Calvary), the site of the crucifixion. Behind John's cross is an elusive shadow of a perpendicular standing cross that could signify the "true cross" of the crucifixion. Symbolically, I would interpret it as the shadow of suffering and memory of the crucifixion that has lingered far too long.

When we adjust our eyes, we discover the first of the many optical illusions in the painting. On the front face of the mound of earth, a spirit face takes shape. First we may notice the eyes and the brows created out of the overhanging ledge and then perhaps the nose. The spirit face resembles Green Man, the pagan fertility deity. The face of this vegetative deity was commonly found carved in wood or stone in churches and on the facades of Romanesque and Gothic cathedrals dating from as early as the 5th and through the 20th century. Green Man has been interpreted to represent, rebirth, resurrection or "Renaissance" because of its association with the vegetative cycle and the arrival of spring. Leonardo included him in the composition to convey something important.

What was Leonardo communicating with these symbolic elements? He is tying two important locations together, Golgotha in Jerusalem and Provence, to remark on the conclusion of one legacy and the beginning of another, a genesis—a new dawn. There atop Golgotha instead of the cross, an evergreen tree stands as the symbol of immortality. The cross has transformed back to its root or original form, an evergreen, which, whether a cedar or a yew, many have suggested was the wood used to construct the true cross. This transformation remarks on a rebirth or a renewal of consciousness. Adding to this interpretation, we notice the evergreen cedar has rich vegetation at its base, signifying abundant growth. Perhaps Da Vinci intended the vegetative growth at the base of the tree to be a part of Green Man's head. Green Man is often depicted in art and sculpture with vegetation growing out of his mouth and head. An example is the Disgorging Green Man on the tomb of St. Abre (c. 4th or 5th century CE), now in the church of St.-Hilaire-le-Grand at Poitiers, France.

Conversely, Golgotha, the place of the skull, was so named because of the unusual naturally chiseled rock formation that still maintains the shape and faces of skulls as a geological feature. It remains a poignant reminder of Jesus' suffering and death on the cross for pilgrims who journey to the Holy Land. It appears Leonardo replaced the skull faces with the face of Green Man to remark on a transformation from death to rebirth, a regeneration theme of renewal. He replaced one mythology for another to mythologize rebirth through resurrection, not the resurrection of Christ but instead the resurrection of the divine feminine—Mary Magdalene. She is resurrected out of the guise of penitent sinner and the shadow of Eve and emerges reborn as the Bride of Christ, but not alone. She is with her son and with him the promise of the continuation of the bloodline. Aix en Provence is the setting where her spirit survives.

Thus far and without a doubt it evident that Da Vinci is speaking to us about the legacy of Mary Magdalene in Provence while at the same time mentioning the crucifixion of Christ and the heretical debate over who was the legitimate lamb of God. This bridge between Golgotha and Provence mentions a renewal of consciousness and of faith, from the suffering of Christ's crucifixion to a renewal with a new focus on his sacred bride, Mary Magdalene. Perhaps even intimating that the New Jerusalem was born through her arrival in Gaul. However, what is even more probable is that Da Vinci is pointing to his own revelations and a shift in his own consciousness achieved through some sort of spiritual experience with the divine feminine, Mary Magdalene. This brings us to what in truth John the Baptist is pointing his finger.

Mary Magdalene as The Lamb of God

If we reexamine the painting, shifting our perspective just enough, we notice that John's finger points to Mary Magdalene (her lap) not to the lamb, as our mind first perceived it out of our expectation. Leonardo's genius created this ambiguity with his knowledge of optics.

In Leonardo's mind, the debate is over and he must admit his mistake in overly identifying with John the Baptist, proclaiming him the Messiah, and dismissing the Goddess. Leonardo as John the Baptist now proclaims a different heresy: Mary Magdalene is the Lamb of God. His choice of the carnation she is holding punctuates this revelation through its symbolic meaning. As we recall, it represents her "coronation," as Queen of the Jews, Queen of the Heavens, Daughter of God, and God made flesh, "in-carnation." For Leonardo, Mary Magdalene is the salvation for the world as the embodiment of wisdom Sophia, the feminine aspect of God and "the one who knew the all." One might wonder if Leonardo reread Isaiah 53 and recognized how if one substituted "she" for "he," the prophecy takes on a whole new meaning. It must be appreciated in its entirety but this portion makes this point:

> "He was despised and rejected – a man of sorrows, acquainted with bitterest grief. We turned our backs on him and looked the other way when he went by. He was despised, and we did not care." – Isaiah 53:3

We must admit that Mary's penitent sinner status certainly could be equated with "a woman of sorrows, acquainted with the bitterest grief", someone whom others would reject as the bride of Christ.

Leonardo might have appreciated this redaction (gender change) of the 16th century translation of John 3:16:

> "For God so loved the world, as to give his only begotten Daughter; that whosoever believeth in her, may not perish, but may have life everlasting."

Why John Has No Foot

A curious element in the painting, John's unfinished foot, leads us to believe Leonardo once again left a masterpiece unfinished, something truly characteristic of his paintings that drew criticism and frustrated his patrons. However, I believe the painting to be near finished and that this missing element was deliberately left unfinished to mention a cripple. Leonardo was pointing out his own physical condition. Furthermore, Leonardo is revealing his identification with John the Baptist by painting him with no right foot, symbolizing his own paralysis. There was no better way to portray a handicapped man without confusing the viewer.

If the painting truly was Leonardo's last commission as proposed by McLaren, then he was in the later stages of his life when he painted it. The last three years of his life were spent in the service of Frances I, the King of France, who offered him the manor house, *Clos Luce*, as his residence in Amboise. While there, in 1517, he suffered a stroke that paralyzed his right side. But, because he was left-handed this disability did not hinder him from painting. It was during this time, between 1517 and his death in May of 1519 that Leonard painted this Magdalene-Madonna. Some twenty years after Leonardo's death, Francis I was quoted as saying, "There had never been another man born in the world who knew as much as Leonardo, not so much about painting, sculpture and architecture, as that he was a very great philosopher."

The Grail Table

John's invisible foot rests and bears its weight on another important element that at first glance merely appears to be a piece of wood in the foreground. To understand what it represents, we must look again to the symbol of the lamb posed lying on it. Considering an alternative meaning for the lamb, we can render it a double meaning. In this case, the lamb represents the Pascal lamb associated with the Passover meal at the house of Simon, the Last Supper. Therefore, the slab of wood is really a table. Though not the same height as the table Da Vinci painted in *The Last Supper*, we do notice that Mary's left knee does fit beneath it, confirming that we are looking not at a slab or plank of wood on the ground but a table as a foreground that extends on three sides beyond the paintings parameters. Leonardo probably shortened it to make the painting work as a composition. Although McLaren didn't recognize the piece of wood as a table, she did mention that Mary's slanted pose is reminiscent of her position in the Last Supper. The angles line up well when the image is superimposed.

The question arises how does the Last Supper table fit into the setting of Provence and what was Leonardo wanting to convey symbolically? Leonardo was mentioning that Mary Magdalene had carried forward Jesus' ministry in Provence, had gathered her own disciples and was the leader of the Grail Church. The table in the painting then represents the Grail Table. As we recall, the Grail Table, as the second table, represented the table of initiation where a dissemination of mystical teachings from master to disciple was accomplished. These rites of initiation and teachings were brought to Gaul by Mary Magdalene and Joseph of Arimathea (Jesus) and represented the second chapter of Christ's ministry, hence the second table. It is unlikely that Leonardo was privy to the Cistercian secret of Joseph of Arimathea's true identity and that Jesus accompanied Mary to Gaul. Therefore, in Leonardo's eyes, Mary Magdalene had taken Jesus' place and was seated in his position. As with the meaning of the mound with the evergreen, Leonardo was referencing two tables in his painting, and two periods in the history of Jesus and Mary Magdalene's legacy, adding his own twist to the mythology laid out in *La Queste del Saint Graal* which we can be sure he would have enjoyed reading for its mythologizing of the high history of the Holy Grail. By seating Mary Magdalene at the Grail table, Leonardo is mentioning that Mary Magdalene carried the covenant forward with her ministry in Provence.

Why does Leonardo rest John's missing foot on the table? The obvious answer is to bring attention to the missing foot. But I can't help but wonder if Leonardo wasn't humbly asking for the power of the Grail, Christ's intercession and Mary's compassion, to restore him to health and for his sins to be forgiven as they were forgiven in the gospel of account of the paralyzed man (Mark 2:1-12). He also could have been pointing back to the legend and account of King David welcoming the crippled son of Jonathan to sit at his table as an act of humility and compassion.

V's and Widow's Peak

To authenticate the painting as a Da Vinci, McLaren points out a number of "V's" in the painting and describes them as representing the divine feminine, the V-shape chalice pointing to the mystery of the Holy Grail. The theory that Da Vinci encoded *The Last Supper* with the V-shape, signifying Mary Magdalene was the Holy Grail, was first introduced Margaret Starbird in *Woman with the Alabaster Jar* and later sensationalized in Dan Brown's *The Da Vinci Code*. Specifically, McLaren points to the noticeable V part-line in Mary Magdalene's hairline as a known characteristic in another of Leonardo's paintings. However, from our perspective the hairline symbol is the inverted V, not the chalice V, and therefore, the interpretation may not be exactly correct. Needless to say, it is only part of an equation being conveyed by Leonardo. After closer examination, we notice the baby has the reverse, the V, as a quite pronounced widow's peak. Da Vinci had encoded this painting with arcane symbols, the V and inverted V that point to a mystery associated with the tenets of the underground Gnostic stream of Christianity. These two symbols fused together form the "X" that can be found in religious art of the Middle Ages and recognized now as a symbol adopted by a secret underground community of Christians. The two symbols further point to the mystery of the sacred union, sacred bride and bridegroom united in the bridal chamber. In psychological alchemy it is referred to as the *sacred marriage*. The V (masculine) and inverted V (feminine) join together as the unification of opposites, male and female, descending spirit and ascending matter, fire and water. This unification principle is also symbolically represented in the Star of David that merges descending and ascending triangles. The same mystery (making the two one) Jesus taught to his disciples as the key to the realization of the Kingdom of God in saying 22 of the Gospel of Thomas.

And what of John the Baptist who has a quite pronounced inverted V in his hairline to complement Mary's? Now that we have established that Leonardo had painted himself as John the Baptist, we can perhaps understand why he would distinguish himself with the inverted V. My thoughts are perhaps Leonardo was in fact gay, as many have concluded from his history and from the androgynous features in the *Mona Lisa's* face and the portraits of John the Baptist. I believe Leonardo identified more with the feminine soul than with the masculine archetype and that he was hinting at a personal secret as cleverly as he could.

Afterlife of Optical Illusions

The day after the photo of the painting was released in a UK newspaper article about the discovery, a comment left by a young man mentioned an illusive image of an animal that he described as a horse in the right hand side of the upper quadrant of the painting. The image emerges from the seemingly blank space as an illusory spirit horse whose profile faces right near the edge of the wooden canvas. Once the nostril opening is noticed, the head of the horse crystallizes. After closer examination, not only does a horse become visible but also two, if not more, superimposed or overlapping faces emerge within the same area. They appear as two bearded men, one a profile facing left, the other a frontal pose. The faces emerge as our eyes and brain adjust and interact to perceive the many optical illusions Leonardo painted into the background. The profile of the man with beard facing left I concluded to be a self-portrait.

For Leonardo, optics was at the foundation of painting. Throughout his life, he observed optical phenomena and recorded them in geometrical diagrams and jotted down lengthy notes, made sketches and drawings within his notebooks. Leonardo studied ancient and medieval optical treatises such as those of Aristotle, Euclid, and Ptolemy to name a few. He imagined and created experiments with colored light sources, projective screens, mirrors and apertures, and investigated optical illusions and their errors. He seemed fascinated by the interaction between sensory information and the intellectual processes of the 'sensus communis' (Aristole's principle), imagination, and memory, in an attempt to explain the role of the senses in the acquisition of knowledge. The genius of Da Vinci should never be underestimated.   He had developed techniques beyond any artist in his time or for that matter in our time to create complex and astonishing imagery with many layers of visual experience all loaded with meaning.

The question arises: What did Leonardo have in mind in painting such an illusory space with layers of faces and to include his own? Was he merely practicing an illusionary optic technique to create supernatural ghostly figures for mere amusement or was something plaguing his mind?

Leonardo had been plagued by ill health the last two years of his life. The paralysis that left him disabled would have surely frustrated him. As his body weakened he probably knew he would soon depart this world for the next. He recognized death was eminent and perhaps welcomed it. His philosophy of death is best expressed by this quotation, "As a well spent day brings happy sleep, so a life well spent brings happy death."

After piecing together the clues, I have concluded that Da Vinci was contemplating his own death, his transition from this world to the next— an afterlife. The ghostly and elusive and illusory faces were painted in a spirit world, heaven, beyond the world we know yet at the same time interfacing it. Perhaps, one of the faces alongside him was his father whom he imagined would be there in a bardo to greet him. And if the other faces are not just creations of the imagination, then perhaps they are friends who had made their transition years before and there now to help him complete his own journey. The bridled horse for the heaven bound traveler mentions another helper on his journey to the other side. We know that Leonardo was an animal lover. Horses were often the subjects of his sketches and he once created a silver lyre in the shape of a horse's head on which he performed an improvisational piece that drew him praise. It would be natural for him to paint a beloved and familiar animal ally to be with him on this journey into the heavenly realms. What's clear to me is that Da Vinci was preparing spiritually for his death and that perhaps the process of painting was helping him make peace with the fact.

Da Vinci's Conversion

The painting now can be accurately named: *Magdalene-Madonna and Child with John the Baptist*.   Painting this masterpiece was Leonardo's way to record and define his awakening, knowledge and revelations, a change and complete transformation in his consciousness and in his thinking. For Leonardo, Mary Magdalene was not the epitome of penitence or merely one of the Apostles. And she was more than the carrier of a bloodline, more than a Hasmonean Queen whose lineage was more regal and priestly than Jesus' and she was more than the bride of Christ. She was the divine feminine through whose heart Leonardo could embrace the afterlife and touch the more divine aspect of his own feminine soul. She had truly become defined in his painting as the feminine face of God and also perhaps as a substitute for his own mother, Caterina, who he was separated from at an early age. He was intimately bonded to the Magdalene in his last years.

The painting remarks on a progression and integration of spiritual knowledge and understanding that he could no longer keep to himself. He left enough obvious and even brazen clues in the painting to demand a more thorough search for additional clues to put the pieces of a puzzle together of a truer legacy for Mary Magdalene as well as for him. A scientist turned mystic who had transcended his arrogance and abandoned his previous spiritual misconceptions in defiance of the Church, he was now a humble man and a determined soul. He was desperate and determined to leave this world having expressed what he knew to be true and what his heart felt. One can't help but wonder if he foresaw a time when his heresy would be more accepted.

There is evidence to suggest that Leonardo had a deep calling, a destiny that he may have been privy to at an early age. Da Vinci reveals in *Selections from The Notebooks of Leonardo da Vinci*, that one of his earliest memories was a dream of a kite. In his own words,

> "Writing about the kite seems to be my destiny since among the first recollections of my infancy it seemed to me that I was in my cradle and a kite came to me and opened my mouth with its tail and struck me several times with its tail inside my lips."

Numerous dream researchers including Freud and Erich Neumann have discussed Leonardo's dream. From a transpersonal and shamanistic perspective of dream interpretation, the kite (Falcon) was an animal ally, a spiritual messenger helping to open the mouth of the young Leonardo before he could even speak. Perhaps, he arrived to signal the time for Leonardo to utter his first words. The dream was to remind him throughout his life that his destiny was to express through his gifts and genius what others could only imagine. He was to express the unspeakable truth.

Jesus Hidden In the Background

In further examining the painting, we see an irregularity with Mary's right hand resting against her son's chest. The thumb and forefinger are recognizably those of a man, not of a woman. When compared to the other three more delicate and slender fingers with long nails they are quite a bit larger and the broad thumbnail is noticeably clipped. This oddity was one of the first clues I noticed in the painting and puzzled me for several days. My first thought was that once again Leonardo was pointing to the androgyny of the soul as he had in so many earlier paintings like the *Mona Lisa*. However, with closer examination, we can see there are really two hands. Mary's hand and arm covers the majority of the man's fingers and her son rests his hand on the man's hand signifying an emotional connection and bond. The three hands together represent a family bond: father, mother and child, as a unit bonded with love. But from where does this hand appear? Would Da Vinci have painted such a surreal anomaly without artistic explanation? No. Figuratively speaking, the hand belongs to the man sitting with them—Jesus Christ.

To find Jesus in the painting we must travel up the canvas back to the arrow created out of the bird's wings. There we may notice that a wing lies adjacent to a cheek and points down to the jaw line of another large illusory face emanating from the background. Its chin rests in the concave dip of the mountain and once our eyes adjust, comes completely into form above and adjacent to Mary's right shoulder.

The face that is in correct proportion to the disembodied hand, I thought at first to be masculine. Someone else who noticed the emanating spirit face mentioned it looked like a Sun god. For a time, I concluded the face must be Jesus, whose hand appeared

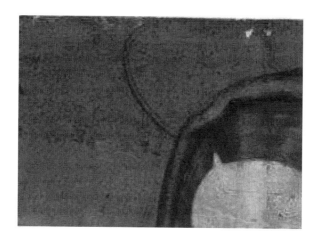

Jesus' illusory face (eyes and nose) within the halo

Mary's Spirit—her chin rests in the concave slope, eye and brow at edge of halo and a veil cascades down the middle of the Madonna's face.

manifest beneath Mary's hand as well as beneath the infant's. However, the feminine features of the face haunted me for several days and because I noticed a shadow of light outlining a veil descending from the figure's head down the bridge of the Magdalene's nose, I decided to take another look with fresh eyes the next morning. What emerged was nothing short of astonishing. Another face emanates from in front and behind as well as just above the feminine illusory face as if the two were partly superimposed. It is another optical illusion and more difficult for the brain to grasp. The eyes and nose of the face are captured within the left side of Mary Magdalene's halo. Once noticed, it takes only a moment or two for the image to crystallize. This face is clearly masculine and because of its proximity to the now clearly defined feminine face with veil, we are delivered to the images Leonardo had in mind.

We can venture a guess that these godly spirit figures are the ascended spirits of Mary Magdalene and Jesus, portrayed as Divine Complements, God and Goddess, Christ and Christa and husband and wife. Apparitions born out of the vision of a genius and put to canvas. Amongst other things, Da Vinci had painted a worldly and otherworldly family portrait. And he had included himself as he envisioned his entrance into the heavenly realm would be. With this in mind, we recognize that Leonardo fully expected to be greeted by Christ and the Magdalene at the end of his life as he made his transition. Now we notice Mary does seem to be looking in Leonardo's direction and that he stands humbly before her and her partner, Jesus.

Seeking to add a bit more so that important connections were made, Leonardo again applied his knowledge of optics to the eyes he painted for the spirit of Mary Magdalene (the woman spirit with veil). With a perceptual shift, the eyes change from glazing downward and towards the right side of the canvas to glancing back in the direction of the evergreen tree, as if to stress the importance of the mound with the tree. And, of course, as mentioned earlier, it is important in conveying the completion of the crucifixion mythology to usher in a period of rebirth and renewal. An old cycle is completed with God and Goddess resurrected together and reunited, reconciling the separation created in a pseudo-myth of a dying God without a partner.

There is a bit more meaning that we can extract from Leonardo's depiction of Jesus. We must first ask why Leonardo painted the hand fully manifest in human form instead of merely carrying forward the entire figure as an illusory spirit. Those already familiar with the discovery of a disembodied hand in Da Vinci's painting *The Last Supper* may see this in the same light—a hand with a difficult to establish hidden meaning. My thinking is that Leonardo had a change of heart and change in position as to whether Jesus was an incarnated god. In combination, the human hand and divine spirit, translates to mean, "God made flesh," something I believe Leonardo was unwilling to accept in earlier years when he became influenced by many conflicting views of other traditions and because of his obvious disdain for the doctrine of the Church of Rome.

The depiction points to a conversion in his beliefs, but one that recognizes both God and Goddess as divine, having served humanity together. I believe this conversion was born out of a spiritual experience that expanded Leonardo's view and turned his old opinions and religious beliefs upside down. It is well documented that Leonardo planned for his own funeral, calling for three major masses and some thirty smaller masses at four different churches. He asked the church deacon and sub-deacon to accompany his body for burial, as well as a procession of sixty paupers to follow the casket. One might conclude he sought absolution for his sins and to be seen as a humbled true Christian, if not by his fellow man then to his heavenly companions, Jesus and Mary.

The painting *Magdalene-Madonna and Child with John the Baptist* may very well be the most brilliantly laid out multilayered heretical painting of all time. I am of the opinion, after considering all the hidden clues found by myself and a few others, that its authenticity is a given: This was Da Vinci's creation, at the very least in its conceptualization, design, and composition. If not all done by his own hand, because of his weakened condition, then completed with the help of his lifelong companion and apprentice, Francesco Melzi, who may have assisted in rendering it to canvas. The expert verification of this fact will unfortunately have to wait until the painting is sent to the labs to be thoroughly examined. Until then there are apt to be those who discover even more hidden symbols, illusory optical images, divine numbers and proportions that could add even more to this interpretation.

Packed with symbolic meaning, the painting summons us to see with new eyes to grasp a secret legacy that few in Da Vinci's time had any knowledge of. Leonardo, I am sure wished everyone could have known what he did and could comprehend what he struggled with spiritually and believed to be true: Mary Magdalene was not the penitent sinner the Church had painted her to be. She was the Bride of Christ and the mother of his son.

This once lost and probably last masterpiece offers the clearest evidence to date that with certainty Leonardo coded his paintings with clues, metaphorical elements with hidden meanings, and arcane symbols to disclose heretical secrets. It should spark new interest and open the door for more thorough analysis of Da Vinci's earlier works. Hopefully this interpretation will reopen what was begun by the authors of *Holy Blood Holy Grail* and dramatized in Dan Brown's *The Da Vinci Code* for serious discussion and debate, not only from conspiracy theorists, but those open-minded individuals who were waiting for some more substantial evidence.

VAN GOGH'S RESURRECTION

Raising of Lazarus- Vincent Van Gogh - 1891

The Raising of Lazarus is one of only a few compositions Vincent van Gogh painted on a religious theme. It was executed while he was recovering from a bout of psychosis at the hospital at Saint Remy de Provence, only 70 kilometers north of Saintes-Maries-de-la-Mer where according to legend Mary Magdalene and others arrived on the shores of the village in France. Like Da Vinci's *Magdalene Madonna with Christ and St. John,* the painting was put to canvas the last year of Vincent's life, a time during which he suffered great emotional turmoil and anguish from mental illness. Some commentators have suggested Lazarus was a self-portrait because he is painted with a ginger white beard and resembles Vincent a great deal. Van Gogh perhaps identified with Lazarus at the time, seeing himself as needing healing and a resurrection of sort.

The painting was based on an etching by Rembrandt that depicts the biblical scene of the raising of Lazarus by Jesus in front of witnesses (John 11:1-44). In Rembrandt's version, Jesus is the central figure performing the miracle while a number of others stand around as witnesses. However, Van Gogh chose to omit a great deal from his painting, depicting Mary Magdalene and Martha as the only two present, as if to remark Lazarus had been raised by Mary. .

This interesting composition remarks on a transcendent experience that so moved Vincent that he felt compelled to convey his lucid awakening to the resurrecting power of Mary Magdalene on canvas. Coupled with his painting *The Angel, a* stellar blue angel with golden halo painted in the same year, *The Raising of Lazarus* is a departure from Van Gogh's usual subjects of nature and reality. It certainly would not have been unusual for someone suffering a psychotic episode to have religious and spiritual ideations, but this painting demonstrates not only Van Gogh's spiritual side, but contains a great deal of psychological insight and sophistication. It is beyond the meanderings of a sick mind.

In my mind, *The Raising of Lazarus* conveys Vincent's own healing process on the road to what would be only a temporary recovery. He may have very well made conscious contact with the divine healing energies of Mary Magdalene's intercession. For Vincent, Mary Magdalene's miracle was greater than Christ's.

CHAPTER TEN
Expectant Magdalene

God gave birth to us all and there was no sin attached to it.

The same heresy Leonardo Da Vinci implied with hidden clues and the use of optics in the *Last Supper* and The *Magdalene Madonna* was made explicit by a Flemish artist a century before: Mary Magdalene was the spouse of Christ and the vessel for the child produced by their union.

A highly revered Flemish primitive painting hangs in Museo del Prado in Madrid one that has been the subject of commentary by art historians, described, analyzed and appreciated for its detail in depicting Christ being brought down from the cross.

The Deposition, as it is titled, was painted by Rogier van der Weyden, a master Flemish painter of the 15th century. The painting was an altarpiece, commissioned for the chapel of the Confraternity of the Archers or Crossbowmen of Leuven. The two small crossbows in the lower spandrels of the tracery in the picture were emblematic for the Confraternity. Mary of Hungary (1505-1558), Regent of the Netherlands, acquired the painting from the Archers of Leuven before 1548. Later it came into the possession of her nephew King Philip II of Spain (1527-1598; king from 1556), who finally placed it in the monastery fortress of the Escorial he had founded near Madrid. At that time *The Deposition* was the centerpiece of a triptych, but there is little indication that the side wings were originally part of the work. It is thought that *The Deposition* was originally a single panel.

The composition is a snapshot of an emotional moment in time, with Jesus' body having been brought down from the cross and nine other figures participating in some role and exhibiting varying degrees of grief. The Virgin has succumbed to a fainting spell and John the Evangelist has leaned over to catch her. The Virgin is depicted as suffering from an unsightly case of goiter because her thyroid and neck appear swollen. Depicting the immaculate Virgin in this light should have raised some eyebrows at the very least, if not perceived as complete blasphemy. The holy women, relatives of the Virgin, are behind her, one in support and the other overcome

Deposition - Rogier van der Weyden – circa 1435

Deposition Close-up - Rogier van der Weyden – 1435

Visitation - Rogier van der Weyden – 1445

Closeup of spiral lacing

Mary Magdalene - Rogier van der Weyden – 1450

by her own sorrow. Visibly, tears stream down her face like pearls. A richly clothed Joseph of Arimathea solemnly carries the torso of the body of Christ while Nicodemus in a fine gold brocade robe supports the legs. Behind him and high up on the ladder leaning against the cross is an unidentified man who holds the crucifixion nails in hand and just over Nicodemus' left shoulder is another man whose sole function seems to be to hold Mary Magdalene's alabaster jar while she leans against him for support.

Mary Magdalene is portrayed as a grief stricken woman with tears of sorrow streaming down her face. She clutches her hand in the "prayer of the heart" position with fingers locked together.

Upon close inspection, details emerge that turn the subject of this painting into a whole other subject than at first glance. By magnifying Mary Magdalene's image, we notice several unusual elements that up until now have gone unnoticed or at the very least were glossed over. Or perhaps, art historians avoided remarking on them because of the implied heresy.

First of all, Mary Magdalene wears a simple gold band on the ring finger of her right hand. At the time this painting was commissioned and executed it was customary for brides to wear a wedding ring on the right hand not the left. It was not until the 16th century that this custom changed to the left hand. Although a few portraits by other Flemish painters have depicted Mary Magdalene as regally dressed and adorned with fine jewelry, even thumb rings, only a few others portray her wearing a wedding ring. An example is a 16th century painting titled *Mary Magdalene Reading* painted by Ambrosius Bensen that depicts Mary with prayer book in hand and a wedding ring on the left hand. For Weyden as well as Bensen, Mary Magdalene was a married woman and we can definitely assume they believed she was betrothed to Jesus. The "prayer heart position" of her hands is one that was frequently used in association with Mary Magdalene. A survey of Renaissance art will prove countless examples such as, George de la Tour's *Penitent Magdalene with Twin Flames*, El Greco's *Penitent Magdalene*, Caravaggio's *Mary Magdalene in Ecstasy* and *Marie Madeleine* at the altar of the chapel at Rennes le Chateau. The hand position not only takes on the symbolism of a heart but also speaks of the binding love of her commitment to Jesus and their union.

Weyden also painted other symbolic elements that not only confirm Mary's position as Jesus' wife but also suggest she was pregnant with child. Looking at Mary Magdalene's clothing, we notice the predominant dress she wears is actually an under dress, a kirtle. Her overdress, mantle, or cloak had slipped down to her hips forming soft folds of fabric all the way to the ground. We recognize that the cloak must have fallen off her shoulder because the pin that once held it up remains. The under dress (kirtle) is in fact a 15th century maternity dress that characteristically laced up the front so that it could be adjusted (let out) as a pregnancy progressed. We notice that below her waist the lacing is loosened and slightly open to reveal a white undergarment beneath. The lacing had been loosened to accommodate her growing pregnancy belly and when we take a closer look it does appear protruding to denote a pregnancy bump.

Spiral lacing that could be adjusted to accommodate a full term figure was characteristic of maternity wear in the 15th century. In the 1445 painting *The Visitation,* again by Weyden, we notice that the red gown on Elizabeth, who was pregnant with St. John the Baptist at the time, had side lacing that is loosened and stretched apart to accommodate her growing figure. The close-up detail shows the separated spiral side lacing to be similar to that on Mary Magdalene's kirtle in *The Deposition*. This would still permit a fairly form-fitting gown that could be tightened afterwards.

Another intriguing element is the belt with two ornamental medallions and a chain dropping down, framing and accentuating her pregnant belly. The belt, referred to as a *girdle*, not to be confused with a chastity belt, was an ornamental fashion statement during the Middle Ages denoting a woman's status. The pendant tag or medallions at the belt end are known as *belt-chape*s. Many such belts had decorative buckles and additional metal mountings and most had a metal chape at the end. The higher a woman's status the more likely her girdle would be rich with ornamentation.

Beginning in the 13th century, girdles were popular wedding gifts given to brides. By the 15th century, girdles were less commonly presented as gifts, but they retained romantic significance. Girdles were often personalized with heraldic motifs or decorations that symbolized ownership, allegiance or love. Some girdles were inscribed with mottoes and sayings personal to the owner, sentiments of faith and love. These sentiments seemed to reflect the symbolism of the girdle itself. A girdle could signify chastity, virginity and fidelity owing to the intimate nature of the object and where it was worn. By removing her girdle and giving it to her husband, a lady symbolically bestowed her love and fidelity.

The most astonishing least hidden clue in *The Deposition* lies in the embossed inscription on the girdle written in Latin. Rather than a motto, it is inscribed with a name. The name is actually two names strung together spelling out— IOESVSMARIA. From Latin to English, the name translates as: "JESUSMARIA". Although the most common spelling for Jesus in Latin is "IESVS", "IEOSVS" is a close variant of that spelling. The "OE" diphthong would be pronounced as a "long E", "JEESUS". What was Weyden hinting at with this inscription on the belt? He wasn't hinting at anything. He was proclaiming loud and clear the sentiments and status of the woman who is wearing it. The two names represent the sacred union of bride and bridegroom, husband and wife. As with the ring, the inscription denotes Mary's faithfulness to the bond of love between she and Jesus. And because the belt frames her pregnant belly it points to the paternity of the child Mary Magdalene is carrying. Weyden spelled it out as clearly and cleverly as he could. Little JESUSMARIA was being nurtured within the womb of his mother, Maria Magdalene. The belt is, therefore, emblematic of Mary Magdalene's status as Jesus' wife and the mother of the child from their union.

The Deposition is only one of two paintings in which Weyden painted Mary Magdalene dressed in a maternity kirtle. The second portrait, *Mary Magdalene* (circa 1450), represents the right panel of the *Braque Triptych* and is considered one of the finest Flemish 15th century portraits in existence. Mary is dressed in a kirtle highlighted by fine red and gold brocade sleeves. The brocade is engrailed with pomegranates, a symbol not only of fertility but one that mentions her priestly lineage as a Hasmonean. Exodus 28:33-34 states that images of pomegranates be woven into the hem of the me'il ("robe of ephod"), a robe worn by the Hebrew High Priest. Her dress therefore is a reminder of her regal status and that she is the dynastic heiress of a Davidic legacy through her marriage to Jesus. Again, as with *The Deposition,* the front lacing on her kirtle is stretched open (separated) and her belly distended to hint at pregnancy. Overall, this portrayal of a pregnant Mary Magdalene is a far cry from the penitent representations preferred and celebrated by the Church. Instead, Mary is presented with her alabaster jar in hand appearing noble, royal, stately and dignified.

Written at the top of the painting on the blue-sky horizon is the passage from Vulgate John, Chapter 12, that describes Mary of Bethany anointing Jesus' feet with expensive spikenard at the house of Simon. In Latin it reads: *"Maria ergo accepit libram ungenti nardi pistici, pretiosi, et unxit pedes Iesu"*. In KJV-English: *"Then took Mary a pound of ointment of spikenard, very costly, and anointed the feet of Jesus"*. Interestingly, Weyden chose the most intimate scene between Jesus and Mary Magdalene in all the Gospels for the inscription of this panel. The inscription ties together the pregnancy elements of the portrait and identifies Mary Magdalene and Mary of Bethany as one and the same. By pointing back to the anointing at the House of Simon, Weyden intimates that more transpired after the meal and anointing ritual. The couple, who were husband and wife, consummated their love and a child was conceived.

Another painting by Rogier van der Weyden contains heretical elements that hint at Mary Magdalene's status as high priestess and as the carrier of the dynastic bloodline and legitimate head of the Church. The painting titled, *The Lamentation of Christ* is an oil-on-panel that is now housed at the Uffizi Gallery in Florence, Italy. It was painted by Weyden between 1460 and 1463 having been commissioned by the Medici, the royal dynastic house of Florence.

The iconographic painting depicts the body of Christ being carried into the tomb with the weeping Virgin Mary and John the Evangelist supporting his arms in a way that mimics Christ on the cross. Christ's body is propped up and supported by the richly dressed biblical characterization of Joseph of Arimathea and by Nicodemus. In the foreground, Mary Magdalene is dressed in a bluish-white overdress, mantle or robe, and is posed kneeling on the ground giving a blessing. Beneath her legs is what appears to be a wooded staff or stave.

The impossibility that the thin wooden rod/staff was inserted in the painting to represent an instrument used to pry open the thick stone door, led me to wonder what it represented in the artist's mind. Its position beneath the door as well as underneath Mary's legs hints that it is connected to her in some way. The most plausible interpretation is that it represents the Rod of Jesse, a symbol of the dynastic succession and divine authority associated with Jesus as foretold by Isaiah 11-1-2.

Lamentation - Rogier van der Weyden - 1460-1463

"And there shall come forth a rod out of the stem of Jesse, and a Branch shall grow out of his roots: And the spirit of the Lord shall rest upon Him, the spirit of wisdom and understanding, the spirit of counsel and might, the spirit of knowledge and of the fear of the Lord"

The biblical origins of the rod as a staff or stave as a symbol of genealogy, divine authority and spiritual power point back to Moses and his brother Aaron. Numbers 17 reads,

"And the LORD spake unto Moses, saying,
Speak unto the children of Israel, and take of every one of them a rod according to the house of their fathers, of all their princes according to the house of their fathers twelve rods: write thou every man's name upon his rod.
And thou shalt write Aaron's name upon the rod of Levi: for one rod shall be for the head of the house of their fathers.
And thou shalt lay them up in the tabernacle of the congregation before the testimony, where I will meet with you.
And it shall come to pass, that the man's rod, whom I shall choose, shall blossom: and I will make to cease from me the murmurings of the children of Israel, whereby they murmur against you.
And Moses spake unto the children of Israel, and every one of their princes gave him a rod apiece, for each prince one, according to their fathers' houses, even twelve rods: and the rod of Aaron was among their rods.
And Moses laid up the rods before the LORD in the tabernacle of witness.
And it came to pass, that on the morrow Moses went into the tabernacle of witness; and, behold, the rod of Aaron for the house of Levi was budded, and brought forth buds, and bloomed blossoms, and yielded almonds."

According to Judaic literature, this same rod that belonged to Moses and his brother Aaron was passed down paternally to King David who was recognized as the first King of Israel. Not only was it symbolic of his spiritual authority, it afforded him the supernatural power and strength to slay Goliath. The great prophecies of the Old Testament, such as Isaiah, clearly foretold of a divine King –the coming Messiah. Jesse was the father of David whose line of kingly heirs would eventually be cut off by virtue of their sins (e.g., Jeremiah 22:28-30; 36:30). But God had also promised David that his seed would, indeed, establish his throne forever (II Samuel 7:6; Jeremiah 33:17).

If the everlasting promise by God was to be fulfilled then there would obviously be other heirs, a continuation of the bloodline throughout the ages. The fact that the Rod of Jesse in the painting is beneath Mary remarks she was the vessel carrying the seed of the Davidic line. In the mind of the artist and as the symbol implies, Mary was the vessel carrying the child of her union with Jesus. She carried the heir to the Davidic throne in her own body.

Mary Magdalene is the only figure in the painting turned away with her back towards the viewer. Perhaps it was Weyden's way of intimating a concealed pregnancy as he had with two other of his paintings. Also, Mary is draped in bluish white linen cloth closely mirroring the burial cloth draped around Jesus. This fact connects the two intimately and elicits the image of bride and bridegroom, complementing each other. Perhaps Weyden derived the linen robe symbolism to signify the Bride from the following passage:

> "Then I heard what sounded like a great multitude, like the roar of rushing waters and like loud peals of thunder, shouting:"

> "Hallelujah! For our Lord God Almighty reigns,
> and give him glory!
> For the wedding of the Lamb has come,
> And his bride has made herself ready.
> Fine linen, bright and clean
> Was given to her to wear." — Revelations 16: 6-8

The robe is characteristically a priests' or priestess' robe. Her kneeling posture mentions her service to Christ and her arms extended out are not that of repentant or lamenting woman but instead conveys a priestess' function to bless the body of the deceased and serve as a spiritual mediator.

Next to Mary, tipped on its side, is an earthen water jug. Curiously, on the opposite side of the painting is a Ciborium, a mass implement made of gold that traditionally holds the host (the bread or communion wafer), signifying the sacred sacrament. Like Magdalene's jar it also represents a sacred vessel. In addition to bringing balance to the composition, the Ciborium symbolically ties the body of Christ with the sacrament of the Church and satisfies the function of the painting as an altarpiece. However, something else is subtly implied by the position of the two vessels in relationship to Mary and the rod or staff. The rod points to and rests with Mary Magdalene rather than pointing to the Ciborium which is placed some distance from the opposite end of the rod signifying a separation or gap and thus minimizing its value and the Church's authority. Was Weyden saying that divine authority was given to Mary and the child she was carrying and not to the Church? For two thousand years, the Church has insisted that it was the Bride of Christ and that references to the Bridegroom and Bride in the Bible were to be interpreted as such. However, for Weyden, Mary Magdalene was the Bride whose union with Jesus culminated in the Wedding Feast.

Difficult as it can be to ascertain exactly what was in the artist's mind, there is little doubt the elements are positioned in a deliberate fashion to make a point. In this case, the point was to disclose through symbolic placement the artist's Magdalene-centered Gnostic beliefs. As a Gnostic heretic and one partially in the know, Weyden had painted the *Lamentation* as a heretical composition in the guise of a traditional Station of the Cross. In it he conveyed an alternative view of Mary Magdalene, one held by a Gnostic community to whom Weyden was probably a member. This Gnostic community believed Mary Magdalene was the legitimate Bride of Christ as well as the authority of the true Church. Amongst themselves, they opposed the doctrine and Christology of the Church that sought to persecute them for heresy.

Rogier van der Weyden was a Northern Renaissance painter who was one of the three most influential Northern European artists of his time. The other two who gained as much popularity were Robert Campin and Jan van Eyck. Most of Weyden's surviving works were religious paintings, however, he produced secular paintings and a few portraits, most of them lost.

Little is known about Rogier van der Weyden from first hand sources, because most records were destroyed or lost in 1695 and then again in 1940. Rogier van der Weyden's birth name was Rogier de la Pasture and he was born in 1399/1400, Tournai Belgium. He was the son of a knife maker and husband to a shoemaker's daughter, and there is indication he was well educated because in 1426 he was honored by the city as "Maistre (Master). He began painting at the age of twenty-seven, his career beginning as an apprentice in the workshop of Robert Campin, who was the dean of the painters' guild. Rogier remained in Campin's workshop for five years, becoming an independent master of the guild on August 1, 1432. From Campin, Rogier developed his style of realism, and so alike, in fact, are the styles of these two masters that experts still do not agree on the attribution of certain works. There is no indication however, Weyden derived his heretical beliefs from Campin.

Weyden later moved to Brussels where he established himself as the official painter for the city. The post of city painter was created especially for him and was meant to lapse on his death which occurred in 1364. His position in Brussels was linked to a huge commission to paint four justice scenes for the 'Golden Chamber' of Brussels City Hall. The acquisition of property and investments that are documented suggest he became quite affluent. The portraits he painted of the Burgundian Dukes, their relatives and courtiers, demonstrate a close relationship with the elite of the Netherlands.

Beyond the heretical subject of the three paintings, *The Deposition*, *The Lamentation* and *Mary Magdalene*, there is no documentation that sheds any light on Weyden's spiritual beliefs or religious affiliations.

Weyden's fearlessness in depicting Mary Magdalene as married and pregnant perhaps had something to do with his patrons the Guild of the Crossbow men who commissioned *The Deposition* or to the Medici, the godfathers of the Renaissance.

There are numerous examples of Renaissance paintings that portray Mary Magdalene as an expectant mother such as Georges le Tour's *Penitent Magdalen in which Mary* sits in front of a candle lit mirror, her belly obviously protruded, and Caravaggio's *Ecstatic Mary Magdalene*. At least one North Netherlandish artist followed the footsteps of Weyden because almost one hundred years later he produced his own pregnant lady in a painting titled: St. Mary Magdalene. It is attributed to an unknown painter who is only referred to as The Master Mansi, named for a painting attributed to him that hangs in the Staatliche Museum in Berlin. The Master was known to have also borrowed from some of the engravings by Durer, one as late as 1511 and was a follower of the Flemish painter Quentin Matsys.

In his portrait, *Mary Magdalene*, Master depicts a very pregnant Mary in the style of other Flemish painters: sophisticated, regally dressed and adorned with jewelry. She holds her signature alabaster jar with an etched design in one hand and the lid in the other.   The open jar, as a metaphor, echoes the topic of the composition.   He is lifting the lid to reveal the secret of her pregnancy and her status as the carrier of the Sangreal, the blood royal. The extended belly and sash around her hip, tied in a loose knot at the front just below her belly, mimics the position of the belt in Weyden's *Deposition*.   It is wholly possible that the Master borrowed the element from *the Deposition* to punctuate Mary's pregnancy in the same way.

The knot formed by the sash is no ordinary knot.   Known as a tiet or Isis Knot, its style has associations with the Egyptian goddess Isis and her priestesses. Also called the *Blood of Isis*, it has been suggested that to the ancient Egyptians it symbolized the power of the female genitalia because of the shape and resemblance to a menstruation cloth. In its connection to the womb of the goddess, Isis, it was considered to have magical properties and protective powers. The attribution of magical powers to the tiet can be traced to the 156th spell in the *Book of the Dead:*

> "You possess your blood, Isis, you possess your power, Isis, you possess your magic, Isis. The amulet is a protection for this Great One, which will drive off anyone who would perform a criminal act against him."

In addition to being tied on garments, the shape was often fashioned into an amulet by ancient Egyptians to be worn as protection.   These amulets were placed around the necks of the deceased, for instance, to protect them on their journey into the afterlife.   Other meanings assigned to the Isis knot are "life", "welfare" and "resurrection".

Two other paintings, *Noli Me Tangere* (1524) by Hans Holbein the Younger and *Madonna with Child and St. John the Baptist and Mary Magdalene* by Giovanni Battista Cima, circa 1510, also depict Mary Magdalene with a sash tied at or below the waist in an Isis knot. They offer further evidence that Mary Magdalene became equated with the goddess Isis in her high priestess aspect in much the same way the Virgin became associated with the Universal Mother aspect of Isis. Because the Isis knot was a protective and magical symbol associated with the Goddess Isis, it lends to the distinction of Mary Magdalene as a High Priestess of her cult.

Mary Magdalene -The Master Mansi Magdalen - circa 1525

The coded symbolism of the Isis knot in Master's painting could communicate a great deal more. The placement of the knot succinctly below her belly highlights that she is with child. Perhaps, it was Master's way of disclosing the concealed pregnancy and mentioning that the true legacy and bloodline was "protected" by the inheritors of the Grail, those connected by blood and oath.

Interestingly, in his painting of *The Last Supper*, Leonardo Da Vinci tied an Isis knot at the bottom right hand corner of the tablecloth. Art historians suggest the knot to represent a cryptic artist's signature because in Latin, the word for a knot is *vincium*. However, that does not explain why the knot is fashioned in the style of an Isis knot. In the novel, *The Secret Supper,* Javier Sierra explains the "gratuitous knot" in the corner of tablecloth had a hidden meaning and symbolized that a painting was dedicated to Mary Magdalene.

Michelangelo Caravaggio (1571 –1610) was another Renaissance artist to paint Mary Magdalene as an expectant mother. Though not as detailed as Weyden's composition, Caravaggio's *Mary Magdalene in Ecstasy*, portrays Mary Magdalene overtly pregnant. She is reclining backwards in an apparent spiritual state of spiritual ecstasy having succumbed to the moment of her deliverance to the heavenly sphere, *"where she heard, with her bodily ears, the delightful harmonies of the celestial choirs"* (Golden Legend). She is wearing a blousy gown with soft folds that gather in pleats over her extremely protruding pregnant belly. A red blanket draped around her just below her hips frames and brings even greater attention the area. Her hands are clutched fingers interwoven together in the "prayer heart" position, the hand gesture associated with the underground Christian Church.

Caravaggio painted two other paintings that express the same heresy, *Penitent Magdalen* and *Flight into Egypt*. *Penitent Magdalen* depicts a very realistic Mary Magdalene sitting in a room on a low chair. Beside her on the floor are her worldly adornments (jewelry) to support the legend that she relinquished her possessions of vanity to serve a penitent life in prayer. Certainly, at first glance, the composition falls within the Church's criteria for depicting Mary Magdalene as a penitent saint. However, all is not as it seems. The

Mary Magdalene in Ecstasy – Michelangelo Caravaggio

Penitent Magdalene- Michelangelo Merisi da Caravaggio – 1594

Flight into Egypt- Michelangelo Merisi da Caravaggio-1594-1595

primary element of interest is the scalloped vessel (terrine) woven as a design on the front of the elaborate skirt of her dress. Magdalene mystery theorists, like Laurence Gardner, have suggested the vessel represents the Holy Grail, supporting the notion that Mary Magdalene was the vessel of the Sangrael—the blood royal. The scallop design in the motif of the Grail vessel associates her again with her mythological counterpart Aphrodite as the goddess of love who emerges out of the sea standing on a scallop shell as represented in Boticelli's *The Birth of Venus*. The scallop shell in and of itself had become an important Magdalene cult symbol and examples can be found, for instance, in the carvings of Rosslyn Chapel in Edinburgh. In classical antiquity, the scallop shell represented a woman's sexuality and fertility because it resembled a woman's vulva. The Church however reassigned the symbol to St. James the Greater and adopted it as a badge for pilgrims visiting the shrine of Saint James of Compostela. Hence, it is called by naturalists the *Pecten Jacobacus*, the comb shell of Saint James.

There is a maternal quality in Magdalene's pose in Caravaggio's composition that takes a bit of imagination to realize. Curiously, Mary Magdalene holds her arms as if cradling a baby, her head tilted down in motherly adoration of an invisible child presumably still in the womb. Her face is somewhat sorrowful, seemingly to mention a penitent demeanor. But in the mind of the artist, it is because she is suffering the loss of her husband, leaving her child fatherless.

In Caravaggio's *Flight into Egypt* (circa 1595), what appears to be a conventional interpretation of the Virgin Mary and Joseph in flight into Egypt with the newborn Jesus (Matthew 2:13-23) is turned upside down when we compare it with his *Penitent Magdalene*. We immediately see that the women in both paintings are the same woman. The hair color and facial features are identical. Caravaggio obviously used the same model and portrayed both women in nearly identical poses, head tilted to the right, arms embracing a child, albeit one is imaginary and presumably still in the womb. Joseph is portrayed as an old man, an identifiable feature more associated with the characterization of Joseph of Arimathea as the Virgin's uncle than of her husband. A further clue solidifies the heresy that the flight into Egypt referred to in this painting's composition refers to the exile of Mary Magdalene a generation after the biblical account of the Virgin and Joseph's flight.

The sheet music that Joseph holds up for the angel with violin to play has been identified as a motet titled "How Fair and Pleasant Art Thou" or "How Beautiful You Are". The piece was composed by the Flemish Renaissance composer Noel Bauldweyn, a contemporary of Caravaggio, who was inspired by the *Song of Solomon in* composing the following lyrics:

O how beautiful you are,
My girlfriend, my dove.
My beautiful one.
Your eyes are those of doves
Your hair is like flocks of goats,
Your teeth are like rows of oars.
Come from Lebanon, come, I will crown you.
Arise quickly, arise my bride
Arise my precious my spotless one.
Arise, come, because I languish in love.

As with the *Song of Songs*, these words are musings between two who are sacred lovers, King and consort and bridegroom and bride. Caravaggio would have chosen the musical score to hint at the real subject of his composition.   His composition was much like a private declaration: Mary Magdalene was the "Bride of Christ" and mothered the child of their union in exile. Members of Andrew Gough's Arcadia Forum have suggested the motet was chosen for verse 12 of Chapter 7 in the *Song of Songs*: "Let us get up early to the vineyard: let us see if the vine flourish, where the tender grape appear, and the pomegranates bud forth: there will I give thee my love". The symbols of the "vineyard" and the "vine" are usually interpreted to represent bloodline genealogy, dynastic succession. The pomegranate, a symbol of fertility also has associations with Mary Magdalene.   An example is the incorporation of the pomegranate into the brocade sleeve of Weyden's *Mary Magdalene*.

The intriguing mysteries and conspiracy theories of Rennes-le-Chateau in the land of Magdalene's light, Languedoc France, are many. A great deal of attention and investigation has been centered on the various symbols and unusual pieces of art that dwell within St. Mary Magdalene's Church perched on the hilltop grounds of

Bas-relief Altarpiece Maria Magdalene- Rennes le Chateau

Rennes le Chateau. The most prominent is the altar bas-relief of a Penitent Mary Magdalene with a beautiful inscription painted below that reads: JESU MEDELA VULNERUM SPES UNA POENITENTIUM PER MAGDALENAE LACRYMAS PECCATA NOSTRA DILUAS. Loosely translated it means,

> "Jesus, you remedy against our pains and only hope for our repentance, it is thanks to Magdalene's tears that you wash our sins away."

This inscription points to a tradition that connects Mary Magdalene's tears with salvation through Christ. She is the intermediary of salvation because she lived an exemplar life and her sorrow somehow touched Jesus so much that he performed the miracle to save us all. Her example of retreat, penitence and sorrow (streams of tears) is the sure path of redemption and salvation for the model Christian. Although a few Rennes-le-Chateau conspiracy theorists have argued the inscription is a blasphemous statement of heresy because it suggests it was Mary's tears washed away our sins rather than the blood of Christ, this inscription is not very far outside the parameters supported by Church. And certainly the composition itself would not raise many eyebrows. In the abundant number of penitent iconic paintings of the Renaissance, like those by Titan, Mary was most often depicted, as she is portrayed in this bas-relief. She is cave bound with a skull and book of scripture to exemplify a penitent lifestyle of constant prayer and spiritual contemplation. According to her mythological legend in *The Golden Legend*, Mary meditated in her cave at St. Baume with a skull and scripture seven times a day as an act of penitence. During her hermitage, angels lifted her into the heavenly spheres daily for a period thirty-three years until her final ascension.

The composition of the altarpiece portrays Mary reverently kneeling with her hands clutched in the signature "prayer-heart" position, fingers interwoven. Conspiracy theorists have taken great pains in examining the relief trying to uncover more symbolic clues but have come up short. However, the tree-cross that Mary kneels before is extremely significant and remarks on a secret legacy, one I discussed in Weyden's *Lamentation*.

The tree-cross is symbolic for the re-rooting and regeneration of the rod of Jesse: "*And there shall come forth a rod out of the stem of Jesse, and a Branch shall grow out of his roots.*" As mentioned earlier, it is the symbol of the dynastic succession and divine authority associated with Jesus as prophesized by Isaiah 11-1-2.

Upon close examination, we notice the tree-cross has sent out shoots of leaves or flowers, symbolic of the marriage between Jesus and Mary Magdalene in the same way that Joseph's (Jesus' father) staff flowered in his hand when the Virgin was betrothed to him.

According to scripture, Jesse's tree was identified as an almond tree that "flowered and yielded ripe almonds" (Numbers 17:8). Interestingly, there is a Greek Orthodox tradition of giving out honey coated or Jordan almonds called "koufeta" in odd numbers in a small bag at weddings. Symbolically the odd numbers of almonds are indivisible, representing how the newlyweds will share everything and remain undivided.

The true cross of the crucifixion has been interpreted by some who reference Acts 5:30, as not a constructed cross but a tree propagated from the same branch—the rod of Jesse. Acts 5:30 reads, "The Elohim of our fathers raised up Yahushua whom you murdered by hanging on a tree. And 1 Peter 2:24 which reads,

"…who Himself bore our sins in His own body on the tree, that we, having died to sins, might live for righteousness by whose stripes you were healed."

The use of the tiny tree-cross in the composition of the bas-relief also evokes a sense of resurrection, regeneration and renewal. It is, therefore, symbolic for the rebirth and continuation of Jesus' covenant through Mary's ministry and the more literal propagation of his royal seed — the continuation of the bloodline through his and Mary's son Josephes.

The composition design of L'abbe Sauniere's altarpiece was probably inspired by if not copied from Johann Gerbhard Flatz's painting, *Maria Magdalene*. The engraved etching is nearly identical in its composition except for the fact that the tree-cross does not appear to be a flowering almond.

The Renaissance was a period marked by a rebirth of humanism and a cultural movement that witnessed many contributions to the arts and sciences. Galileo, Kepler and Bruno changed our way of looking at the world from a geocentric to a heliocentric model, producing a scientific revolution. Libraries of literature and ancient texts were established by benevolent patrons such as the Medici. And the art world produced artists of pure genius like Caravaggio, Weyden and Da Vinci. It was a time of genius that could not be contained and although there are those art historians who have insisted artists strictly observed the parameters of the religious doctrine of the Church and the desires of their patrons, there were the notable exceptions set forth in this chapter. Amongst the hundreds of artists of the Renaissance there were a few brave souls who would not submit to censorship and the authority of the Church. Whether out of shear defiance or out of a deep need to express the core of their beliefs, a handful of artists discovered interestingly clever ways to communicate what they believed. The subject of their heresy was one woman who would become the most painted woman in history — Mary Magdalene.

CHAPTER ELEVEN
The Gnostic Mary Magdalene:
Petites Heures

All this worldly wisdom was once the unamiable heresy of some wise man.
—Henry David Thoreau

The propaganda and agendas of the Church of Rome had crested as a wave of tyranny over the spiritual environment in the Middle Ages. Amongst the casualties of this tyranny were the Cathars, the "pure ones", also known as the *Bon Hommes,* which translates as "Good Christians". The Cathars had their own brand of Christianity rooted in Gnosticism and flourished for three centuries in communities of Southern France and Northern Italy. Little of the specifics are known about the beliefs of this large spiritual movement because the vast majority of the documents pertaining to their doctrine were burned and over twenty thousand of its members massacred by order of Pope Innocent III during the Albigensian Crusade beginning in 1209. Only three sacred texts have survived. Scholars have drawn links between the Cathars and the Paulician movement in Armenia and the Bogomils of Bulgaria whose dualistic Gnostic ideology was somewhat similar. From the bits and pieces of evidence that can be found in the Languedoc area of Southern France and in Northern Italy, it appears the Cathars venerated John the Baptist, and Mary Magdalene above the other Apostles and that they held the Gospel of John as their most sacred text. Pier vaux de Cernay, in his chronicle of the Albigensian Crusade wrote that townspeople of Béziers were burned alive on the feast day of Mary Magdalene (22 July 1209) in retribution for *"their scandalous assertion that Mary Magdalene and Christ were lovers."*

In the area of the Southern Pyrenees, a form of heterodox mysticism coincided with the Cathar movement. This mysticism had archetypal roots in the gnosis and the Gnosticism of late antiquity. The region also saw the first flowering of the Troubadour traditions and of the Jewish Gnosticism of the Kabbalah. In addition, a mystical tradition in Spain, rooted in a Gnostic school of Islam took form, one attributed to Ibn 'Arabī (1165–1240), the seminal figure in Turkish, Persian and Sufi Gnostic traditions. The milieu in which all these traditions arose represented an obvious resurgence of a Gnostic tradition, one that was preserved from its roots in the Gnostic Christianity of the 2nd and 3rd centuries. There was a spirit of gnosis in the air that the Church deemed heretical and proceeded to stamp out.

The Church's campaign to stamp out free religious thinking was extremely successful through its inquisitions of the 12th and 13th centuries, driving underground those who might challenge the Church's doctrine and authority and who subscribed to Gnosticism instead. Gnostics met in secret, behind closed doors, and the tenets of their beliefs were not made available to the masses. As a result, there is little evidence to point to a Gnostic revival after the 13th century with the demise of the Cathars. But Gnostic groups of elite intellectuals continued their tradition in secret.

How the Gnosticism of the 2nd and 3rd centuries survived and its tenets were carried forward into the Middle Ages is a question difficult to answer. There is no hard evidence to suggest Gnostics in the Middle Ages possessed ancient copies of the only recently unearthed Gnostic gospels that make up the Nag Hammadi Library. It has been assumed, gospels such as the *Gospel of Thomas*, *Pistis Sophia*, the *Gospel of Philip*, the *Gospel of Mary* and *The Dialogue with the Savior* were unknown to the Gnostics of the Middle Ages in Europe. Most scholars have concluded that the tenets of their spiritual beliefs were probably preserved and disseminated through oral tradition instead.

In brief, the Gnostics of the Middle Ages, like those of early Gnostic Christianity, believed salvation was a personal accomplishment, achieved through "knowledge" and transcendent and intuitive experiences rather than through worship, faith (pistis) and belief. In Valentinian Gnosticism, this knowledge is attained through the heart, *Gnosis Kardias,* affording the initiate a heightened experience of his relationship to the cosmos, the Pleroma (the fullness). First and foremost, the Gnostics of the Middle Ages were Christians who believed Jesus, as a perfected God-man (human and divine), lit the path of "gnosis" and transcendence from the constraints of the flawed material world. For them, he was a light-bringer whose path was self-knowledge with the aim of spiritual and human perfection. This same Gnostic tradition held up Mary Magdalene as a wisdom teacher, a mystic in her own right and

Jesus' closest companion, if not wife. This religious view countered the Church's propaganda that bolstered an image of penitent sinner, one whom Jesus pitied enough to cast out seven demons (Luke 8:2) and a reformed prostitute who could become their model of penitence. Once more, the Gnostics viewed Mary Magdalene as the head of their church in much same way Peter was "the rock" on which the Church of Rome was built. And they venerated her as the Goddess and Divine Feminine, dethroning the Virgin from that status.

Unfortunately, there is scanty evidence of the existence of the Gnostic underground stream of Christianity in the Middle Ages because of its suppression by the Church. But if we dig deeply into the art of the Middle Ages, surveying paintings, sculpture, and illuminated manuscripts we find fossils of proof in their compositions and reflected in their symbols. One discovery offers substantial proof that a Gnostic tradition was very much alive amongst groups of elite intellectuals including the royals of France in the 14th and 15th centuries.

By divine providence, I stumbled upon a fascinating illumination (spiritual illustration) of a Station of the Cross from the late 14th century Book of Hours, Petites Heures de Jean de Berry, just as I was about to complete this book with a final chapter. It had such an impact on me that I immediately moved my research into a new direction. I consumed, analyzed, compared and pondered the meaning behind some 119 miniature illuminations decorating the 600-page manuscript. I soon realized that this personal prayer book belonging to John de Berry was unlike any Book of Hours or Psalter of its time.

Petites Heures (small book of hours) de Jean de Berry is housed at the Bibliotheque nationale de France. It is an elaborately decorated devotional Book of Hours created by as many as five illuminators for Duke of Berry, Jean de France — The Magnificent. It was begun in about 1372 and wasn't completed until about 1385 to 1390. The illuminator responsible for executing the majority of the illustrations was probably Jean le Noir, a student of the great illuminator Puecell and inheritor of Puecell's workshop after his death in 1334. Documents show that Jean Le Noir was successively in the service of Yolande of Flanders, Charles V, and Jean de Berry. A document of 1358, states that Jean Le Noir left the service of Yolande de Flandre and along with his daughter Bourgot entered the service of King John the Good and his son the dauphin Charles, Jean du Berry's father and brother. This document also records the gift of a house to Jean in Paris on the Rue Trousevache. In 1372 and 1375, there are records in the accounts of Jean de Berry of gifts of cloth and payments to Le Noir. In this document, he is listed as "enlumineur du roy et de mon dit seigneur." By 1375, Le Noir had moved from Paris to Bourges. The correspondences between this documentary record of Jean Le Noir and the patronage of these manuscripts create a compelling argument to identify Jean Le Noir as the primary illuminator of Petites Heures. Another contributor was Jacquemart de Hesdin, a Franco-Flemish manuscript illuminator. Influenced by Sienese painting, his illustrations included elaborate architectural interiors used to place figures in a realistic space. Jacquemart was known for his marginalia — intricate and elaborate foliage and animal shapes forming a sort of frame to encompass the manuscript page.

Petites Heures is one of the richest examples out of some thousand or so illuminated manuscripts still preserved in museums and private collections. The Latin text is written in gold leaf and ornamented with elaborate borders of tree branches, songbirds and butterflies. Each of the 119 miniature illustrations, beautifully highlighted with gold leaf, complement and embellish the prayers, devotional hymns, biblical scripture and calendar contained within the 600-page prayer book.

But when we examine the sets of illuminations we discover something very odd. There are two sets of illuminations for many of the cycles of the Passion of Christ and Stations of the Cross as told from two very distinctly different perspectives — Orthodox and Gnostic. The scene compositions are similar but the characters and their roles switch in some cases, as I am about to describe.

The One Who Knew the All

Our first illustrative examples with the purpose of comparing two distinctly different traditions, Gnostic and Orthodox, are two illuminations titled *Pentecost*, presenting a composition depicting the descent of the Holy Spirit on Apostles on the day of the Pentecost as described in Acts 2:1-21. Acts reads,

"And when the day of Pentecost was fully come, they were all with one accord in one place. And suddenly there came a sound from heaven as of a

Penecost—Gnostic Version—Petite Heures

Pentecost – Orthodox Version – Petite Heures

rushing mighty wind, and it filled all the house where they were sitting. And there appeared unto them cloven tongues like as of fire, and it sat upon each of them. And they were all filled with the Holy Ghost, and began to speak with other tongues, as the Spirit gave them utterance. And there were dwelling at Jerusalem Jews, devout men, out of every nation under heaven. Now when this was noised abroad, the multitude came together, and were confounded, because that every man heard them speak in his own language."

What is unusual about the composition of the first illumination is that Mary Magdalene is present, seated amongst the Apostles and in a central position. She wears a red robe (mantle), the color most often associated with her in iconography of the Middle Ages and Renaissance. While the Apostles are depicted hands together in prayer, Mary has her hand to her heart to mention "gnosis kardias", spiritual knowledge attained through an open heart.

Mary Magdalene appears as the one to have the deepest connection to the Holy Spirit and to the event. In this sense, she receives the spirit through her body and seems to appreciate and understand through her wisdom that the Holy Spirit is housed within her own heart. The other Apostles must look outward and upward to summon the Holy Spirit through their prayers. Therefore, her position and knowledge is conveyed as superior, reminiscent of a passage of Pistis Sophia, a Gnostic apocryphal text. It reads:

"Now it happened when Mariam heard these words as the Saviour was saying them, she stared for one hour into the air and said : 'My Lord, command me that I speak openly.'
Jesus, the compassionate, answered and said to Mariam: 'Mariam, thou blessed one, whom I will complete in all the mysteries of the height, speak openly, thou art she whose heart is more directed to the Kingdom of Heaven than all thy brothers'."

The description in Acts 2 of the event on the Pentecost makes no direct mention of Mary Magdalene as attending the feast. In fact, most of the artist representations, whether those found in Psalters, books of hours, or in Byzantine iconography, hold that place and position for Mary, the mother of Christ.

The Vatican makes clear the fact that it was Mary, the mother of Jesus, who was present (front and center) at the Pentecost and they claim this event as the birthday of the Church. In the following excerpt from a proclamation written in 1989, the Vatican presents this position:

> "In the upper room in Jerusalem, as the Paschal Mystery of Christ on earth reached its fulfillment, Mary together with the other disciples prepared for a new coming of the Holy Spirit which would mark the birth of the Church. It is true that she was already a "temple of the Holy Spirit" (LG 53) by her fullness of grace and by her divine motherhood. But she took part in the prayers for the Spirit's coming so that through his power there should burst out in the apostolic community the impulse toward the mission which Jesus Christ, on coming into the world, had received from the Father (cf. Jn 5:36), and on returning to the Father, had transmitted to the Church (cf. Jn 17:18). From the very beginning, Mary was united to the Church as a disciple of her Son and as the most outstanding image of the Church in her faith and charity (cf. LG 53).

Sorting through the 119 illustrations contained within Petites Heures de Jean de Berry, we curiously discover another depiction of the *Pentecost* that is almost identical to the first except for four significant differences. First and secondly, the woman in the foreground is now wearing blue mantle and instead of hand on her chest, one hand is held outward and up as if she must summon the Holy Spirit. The other hand rests on her belly, which appears a bit protruded. This Mary is also holding a book of prayers or scripture and the dove symbolizing the Holy Spirit descends without its power. The element of fire from its beak is not depicted.

Firstly, why the change in color of Mary's mantle? As far back as 500 AD, the blue mantle or robe has traditionally been associated with the Virgin Mary. Dark blue (coeruleus) according to Catholic sources is the color of humility. Its Byzantine connotation was the mark of royalty and was associated with the attire of the Empress. The blue mantle was transferred from the Empress to the Virgin Mary in the many representations of her as Our Lady, Queen of the Heavens and Virgin Mother to signify her divine status and her humility. Therefore, this depiction of the same event places the Virgin Mother in the central apostolic position instead of Mary Magdalene, a position somewhat supported by narratives of Acts and definitely the position of the Church of Rome. Now we have the exact same scene portrayed with different leading characters and we will see why as we continue with the interpretation.

As to the change in hand position (hand resting on her belly), it connects the scene to the mythology of the Virgin birth, her womb having given birth to the Son of God through God's insemination. In the first illustration, the event is connected instead to Mary Magdalene's heart, her spiritual center, and presents an altogether different mythology, that of Sophia and tenets that are more in line with Gnostic Christianity.

The third obvious difference is that the Virgin Mother now requires scripture or a book of prayers as do a number of the other disciples pictured. This interesting difference between the two renditions remarks that two different ideologies are being presented. In the Virgin Mary version, the artist is communicating on a reliance on scripture, the so-called word of God as the requirement for participation in the mystery. The former version conveys that participation only requires an open heart, opening one's vessel to receive the Holy Spirit, knowledge and wisdom.

The last difference in the two renditions is the appearance of the descending dove. In Valentinian Gnosticism, the dove represents the "Spirit of the Thought of the Father" which first descended into Jesus' consciousness at his baptism. As we examine the first illustration both fire and water emerge with the presence of the Holy Spirit. In the second illustration with the Virgin Mother, the dove has no fire coming out of its beak. What does the fire symbolize? For the Valentinian Gnostics, the fire represents the chrism, the anointing fire of God that transforms the initiate within the Bridal Chamber.

As we recall from an earlier discussion of the mystery of the Bridal Chamber, the Gospel of Philip explains,

> "It is from water and fire that the soul and the spirit came into being. It is from water and fire and light that the son of the bridal chamber (came into being). The fire is the chrism, the light is the fire. I am not referring to that fire which has no form, but to the other fire whose form is white, which is bright and beautiful, and which gives beauty." — Gospel of Philip

With the omission of the symbolic element of the fire in the Orthodox version, the illuminator cleverly conveyed ideas that were held by his Gnostic community. He mentions that the "holy" in this Pentecost scene cannot attain the spiritual light (fire) by virtue of faith alone or by relying on scripture and other intellectual means.

They have not achieved "gnosis", wisdom, though initiation and direct conscious contact with the Holy Spirit and its anointing fire, because they are worshiping the wrong way. They are not choosing the path of the heart, "gnosis kardias". In other words, the Church has presented an inferior spiritual path, venerated the wrong goddess and thus denied the true bride of Christ who is integral to the mythos of the reconciliation of the Fall wherein God and Goddess are united in the bridal chamber through a sacred mystical marriage.

Proverbs 8:22-31, part of the Wisdom literature in the Hebrew Bible, that includes also Job and Ecclesiastes, Wisdom (Sophia) is Yahweh's (God) intimate companion in creating the world. For early Christians, Sophia, whose symbol is the dove, serves as God's channel of communication with humanity. Therefore, the Holy Spirit is the feminine wisdom aspect of God descending amongst the disciples on the Pentecost and initiating them into her wisdom and mysteries. For many of the Gnostics, Mary Magdalene, was the embodiment and incarnation of Sophia and was paired up with her Divine Complement, Jesus Christ, as his bride just as Yahweh, (God and Logos) was paired with Sophia (Wisdom). What the illuminator also conveyed by placing Mary Magdalene in the center was that she was the inheritor of Jesus' ministry and the leader of the early Christian movement. The *Gospel of Mary*, a Gnostic text from the 2nd or 3rd century, of which only a fragment remains, supports the interpretation of the first composition of the Pentecost. In it, Mary Magdalene's role is to give voice to the words of the risen Christ. She is also the voice of her own wisdom. She stands before the disciples as the new leader, conveying the dialogue she had with the risen Christ. The Gospel of Mary reads,

> "Then Mary stood up and greeted all of them and said to her brethren, "Do not mourn or grieve or be irresolute, for his grace will be with you all and will defend you. Let us rather praise his greatness, for he prepared us and made us into men." When Mary said this, their hearts changed for the better, and they began to discuss the words of the [Savior]."

The two illustrations of the Pentecost in combination present the ideologies of two competing Christian traditions: one venerating the Mother of Christ (Cult of the Virgin Mother) and the other venerating Mary Magdalene, arising out of the Cult of the Bride of Christ and Gnostic tradition.

In examining and comparing both illustrations, it is difficult to ascertain if the same artist painted both miniatures. If we presume it was one artist (my own supposition), we would assume he wished to bring to light two different traditions, differentiating the two symbolically in a meaningful comparison. He was, therefore, instructing through comparison. His contrasting comparisons mention that the path of salvation through knowledge (gnosis) was the superior and preferred path and that the Church's doctrine represented ignorance of the truth. Another possibility is that two different artists painted the illuminations. It could be argued that another artist painted the Gnostic version in response and in rebuttal to the Orthodox version. A third possibility is two or more artists collaborated.

The two contrasting versions of the same event depicted in the illustrations, offers clear evidence that two Christian communities existed simultaneously and in opposition to each other in the 14th century. The main subject of their differences was the position and status given to the two Mary's. To the Gnostic underground stream, it was Mary Magdalene as the Bride of Christ who had carried forth Jesus' ministry. She was the one "who knew all" and whose wisdom was connected to her heart and to the Goddess Sophia. To the Church, the Gnostics were heretics for their veneration of Mary Magdalene over the Virgin Mother and for denying the Church's doctrine and defying their authority. According to their Mariology, it was Our Lady (Virgin Mother), who must be glorified for her participation in the mystery as Mother of the Son of God. However, the mythology of the Church of Rome, as I said in a previous chapter, is a pseudo-myth because it fails to culminate in the Sacred Marriage and Wedding Feast. This Orthodox mythology limits Jesus' maturity and manliness. Forever Jesus would be seen as tied to the Virgin womb, unable to individuate (become whole) and unite with his Sacred Bride in the Sacred Marriage. This represents an aborted reconciliation myth with no promise of personal reconciliation of the division within the soul.

Besides venerating Mary Magdalene as the bride of Christ, it is difficult to speculate on what sect of Gnosticism the illuminator was identified with. We can only glean out that he believed wisdom is not attained through reading scripture or through prayer but through "gnosis kardias", the knowledge of the heart, a more intuitive understanding of the divine, based on Jesus' authentic teachings such as,

> "If you do not fast from the world, you will not find the (Father's) kingdom. If you do not observe the sabbath as a sabbath you will not see the Father."—Saying 27, Gospel of Thomas.

The Gnostic path is a contemplative one that delivers the initiate into transcendent experiences through which he or she is transformed, realizes himself or herself as a child of God and enters the Kingdom inside his heart to awaken to the Kingdom that is "spread upon the earth." And that path, as the depiction of Mary Magdalene on the day of the Pentecost portrays, is accessed through the heart of feminine wisdom.

In the *Song of Songs,* of his consort, Sophia, Solomon writes, "She is the fountain of the gardens, a well of living waters." Sophia connects us to the primordial paradise of the garden as the Shekinah of Jewish tradition and to the water of the living spirit. While Peter was identified as the rock on which the Church was built, Mary Magdalene was the water of the living spirit by virtue of her Aquarian nature. Conjoined with her Aries consort, Jesus, they are united as fire and water, the alchemy of spiritual unity.

The One Who Shared the Burden

Another set of two illustrations, one with Mary Magdalene in the leading role and the other starring the Virgin, tell different stories about the journey on the road to Calvary. Titled, *Carrying the Cross,* the Gnostic version depicts Jesus carrying the cross across his shoulders followed by a group of disciples on the road to Calvary. And who is helping him to lift and carry the load of the cross but Mary Magdalene. She stands right behind Jesus lifting and supporting the horizontal bar of the cross sharing in the struggle and in her beloved's burden. Jesus' head is turned towards her affectionately, seemingly appreciating her help in carrying the load. Mary is depicted wearing a pink mantle, which as we will see was her dress in the majority of the illuminations in which she is a figure of prominence to the scene. The Virgin Mother, dressed in her traditional blue mantle, is a short distance behind amongst a crowd of followers.

In this illustration, Mary Magdalene is portrayed as Jesus' most faithful companion, accepting Jesus' burden and doing what might have been easier for one of the able bodied male disciples to do. In this role Mary is represented as an equal complement, an equality that is echoed in Saying 114 in the *Gospel of Thomas* when Jesus says, "I myself shall lead her in order to make her male, so that she too may become a living spirit resembling you males."

And *The Gospel of Philip* describes her important role as companion:

> "There were three who always walked with the Lord: Mary, his mother, and her sister, and Magdalene, the one who was called his companion."

Who would have taken such an important position? A wife, just as the meaning of the word "companion" translates from Greek. The illuminator has depicted Jesus and Mary Magdalene as intimate partners who share a deep affection and in each other's burdens during difficult circumstances.

As with the illustration of the Pentecost, the Orthodox version makes a cast change. Mary, the Virgin Mother, is substituted for Mary Magdalene. Mary Magdalene, dressed this time in a red robe, is standing tightly adjacent to the Virgin Mother who is in her all too familiar blue mantle. She is depicted as merely amongst those in the procession and more in support of the Virgin Mother than Jesus. The Virgin Mary is helping to carry the cross and Jesus' head is turned in adoration of his mother. This illustrative interpretation is more in line with Orthodox tradition, differentiating the two Mary's through the most common and familiar red and blue robes and in remarking that Virgin and Son are a spiritual unit as with the proclamation: "Jesus Maria". Again, the artist presents two versions to be contemplated on. The question he seems to be presenting is: Which Mary was the most important goddess in Jesus' life and to Christian mythology — wife or mother?

The One Most Intimately Connected

Two illuminations in Petite Heures are devoted to the portrayalof the *Entombment*, the laying of Jesus' body to rest, each

Carrying the Cross — Gnostic Version

Carrying the Cross – Orthodox Version

Entombment— Orthodox Version

Entombment – Gnostic Versio

again conveying distinctly different traditions. The first is extremely suggestive of the intimacy between Jesus and Mary Magdalene as I am about to describe. As an *Entombment* portrayal, it illustrates the attention given to Jesus' body at the tomb by a group of thirteen mourners hovering around, the vast majority women. The illumination is a *lamentation*, bringing to life and embellishing the events described in the Gospels after the preparation of the tomb and the retrieval of Jesus' body by the biblical Joseph of Arimathea.

Mother Mary, dressed in blue mantle, is depicted pressing her face against Jesus' cheek as she cradles him with one arm. Next to her is Mary Magdalene in pink, just as she is dressed in the previous illustration, *Carrying the Cross*. What is highly suggestive is the placement of Mary Magdalene's hand. We notice it is placed at Jesus' genitals and that she either appears to be resting her fingertips there or perhaps covering the area with the cloth.

The more bizarre element is another hand that at first glance does not appear to belong to anyone in the foreground. But after closer examination, it can be identified as belonging to the Virgin Mother. It emerges out from under her right side, then underneath her left arm to encroach on the position of Mary Magdalene's hand. What did the artist intend to communicate? One can only wonder. Perhaps, it is one artist's imagination gone wild, a fantasy of competition between a pious Virgin mother-in-law and a lascivious sinful daughter-in-law. It may have been an artistic way of conveying the early inferences by the Church that Mary Magdalene had a sinful tainted past as a harlot. Its does appear to be a commentary or parody on the Church's position on Jesus' sexuality with the "repressive hand" of the Church denying Jesus his humanness and sexuality and casting Mary Magdalene in the role of prostitute and sinner rather than wife.

This illustration, first and foremost, is a statement about how important women were to Jesus' life and ministry in the view of the underground stream of Christianity. Women were not relegated to the role of subservient followers and were more than merely the wives of other disciples. Nor were they depicted as penitent sinners, clutching scripture. Instead, the majority (seven out of ten) are with halos, identifying them as saints. The Gnostics considered women high-ranking members of Jesus' community, those most faithful to his mission and devoted to him. Only one man is crowned with halo and most likely represents John who to the

Gnostics was the "beloved disciple". Again the illustration, points to Mary Magdalene's role as far more important than merely one of Jesus' many women followers. She is intimate with Jesus as a sexual partner, suggested by her hand placement at his genitals.

Another important figure in this illustration is the woman in the back with arms up over her head. This posture is not a lamenting pose but is called the *orans* pose, meaning "prayer" in Latin. The archetype of the woman with arms raised is referred to as *Orantes*, and may have been a borrowed image from ancient Goddess worshipping societies such as those in ancient Sumer and Crete. Orantes figures prominently in funerary art dating back to the Roman catacombs of the 2nd and 3 rd centuries, AD. She is always feminine in gender and has been interpreted in a variety of ways such as denoting prayer, the soul in a state of peace in paradise, or as a figure transmitting peace to the bereaved. Margaret Starbird suggests she probably represented the Goddess as *psychopomp*, one who acts as mediator between heaven and earth assisting the soul on the journey into the afterlife. Her spiritual power and purpose arises out of her role as a high priestess. Mary Magdalene is often depicted as Orantes. She is depicted in the orans pose in numerous representations of the crucifixion and entombment in iconography and paintings of the Renaissance. As an example, a painting by Simone Martini on wood, one piece of a number of panels comprising the *Orsini Polytych* (circa 1333-1335), depicts Mary Magdalene in red robes in the orans pose amongst a crowd following Jesus who carries the cross. It is titled, *Way to Calvary*. Another panel of the *Orsini Polytych* depicts a similar but more colorful scene of the entombment with an Orantes priestess amongst the witnesses surrounding the tomb. Painted some 50 years earlier, the painting's composition may have inspired Jean le Noir because it is extremely similar.

Because Orantes in our illumination is with halo (a saint), it is reasonable to conclude that she may represent a high priestess aspect of Mary Magdalene, adding spiritual definition to her more human role as Jesus' wife and sexual partner.

As no surprise, a second version of the *Entombment* switches the roles of Mary Magdalene and the Virgin Mother. Distinguished by her pink mantle, this time it is Mary Magdalene who cradles Jesus in her arms. Mary Magdalene is portrayed as the grieving widow who is holding her beloved husband for the last time and looks about to kiss his lips. She is in the right position and station for her status as wife. The Virgin stands behind Mary's back, hands folded in prayer along with a group of eight disciples. Joseph of Arimathea and Nicodemus, at each end of the ossuary, interestingly, depicted without halos. The Virgin's position now is to reside in the background praying for Jesus' ascension rather than in the role of the most intimately connected participant. Like the *Pentecost* and the *Road to Calvary*, the two *Entombment* illustrations contrast the positions of the Orthodox tradition with a more Gnostic Mary Magdalene tradition in which Mary Magdalene was viewed as Jesus' significant other and divine complement.

Wife of Sorrows

A single illustration, with no second version, depicts what one would presume to be a *Pieta,* one of three common representations of the "sorrowful" Virgin Mary. Pieta in Italian literally means pity. This classic representation of the Virgin Mother was made famous by Renaissance Master, Michelangelo, who sculpted his *Pieta* initially as a funerary monument and which now is housed at St. Peter's Basilica in Vatican City. The other two most popular rendered poses for the Virgin Mother in art and iconography are *Mater Dolorosa (sorrowful mother)* and *Stabat Mater* (here stands the mother).

At first glance and because Christianity has molded and colored our perceptions, the *Pieta* in Petites Heures would appear to be just that—a traditional *Pieta* to include in the Hours of the Virgin. However, it should be more appropriately titled "Wife of Sorrows", because it is Mary Magdalene in pink mantle worn over a blue dress who cradles Jesus' limp completely naked body across her lap. Her arm and the Apostle John's hand cover the genitals and John is positioned supporting Mary Magdalene as the second most beloved disciple. Two other male disciples are present at the scene adding balance to the composition. The "Mother of Sorrows" (the Virgin) stands in the background wearing light blue, another traditional hue of blue associated with the Virgin Mother found in iconography and other religious paintings from the same century. Again the artist has substituted Mary Magdalene for the Virgin because his community of Gnostic Christians venerated Mary Magdalene with the same passion as the Church of Rome venerated the Madonna.

Pieta— Petite Heures

Pieta— Angers Book of Hours

Raising of the Cross— Gnostic Version

Crucifixion—Orthodox Version

In contrast, a *Pieta* in a Book of Hours from Angers, France, circa 15th Century, depicts a more traditional representation and interpretation of the *Pieta*. We notice the Virgin Mary as the *Pieta* and Mary Magdalene in her signature red mantle holding her familiar alabaster jar. She is reverently kneeling behind in her traditional supporting role.

The Stations of the Cross

Another grouping of illustrations depict three stages of the crucifixion known as the "Stations of the Cross". They include: *The Raising of the Cross, The Crucifixion*, and *The Descent off the Cross (Deposition)*. In the *Raising of the Cross*, only one version is offered and it is quite an embellished description of one of the Passion scenes. Roman soldiers are hammering the cross into place and Jesus and Mary Magdalene are paired as Divine Complements with Jesus leaning against Mary Magdalene's body for support. The posture of leaning in sharply contrasts the *Noli Me Tangere* (don't touch me) pose of Renaissance compositions from such artists as Correggio, Holbein, and Titan. Again in this Gnostic illumination, there is an obvious tone of intimacy between Jesus and Mary Magdalene. As a mythic poetic composition of the love between sacred bride and bridegroom, it echoes the vow, "Till death do us part." We notice Mary holds her hand near her bosom, a nurturing gesture. She is composed, conveying strength in expectation of enduring the hours ahead. She is not weeping, pleading or praying but content to stand in unity with her beloved Jesus, resolute in the knowledge that she is helping to fulfill Jesus' destiny.

Sethian Gnostics, from whom the recently discovered *Gospel of Judas* is attributed, believed the crucifixion was Jesus' chosen destiny and that the players in the Passion scenes such as Judas in betraying Jesus were really collaborating to help Jesus fulfill his destiny. The resolute and even cheerfulness conveyed in the illustration supports a Gnostic concept about death. Death is considered a happy occasion because the spirit is liberated from the prison of this world of ignorance.

The crucifixion, specifically, the hours on the cross, is depicted in five illustrations, two of which are of particular interest because they depict a Gnostic perspective on Jesus' final hours. In the first, Mary Magdalene and another female figure, probably Mary the sister of the Virgin Mary, are depicted holding up the Virgin Mother who is hunched-over grief stricken. On the opposite side of the cross is the Apostle John, hands clenched in prayer. Longinus holds his lance having just pierced Jesus' side. He kneels before Christ in full realization of what he has done and the significance of his role, signified by his finger pointed at his own head. This gesture represents an illustrative sign that Longinus was cognizant of Jesus' plan, playing an important part in Jesus' transition from this life to the next. He is a figure of mercy, possessing the "gnosis" that he was a liberator in Jesus' plan to move onward, leaving behind his physical form in favor of his garment of light. Although Longinus is not mentioned by name in Gospel accounts, a legend developed in the Middle Ages that Longinus testified, "*In truth this man was son of God.*" The majority of the Gospel accounts are unclear as to who was present at the crucifixion with the exception of John 20:25 that identifies the women as his mother, his mother's sister, Mary, the wife of Cleophas, and Mary Magdalene. Outside of Longinus' hand gesture, the composition appears to be traditional depiction holding true for the most part to Gospel accounts.

A second composition, the *Crucifixion Trinity*, depicts Mary Magdalene and the John the Evangelist as the only two beneath the cross. Conveying grief, Mary's head is turned away and her hands extended in a blessing gesture. Her pose suggests she is a conduit for the Holy Spirit, assisting Jesus in his transition. Unafraid of death, John gazes upward in expectation of his own spiritual deliverance as he bears witness to Jesus' moment of ascension. The absence of others from the scene is a poignant Gnostic reminder that John, as the beloved disciple, and Mary Magdalene, as Jesus' wife, would be considered the most faithful and enlightened, "towering over all" the other disciples. Pictorially, the composition perfectly conveys Jesus' proclamation in *Pistis Sophia* that awards John and Mary this spiritual authority:

> "Christ says, 'Where I shall be, there will be also my twelve ministers. But Mary Magdalene and John, the virgin, will tower over all my disciples and over all men who shall receive the mysteries in the Ineffable. And they will be on my right and on my left. And I am they, and they are I'." –Pistis Sophia

As leaders of the true Christian Church they are united with Christ in purpose by a sacred covenant. According to Gnostic tradition, they were the two who understood completely the consciousness and mysteries Jesus conveyed.

Interestingly, the two along with Jesus on the cross form a trinity, an iconic depiction with a special meaning in Gnostic theology. The Gnostic tradition has its own rhetoric for the Trinity that on the surface resembles the hypostases of Orthodox Christianity — "Father, Son and Holy Spirit." The reason for this resemblance is that Valentinus, a Gnostic theologian, was credited as the first to conceive of the Trinity in his lost works "On the Three Natures.'

In Valentinian Gnosticism, the origin of the universe is an evolution of emanation from the godhead. God is both Father and Mother, masculine and feminine, a creative intelligence expressing this unity. The aspect through which the Father provides the universe with substance is considered feminine. In this aspect he is called *Silence, Grace* and *Thought*. The masculine aspect of God gives the universe form and is named: *Ineffable, Depth* and *First Father*. Depth represents the incomprehensible all-encompassing aspect of the Godhead. The male and female aspects of the Father, acting in unison, manifested themselves in the Son. The Son is also often depicted by Valentinians as a male-female dyad with twenty-six spiritual entities or Aeons arranged into male-female pairs. Like archetypes, they represent the energies immanent within the Son and were seen as part of his personality. Together they constitute the pleroma (Fullness) of the Godhead.

In the *Trimorphic Protennoia,* the trinity is referred to as, "Father, Mother, Son" (37:22). The iconic representation of the illumination beautifully echoes this triune nature of God.

The three natures in Gnostic doctrine also represented the Spirit, Soul, and Material. In the Gnostic treatise *The Tripartite Tractate* a three-fold order emerges as the result of a fallen deity, "Logos", which corresponds to Sophia in other Gnostic traditions.

As part of his repentance Logos must bring the chaos of the fall into order. This order is divided into three natures: the "Spiritual", the "Psychic" (soul) and the "Hylic" (material). The Spiritual level represents all the purely righteous thoughts of the Logos that existed in the beginning, and which reflects the Pleroma (fullness) above. The Psychic or soul level belongs the Logos' conversion, memory of the Pleroma and judgments against the wrong thoughts and emanations. The Hylic level belongs to the Logos' thoughts and emanations of fear and ignorance. In other Gnostic traditions, the

Gnostic Holy Trinity – Petite Heures

Descent From the Cross— Gnostic Version

Descent From the Cross— Orthodox Version

Hylic level came about as a result of Satan and was considered the evil that was mixed with the other levels at the time of creation.

From the Gnostic perspective all three levels exist in humanity. The Tripartite Tractate reads,

> "Mankind came to be in three essential types, the spiritual, the psychic, and the material, conforming to the triple disposition of the Logos, from which were brought forth the material ones and the psychic ones and the spiritual ones. Each of the three essential types is known by its fruit. And they were not known at first but only at the coming of the Savior, who shone upon the saints and revealed what each was."

In more modern terms, these three levels are all pieces of awakened human consciousness and represent: consciousness of spirit, consciousness of soul and human reality. According to the Gnostics, these were Jesus' true teachings. He enlightened his disciples elevating their consciousness to touch upon the memory of their spirit and soul.

The last Station of the Cross, the *Deposition*, has two versions. The first version positions Mary Magdalene next to the cross caressing Jesus' arm and hand with her face as he is brought down from the cross. Again, Mary Magdalene is the central woman figure with the other women standing behind her. The illuminaire is strikingly similar in detail to the illumination *Crucifixion and Deposition* from the Psalter of Blanche Castille, circa 1230.

In the second version of the *Deposition* Mary (the mother of Christ) usurps the position of Mary Magdalene of the previous version. The Virgin makes what has been recently coined the *John gesture*, index finger pointing up. This gesture is thought to represent the proclamation: "He is the one Son of God", a proclamation that is central to the Christology of the Church of Rome. In contrast, the first version of the *Deposition* has the Apostle John pointing to his own head. This gesture seems to mimic and counter the Virgin Mary's gesture, communicating something altogether different. It signifies that he has attained gnosis and affirms it as the true path of salvation. The artist has beautifully conveyed with these two illustrations the differences between two Christian paths, one in which salvation is accomplished through the sacrifice of the Savior and the other, a path of self-perfection, wisdom and knowledge.

From caressing, fondling, leaning, and supporting to her place amongst the other Apostles on the day of the Pentecost the majority of illuminations depict Mary to clearly be Jesus' significant other, his wife, lover, companion, most beloved disciple and Apostle. The artist of these illuminations was painting a love story in miniature, a complete cycle of the Passion scenes, not in accordance with the narratives of the Gospels or the position of the Church of Rome, but one held by his community of Gnostic Christians. He would have known full well that if not confined to Jean de Berry's personal collection it could have landed him before a tribunal of inquisitors who might have condemned, tortured and burned him at the stake for such heresies. As we now know in consideration of my discoveries, his love story is a truer one.

Resurrection of Christ

The most celebrated moment in the Passion narratives of the Gospel of John is the Resurrection of Christ. Mary Magdalene arrives at the tomb on the third day after the crucifixion to find the stone moved away and is surprised to see the resurrected Jesus whom she initially mistakes for a gardener. Mary reaches out to touch Jesus and according to the Gospel of John (20:17) Jesus said to her,

> "Do not hold me, for I have not yet ascended to the Father; but go to my brethren and say to them, I am ascending to my Father and your Father, to my God and your God."

According to the Christology of the Church, this scene represents the culmination of the Christian mythology of the resurrected Savior, Jesus Christ, who through his resurrection guaranteed our salvation from sin. And as Paul claimed, belief in the death and resurrection of Jesus is so central to salvation that "*if Christ has not been raised, your faith is futile; you are still in your sins. Then those also who have fallen asleep in Christ are lost. If only for this life we have hope in Christ, we are of all people most to be pitied.*" (1 Cor. 15:17-119)

John's account, a favorite of the Cathars, surprisingly is nowhere to be found amongst the some 119 illuminations within Petites Heures. In its place are two renderings of two other Gospel

Resurrected in the Flesh – Orthodox Version

Empty Tomb— Gnostic Version

accounts, one depicting a Gnostic perspective on the Resurrection and the other Orthodox, spun off from the testimony of Matthew.

The Orthodox version, *Resurrection in the Flesh*, is drawn from Matthew's account (Mt. 27. 62-66; 28. 4, 11-1 5); the only version to suggest the tomb had been guarded by Roman centurions. Jesus is depicted as raised from the dead and in the flesh, standing up in his tomb very much alive. He holds the staff of authority, symbolizing "victory over death" and his other hand gives the sign of the Benediction. The centurions are in a state of shock and awe, in disbelief and seemingly afraid for their lives. Two have fallen to the ground while the third remains frozen standing with a shield in hand. The illumination is not exactly true to Matthew's testimony, which tells us the guards only saw the stone in front of the tomb rolled away to reveal the tomb was empty. The illuminator sacrificed accuracy to better portray the Church's contention that Jesus had resurrected in the flesh. Matthew's differing account of the witnesses is believed to be based on an apologetic legend aimed at substantiating the myrrh bearers' testimonies of the resurrection in the other Gospel accounts.

A Gnostic would have considered the resurrection story in the Canonical Gospels a fabrication and mythologizing of Jesus' post-crucifixion story. Gnostics had an altogether different ideology of the resurrection, one conveyed by the illuminator of Petites Heures in *The Empty Tomb*. This illumination echoes the testimony of Luke or Mark because there are three women at the tomb, not two or one, as there are in the accounts of Matthew and John. In the Gospel of Mark, they were identified as: Mary Magdalene, Salome and Mary, the mother of James. In Luke, the myrrh bearers we are told were Mary Magdalene, Joana, and Mary, the mother of James. However, both of those accounts mention an angel or man in white robes (Mark) who appears and announces Jesus had risen and had gone ahead to Galilee. Mark 16:6-7 reads,

> "Don't be alarmed," he said. "You are looking for Jesus the Nazarene, who was crucified. He has risen! He is not here. See the place where they laid him. But go, tell his disciples and Peter, 'He is going ahead of you into Galilee. There you will see him, just as he told you.'"

In this illumination, two lamps have been hoisted up in the tomb to signify an important illumination or revelation about the empty tomb. Jesus reveals himself peeking down from a heavenly realm and two of the three eyewitnesses gaze upwards to see him. He has not risen in the flesh and gone on to Galilee to prove his resurrection to his disciples. According to the Canonical Gospel accounts, Jesus does not appear to the myrrh bearers as a heavenly spirit. He makes no appearance at all, except in John when he appears in the flesh to Mary Magdalene. He later makes several appearances in the flesh as the resurrected Christ to his disciples. But the illumination tells us he has ascended only in spirit and returned to the pleroma as an "imperishable Aeon".

It was the belief of the Gnostics that Jesus did not die and then resurrect in the flesh. The resurrection occurred before he died and was instead a transcendent experience, a rebirth to embody his divine-self.

The Gospel of Philip explains, *"Those who say that the Lord died first and (then) rose up are in error, for he rose up first and (then) died."* This idea is better defined in the *Treatise of the Resurrection*, a second century Gnostic letter:

'Everything is prone to change. The world is an illusion! The resurrection is the revelation of what is, and the transformation of things, and a transition into newness. For imperishability descends upon the perishable; the light flows down upon the darkness, swallowing it up; and the Pleroma fills up the deficiency. These are the symbols and the images of the resurrection."

It goes on,

"The Savior swallowed up death - (of this) you are not reckoned as being ignorant - for he put aside the world which is perishing. He transformed himself into an imperishable Aeon and raised himself up, having swallowed the visible by the invisible, and he gave us the way of our immortality. Then, indeed, as the Apostle said, 'We suffered with him, and we arose with him, and we went to heaven with him'. Now if we are manifest in this world wearing him, we are that one`s beams, and we are embraced by him until our setting, that is to say, our death in this life. We are drawn to heaven by him, like beams by the sun, not being restrained by anything. This is the spiritual resurrection which swallows up the psychic in the same way as the fleshly."

Part of what this treatise conveys is that Jesus conquered the fear of death recognizing the immortality of his spirit and choosing a spiritual identity over human identifications. He had awakened, integrated and embodied his divinity to become an "imperishable Aeon" (an immortal spirit). In other words, he showed us what was possible through gnosis. He was, therefore, the prototype of the spiritually perfected man, both human and divine through his achievement in fulfilling his destiny to do so. From the Gnostic point of view, each initiate is then responsible for raising himself up to embrace the consciousness of the pleroma and be reborn anew — resurrected. He must first "flee the divisions and the fetters" of the material world to achieve a higher consciousness of himself. He can then realize the truth and wisdom in Jesus' words,

> "… the kingdom is inside of you, and it is outside of you. When you come to know yourselves, then you will become known, and you will realize that it is you who are the sons of the living father." — Gospel of Thomas Saying 3.

The Versions of the Arrest

The *Arrest of Christ* is another Passion event with two versions, one orthodox and the other belonging to Gnostic Christianity. According to the narratives of the canonical Gospels, after the Passover meal (the Last Supper) Jesus and his disciples traveled to Gethsemane. From there, Jesus split off from the group into a grove of olive trees to pray. Knowing full well his fate, he prayed for strength and God's will to be done. He returns to his disciples who are asleep and scolds them for not knowing the hour had come. Again, he separates himself to pray and again returns to find his disciples asleep, again scolding them. The scene is repeated for a third time before Judas appears while Jesus is speaking to his disciples.

Mark's narrative reads,

> "And immediately, while he was still speaking, Judas came, one of the twelve, and with him a crowd with swords and clubs, from the chief priests and the scribes and the elders. Now the betrayer had given them a sign, saying, "The one I shall kiss is the man; seize him and lead him away under guard." And when he came, he went up to him at once, and said, "Master!" And he kissed him. And they laid

The Arrest— Orthodox Version

The Arrest -- Gnostic Version

hands on him and seized him. But one of those who stood by
drew his sword, and struck the slave of the high priest and cut off
his ear. And Jesus said to them, "Have you come out as against a
robber, with swords and clubs to capture me? Day after day I was
with you in the temple teaching, and you did not seize me. But let
the scriptures be fulfilled." — Mark 14:43-49

True to the Gospel narratives, the Orthodox illustrative version
of the *Arrest* depicts the scene with Judas on Jesus' right side about
to give him the infamous kiss of betrayal. Simultaneously, Jesus is
blessing and healing a scribe's ear that was just cut off by Peter's
weapon. Jesus and a couple of the disciples hold the Gospels in
their hands to denote the composition holds true to the Gospel
narratives and fulfills the Old Testament prophesies. The account
points out that the kiss was meant to identify Jesus as the Messiah
because a band of priests, scribes, elders and soldiers stand poised
to seize him. In Matthew's account, Jesus responded by saying,
"Friend, do what you are here to do." But in Luke's account the kiss is
never delivered and Jesus says in a self-effacing way, *"You would use
a kiss to betray me?"*
    As with so many of the other comparative illustrations, the
second version seems misaligned with scripture narratives. Judas,
rather than delivering the kiss of betrayal, stands leaning in and
takes Jesus' hand. An expression of sincerity and even love is on his
face, especially as compared to the sinister looking depiction of
Judas in the Orthodox version. The scene seems to convey that
Judas was acting on behalf of Jesus in his role as the betrayer in
order to fulfill the role of a heroic helper of sorts. Therefore, as with
Matthew's account he is there to do what he "must " do. In the
Gospel of Judas, the most recent Gnostic gospel to have been
discovered, Jesus asks Judas to betray him and pulls him aside as
the disciple who displayed the most knowledge (gnosis). The
ideology behind the betrayal was that Judas was merely following
Jesus' orders and that Jesus, as nonsensical as it sounds, had
planned his own execution.
    From Irenaeus' writings in *Against the Heresies* and with the more
recent discovery of the *Gospel of Judas* in 2006, a very different view
of Judas emerges, one belonging to the ideology of a first century
Gnostic sect. Of the Gospel of Judas Irenaeus wrote,

" Others again declare that Cain derived his being from the Power Above, and acknowledge that Esau, Korah, the Sodomites, and all such persons, are related to themselves. On this account, they add, they have been assailed by the Creator, yet no one of them has suffered injury. For Sophia was in the habit of carrying off that which belonged to herself. They declare that Judas the traitor was thoroughly acquainted with these things, and that he alone, knowing the truth as no others did, accomplished the mystery of the betrayal; by him all things, both earthly and heavenly, were thus thrown into confusion. They produce a fictitious history of this kind, which they style the Gospel of Judas." – Against the Heresies

Whether or not the illuminator was privy to the tenets set forth by this particular Gnostic sect cannot be gleaned out from this illustration. However, what is most striking when we compare the two portrayals of Jesus side-by-side is the difference in his mood. In the Orthodox version of the arrest, his facial expression appears happy, if not euphoric, in response to Judas kiss and the understanding that the hour had come. However, in the Gnostic version, Jesus appears distressed and worried, a more natural "human" response to the event. This contrast mentions that to the Gnostics Jesus was both human and divine. Therefore, he was capable of human emotions. He was not pure divinity, God made in the flesh, as Orthodox Christology has persuaded us to believe.

Reviewing the Passion scenes of the Gnostic versions in Petites Heures we have visited thus far, with the exception the *Arrest*, we notice the mood of the characters is not somber. In fact, the characters, in some instances, appear to be smiling as if to mention spiritual contentment and confidence. In contrast, the participants in the Orthodox versions are more somber shaken, grieving or lamenting. This disparity in mood between the two versions remarks on the Gnostic belief that the crucifixion fulfilled Jesus' divine purpose and that those closest to him were collaborating to assist him in shedding his earthly embodiment to return to the pleroma, the fullness of the light. Since the spirit of Jesus (his divinity) did not die on the cross there was no need to grieve and to suffer. The author of the *Apocalypse of Peter* writes that the "living Jesus" was above the cross laughing while the fleshly body was crucified. Jesus thought it hilarious that the people crucifying him did not realize that it was not He on the cross. He rejoiced in his liberation and laughed at their ignorance.

Gnosticism has nothing to do with sin but more to do with mystical knowledge and self-actualization. Gnostics believed we hold a piece of God's light and God's unity (male and female) within us, as symbolized by the light of the cross. They also held that we do not belong to this earth despite the fact that we are in it. The earth is a prison of disharmony and dualism, a mixture of good and evil, and a place of ignorance. The spirit within each person is a spark of "Ineffable God", and Christ's teachings were aimed at awakening those who had separated from this knowledge. Once his initiates had received this illumination and realized who they really were (sparks of the divine) they could understand that they were "living spirits" (Sons of God) who no longer needed to dwell in poverty.

> "...When you come to know yourselves, then you will become known, and you will realize that it is you who are the sons of the living father. But if you will not know yourselves, you dwell in poverty and it is you who are that poverty."— Gospel of Thomas.Saying 3.

The Early John Debate
Petites Heures also presents two versions of the Baptism of Christ that convey two different traditions relating to the position of Jesus to John the Baptist. In both versions, Jesus stands in the rushing waters of the Jordon flanked by an angel on one side holding a cloth. On the other side is John the Baptist pouring the baptismal water over Jesus' head. In the Orthodox version, the dove, symbolizing the Holy Spirit, descends over Jesus' head while in the second version it is absent. Instead, a lamb on its hind legs rests its forelegs on John's bent arm. John is holding a holy book signifying his status as a priest. When we compare the illuminations further, we also notice the angel's wings in the Gnostic version are crossed forming an "X", the significant symbol representing the unification of opposites and tri-unity in the bridal chamber. The symbol as mentioned previously was important symbolic emblem of the Gnostic Church, the underground stream of Christianity.

According to some Gnostic traditions, Christ's baptism marked not only the birth of his ministry but was the event that endowed him with spiritual power ("the living waters"). The Ebonite, an

Baptism of Christ— Orthodox Version

Baptism of Christ—Gnostic Version

early Gnostic sect, believed the baptism marked Jesus' spiritual birth, synonymous with an awakening of consciousness. The Sethian Gnostic sects conceived the baptismal rite as a series of visionary experiences termed the Five Seals, a progression leading to complete enlightenment. Rather than designating a fivefold immersion in the "living water", the Five Seals are interpreted as a five-stage ritual of ascension, which serves to strip the inner spirit of its chaotic psychic and material garments and re-cloth it with shining light. Therefore, through his baptism, Jesus would have been purified and reborn to his more divine expression.

Jesus would have achieved complete gnosis and unification of his "three natures" and with God not through baptism but through the mystery of the bridal chamber as I have mentioned in a previous chapter. As we recall in Valentinian Gnosticism, more specifically and according to the Gospel of Philip, there are three stages and initiations that each initiate must engage in to realize his true nature as a Son of God and Son of Man. They are: baptism, redemption and bridal chamber.

According to the Canonical Gospels and Orthodox Christianity, Jesus' power descended from God on that day as symbolized by the descent of the Holy Spirit in the Orthodox illumination. The account as told by Luke 3:22 reads,

> "And the Holy Spirit descended in a bodily shape like a dove upon him, and a voice came from heaven, which said, 'You are my beloved Son; in you I am well pleased'."

But according to our Gnostic illustration, the heavens did not open up and the Holy Spirit (dove) did not descend on the occasion of his baptism. Was this omission suggesting Jesus was not worthy? Some groups of Gnostics such as the Mandaeans believe Jesus was John's disciple and that John's ministry was more important than that of Jesus. The lamb climbing on John's arm in the illustration perhaps signifies John's status as the "Lamb of God", the legitimate Jewish Messiah. This same motif, theme and debate we see in later centuries in the work of Leonardo Da Vinci, who, as we discussed in the previous chapter, portrayed the John debate in *Virgin on the Rocks*. Perhaps the ideology communicated in Petites Heures was borrowed from the Mandaeans or perhaps another Gnostic sect that venerated John the Baptist in a similar way. Although the Mandaeans consider John the Baptist their most important prophet and teacher and criticized Jesus accusing him of having robbed John of his status and teachings, they did not believe in a Messiah per say.

The absence of the Holy Spirit in the Gnostic version poignantly mentions God made no announcement that Jesus was his Son at Jesus' baptism as Gospel accounts attest. In this illustrative version, it appears Jesus was merely being baptized, symbolic for the washing away of sin as well as affirming his commitment to serve through a ministry. The version also supports the idea that Jesus was viewed as John's disciple.

Gnostic Baptism

As described at length in the chapter, *Twin Soul Legacy in the Bridal Chamber*, the Valentinian Gnostics practiced an initiatory sacrament of a five-stage resurrection. Through the five stages described in the Gospel of Philip, *Baptism, Anointing, Eucharist, Redemption and Bridal Chamber*, the initiate realized his original state of tri-unity with God and the androgyny of his angelic perfection. This self-realizing event was best described in Saying 22 of the Gospel of Thomas on "making the two one."

The illumination, *Gnostic Baptismal Sacrament*, beautifully encapsulates the baptismal sacrament and mystical marriage expounded on by Valentinian Gnostics. Within a baptismal urn are two naked youths, male and female, representing images of the internal unity (male and female polarities) within the heart of our spirit – our Stellar Heart. From above the Holy Spirit (dove) descends, representing the fire of the chrism in the anointing stage of the sacrament.

The saints performing the baptism would most likely have been the Apostles John and Philip, both of whom to the Gnostics were the apostolic leaders of their faith.

The Gospel of Philip reads, *"Baptism is a great thing, because if people receive it they will live."* The spiritual awakening ("great thing") is accomplished through the gnosis of the "resurrection from the dead" (Treatise on the Resurrection). As a result of the resurrection through baptism and the other stages of initiation, the initiate was seen as having undergone a complete restoration to his or her original state of unity, male and female intelligences united, and the reclamation of the original state of unity with God and God's fullness (pleroma). The person is no longer of the world, but

Gnostic Baptismal Sacrament

Creation of Adam

reborn to his spirit, symbolized by the anointing in the bridal chamber.

"Allow the seed of light to take up its abode in your bridal chamber. Receive your bridegroom from me and take him into you, and be taken by him." (Irenaeus Against Heresies 1:13:3)

The gesturing and poses of the naked youth (male and female) echo Irenaeus' description of the teachings of Marcus, a Gnostic disciple of Valentinus. One figure bows to the other (hands pressed together) and the other crosses his hands at his heart. What is truly remarkable is that this figure's crossed hands, arms, shoulders and elbows, perfectly create the signature, ><, which is the hidden code for our tri-unity with God in the Bridal Chamber of the Stellar Heart. As I have mentioned several times, the X was an emblem used by Gnostic underground stream of Christianity of the Middle Ages and was probably adopted from the tradition of the bridal chamber that was passed down from Jesus and Mary Magdalene to their disciples. This X was even incorporated into the elaborate attire (robe) that Jesus wears in Leonardo Da Vinci's most recently authenticated painting, *Savaltor Mundi,* a painting yet to be recognized for its Gnostic portrayal of Jesus.

The Creation of Adam

The creation story of Adam illumination in Petites Heures is of particular interest, as it seems to combine the two versions of Genesis as well as expressing a theology of the triune nature of God. One would expect some rendition of one God as the one source of creation molding Adam in his own image. But instead, identical twin gods stand side-by-side blessing their creation while Adam lies on the ground beneath the Tree of Life seemingly before God breathed life into him. The first question is: Why are there two seemingly identical gods tending their creation? The answer may be that the artist translated Genesis to depict a uniplurality of the Godhead, as in when God says,

"Then God said, "Let us make man] in our image, after our likeness. And let them have dominion over the fish of the sea and over the birds of the heavens and over the livestock and over all the earth and over every creeping thing that creeps on the earth." — Genesis 1:26.

Scholars have debated over the reasons why there appear to be two versions of Genesis, compiled as one, in the Old Testament. In the first, God is the plural, Elohim, suggesting more than one God was responsible for creating the world. In this version, the Elohim create man and woman together. But in the second version, he is "one" God, who puts Adam to sleep to remove his rib to create Eve. The illumination in Petites Heures seems to have incorporated both versions, depicting two Gods (Elohim) but creating Adam only, which is more in line with the second version of Genesis.

Trinitarians and others claim that the Hebrew noun 'Elohim', rendered 'God' in the first clause of Genesis 1:26, as more than one God person, typically thought of or explained as "3 in 1" or "2 in 1" as in a unity of consciousness. In the composition, all three faces are the same, suggesting tri-unity, with Adam having been created out of Gods' image. This would be an unusual representation for the Gnostic Holy Trinity in that we would expect to see a feminine (mother) aspect of God represented, "Father, Mother, Son".

The illustration could instead be hinting at a dualistic view of creation, characteristic of some Gnostic traditions such as the Manicheans whose mythology is thought to have been derived from Zoroastrian mythology. Many of the Gnostic traditions believed that the Abrahamic God of the Jews was an imperfect and jealous God referred to as a demiurge. He was contrasted to the more perfect rival, the more unknowable and supreme being who was inherently good. In the *Apocryphon of John*, a Gnostic text of the 2nd century, this demiurge was named Yaldabaoth. The arrogant and imperfect Yaldabaoth sought to recreate the image of God (Spirit) from the reflection of the water, and many archons and angels pitched in to create this image. Yaldabaoth tried to create a being, the First Man, whom he called "Adam" or "Adama", so he could steal the light (spirit). But his creation was lifeless and without a soul. One might wonder if the three bodies of water and the lifelessness of Adam in the illustration allude to this Gnostic myth. If so, the illustration may be added to the list of illustrations I discussed as heretical and representative of the underground Gnostic stream of Christianity.

The series of comparative illustrations conveying a Gnostic Mary Magdalene tradition in Petites Heures de Jean Berry, those that include the Pentecost, Cycles of the Passion, Stations of the Cross, Office of the Virgin, Office of John the Baptist and Creation of Adam have remained undiscovered till now for reasons that are difficult to grasp. Perhaps, no one noticed, or if they did, even questioned why there were two versions interchanging the roles of the Virgin and Mary Magdalene. Perhaps, it was because of how the Petites Heures was organized that they were overlooked or because no one before myself had the desire to interpret each illustration, to examine them closely enough to see anything Gnostic in the compositions. The fact is art historians missed what to me was obvious. A bigger question, however, is: Why was a Book of Hours saturated with Gnostic theology and ideology commissioned as a personal devotional prayer book for Jean de Berry, third son of King John II, the Good of France? Was Jean de Berry a member of the underground stream of Christianity that venerated Mary Magdalene above the Virgin and one who sought "gnosis" as a means of salvation? Was he a heretic? These questions seem unanswerable and the necessary research is beyond the scope and purpose of this book. However, there is one more illumination from Petites Heures as well as elements to Jean de Berry's genealogical legacy and history that deserve mention.

The illumination in Petites Heures of interest to this inquiry depicts Jean de Berry in cloistered prayer kneeling before an altar with an open book of prayers. Above him on a heavenly platform reside the King and Queen of the Heavens, signified by their crowns and thrones. Christ the King's hand gesture directs a blessing at his Queen and the orb he holds would traditionally be the *globus cruciger* (cross-bearing orb), a Christian symbol of authority. Depictions such as this one signified that Christ had dominion over the world as *Salvator Mundi* (Savior of the World). But in this case, the orb is without a cross, and therefore would be termed *globus terrarum* (world of the lands).

Jesus shares his dominion over the world with a feminine counterpart, the Queen, who traditionally would be identified as the Virgin (his mother) in her position as Queen of the Heavens. Then again, the Church tradition often held up a woman personification, *Ecclesia,* as Christ's counterpart. The church was, in this context, sometimes conflated with the Virgin Mary leading to the concept of "Maria Ecclesia" (Mary as the church), which is an

Jean de Berry in Prayer — Petite Heures

element of Mariology that is behind much of the art showing the Virgin as a queen.

In light of the fact that Mary Magdalene is usually the one dressed in pink robes or mantle in Petites Heures, it seems more likely that it is she sharing dominion with Jesus in this illumination. The Gnostic interpretation of this scene would be that Jesus and Mary Magdalene are now "Imperishable Aeons", who after their incarnation transitioned into their heavenly roles to serve humanity as a unit. The omission of the cross on the globus (orb) presents the view of a Gnostic tradition in which Jesus' suffering (the cross) was not the key to salvation nor did it award him his authority. For the Gnostics, salvation was viewed instead as an individual accomplishment through redemption and self-perfection. Its omission is a sign of renunciation of the Church's authority and doctrine. Instead of the cross, Jesus' hand rests on top of the *globus* eliciting the idea of a more personal relationship to the world through his continued service and intercession in human affairs. As a Gnostic, Jean de Berry would have prayed to Jesus and Mary Magdalene to guide him on his quest for gnosis.

Jean de France, duc de Berry, (born November 30, 1340, Vincennes, France—died June 15, 1416, Paris), was the third son of King John the Good of France and brother of King Charles V (1338-1380). His bloodline pedigree was the House of Valois a cadet branch of the Capetian dynasty, succeeding the House of Capet (or direct Capetians) as kings of France from 1328 to 1589. A cadet branch of the family reigned as dukes of Burgundy from 1363 to 1482. This Capetian linage wound back through the Merovingian kings whose bloodline has been identified as connected to the vine of Jesus and Mary Magdalene. Therefore, Jean de Berry could very well have been a bloodline descendant and inheritor of the legacy of the Grail.

Jean de Berry controlled at least one-third of the territory of France during the middle period of the Hundred Years' War. He was assigned the position as king's lieutenant in 1358 for Auvergne, Languedoc, Perigord and Poitou during the time his father was in captivity in England. In Languedoc, as we know, there was a rich Mary Magdalene and Gnostic tradition. Therefore, it is possible that Jean de Berry participated in the celebrations and pilgrimages honoring the three Mary's whose legends told of their missionary journeys in the South of France. He may have been introduced to

Gnosticism from exposure to this milieu and moved by the spiritual light of the land of the Magdalene.

Jean de Berry lived an opulent life style and was the medieval world's greatest connoisseur of arts, collecting jewels, castles, works of art and exotic animals. Among his extraordinarily varied collection were chateaux such as Saumur and Bicetre, rubies weighing up to 240 carats, a collection of ostriches, bears and camels and most importantly a magnificent collection of books. He owned astronomical treatises, mappa mondes, and a large number of religious books that included: 14 Bibles, 16 psalters, 18 breviaries, 6 missals and some 15 Books of Hours, including Tres Riches Heures illustrated by the Limbourge brothers and Petites Heures. With so many sacred texts and prayer books in his collection, one might suggest he might not have had the opportunity to study the illuminations in his own Books of Hours. It is conceivable that he didn't even know that a Gnostic tradition had been included in Petites Heures. However, because Petites Heures was commissioned to be his own personal devotional tool, it seems reasonable that he was full aware of the heretical nature of some of the illuminations.

Throughout his life, Berry had spent so lavishly to promote the arts that at his death there was not enough money to pay for his funeral. He had invested his fortune in a treasure trove of paintings, tapestries, jewelry, and illuminated manuscripts that are now in private collections and in museums.

In conclusion, the artist Jean le Noir and others who collaborated in secret to put together Petites Heures illustrated and designed more than a generic Book of Hours with elaborate decoration for a single patron. They created and left the most substantial piece of evidence that a Gnostic stream of Christianity survived the brutal campaign to eradicate believers from Europe by the Church of Rome. Through pictorial representations of the passion scenes and Stations of the Cross, we are offered to compare with the traditional accounts of the Gospels, a Gnostic view of Mary Magdalene's role. We are introduced to a Gnostic Mariology that recognized Mary Magdalene's divinity as much as Jesus', one that raised her above her sinful status and penitent persona to stand as an equal—as Jesus' Divine Complement. She was the perfected feminine whose heart was the chasm of unity with the Holy Spirit at the Pentecost and "the one who knew the all". She was the one who helped Jesus carry the cross, accepting her beloved's burden. The one he leaned on most as he faced his destiny. She was seated at the cross, was the first to touch him as he was brought down, the one who cradled him in her arm as the Pieta and the most connected to him at the tomb. She was his companion and wife.

CARAVAGGIO'S GNOSTIC HERESY

Mary and Martha - Michelangelo Caravaggio - circa 1598

During the Middle Ages, a popular milieu of religious piety began to identify Mary of Bethany (Mary Magdalene) as a sinful woman whose vanities were amongst her many sins before her conversion. A number of paintings emerged by Renaissance artists, such as Luini and Gentileschi, depicting Martha reproving Mary for her preoccupation with her own beauty.

Michelangelo Caravaggio painted his own rendition of the relationship between Mary Magdalene and Martha. Although at first glance, the composition seems to present the same theme as other artists, in truth, it depicts something entirely different. Caravaggio's religious theme is not a pious remark on the sins of vanity, but a Gnostic remark on the spark of God that lies within one's own reflection.

Notice Mary Magdalene points to the reflection of the light in the mirror. She is pointing out to her sister Martha that God's light is contained within her own reflection, an important tenet of Gnostic Christianity. She holds a delicate white flower with five pedals, the symbol of feminine beauty and purity (white). The five pedals denote esoteric wisdom as the sacred number of the Goddess and her mysteries.

The symbol of the mirror transforms from a tool of vanity to a symbol of the Gnostic path of introspection, self-reflection, and self-realization. For the Gnostics, these practices led to self-perfection and the realization of the god-self.

Martha's pose is not one of reproving Mary nor is she imploring her to cease her vain obsession. Instead, she is listening intently and by the expression on her face is trying to understand the lesson Mary is imparting. She is seeking "gnosis", the wisdom of an enlightened heart and she holds her sister in highest esteem as her wisdom teacher. The way Martha holds her index finger with her right hand is a sharp contrast to the hand positions in Luini and Gentileschi paintings in which Martha demonstrates the upper hand of religious piety. In contrast, Caravaggio's hand pose seems to convey that Martha now understands Mary's point—the truth.

As with the majority of Caravaggio's portraits of Mary Magdalene, this painting also hints at Mary Magdalene's pregnancy. The gold sash while concealing a part of her belly at the same time brings attention to the slight protrusion.

Martha and Mary was painted while Caravaggio was living in the palazzo of his patron, Cardinal Franceso Maria Del Monte. His paintings for Del Monte included *Rest on the Flight into Egypt* and *Ecstasy of Saint Francis*. Of his religious paintings with heretical elements and underpinnings, this one stands out for its disclosure of his religious affiliations with a Gnostic Mary Magdalene tradition.

END NOTE

I grew up at a house of figs. And I love to imagine it somehow connected to Mary Magdalene's house in "Bethany" which meaningfully translates as — "House of Figs". That giant fig tree in my backyard held great significance throughout my life because as a child it was a safe haven where I would climb its branches to relax out on a limb. There I imagined all sorts of things: How I was in a space ship journeying to the stars or a jungle hideout concealed by leaves and where my family couldn't find me or in a paradise like the Garden of Eden. There I found repose. It was also a tree of plenty, full of ripe luscious black figs and during the hot summer months, I would eat them by the handful. I never seemed to get enough. They were all good figs.

When I first heard the parable of Jesus cursing the fig tree, I couldn't imagine how he could do such a thing. And more recently, I wondered the source of that parable and what it was meant to convey. Mark reads,

> "The next day as they were leaving Bethany, Jesus was hungry. Seeing in the distance a fig tree in leaf, he went to find out if it had any fruit. When he reached it, he found nothing but leaves, because it was not the season for figs. Then he said to the tree, "May no one ever eat fruit from you again." And his disciples heard him say it."

This parable of condemnation, constructed by the Gospel writer

Mark, was an anti-Semitic statement against Jews, because what
followed was Jesus' disruption of the moneychangers at the Temple.
Most biblical scholars interpret the fig tree as emblematic for the
Jewish nation, which seemed to be thriving with an abundance of
leaves (growth) at the time but which spiritually was producing no
fruit—no true spiritual sustenance. The parable, in truth, wasn't
anything close to what Jesus may have said. Like most of Jesus'
sayings in the four canonical Gospels this parable was drawn from
The Gospel of Thomas, modified and corrupted to express an
altogether different ideology, philosophy and doctrine. Saying 43 of
the Gospel of Thomas reads,

> "His disciples said to him, 'Who are you to say these things to us?''
> 'You don't understand who I am from what I say to you.''Rather,
> you have become like the Judeans, for they love the tree but hate its
> fruit, or they love the fruit but hate the tree."

With this saying, Jesus was first and foremost responding to his
disciple's failure to recognize and appreciate him (the tree) and his
wisdom words (the fruit). He is saying you, like the Judeans, either
love the nourishment of my wisdom but reject its source (me) or
embrace the source but find the wisdom difficult to comprehend
and appreciate. Mark took this saying a wild step further to
condemn the Jewish tradition for bearing no good Christian fruit
and for rejecting the tenets of Jesus Christ.

For the Gospel writers, Jesus authentic sayings were
incomprehensible and in need of redaction (revision) to fit into the
doctrine of a new religion that was already emerging through the
propaganda of the Apostle Paul by 60 AD. They liked neither the
tree nor the fruit and sought to refashion Jesus from a wisdom
teacher into a Son of God who was at times an arrogant
revolutionary, at other times a miracle worker, but always a dying
god. As a result, we have been denied figs, the "gnosis" that Jesus
and Mary Magdalene came to offer through their teachings and
their example. The forbidden fruit from the Tree of Good and Evil
was the fig, just as Michelangelo painted it on the ceiling of the
Sistine Chapel. What was forbidden and omitted by the Church
was gnosis (knowledge) of the mystery of the Bridal Chamber, our
internal unity with God and the knowledge of our God/Goddess
nature. But we are now all welcome to enter the House of Figs

whenever it suits our desires. It takes only repose and meditation in our stellar hearts.

APPENDIX 1
A Divine Emanation:
The Secret in Mary Magdalene's Rose

I bought a beautiful bouquet of long-stem red roses for my best friend, Laura, who was in the hospital last autumn. Cancer and the complications of surgery and chemotherapy had pushed her to the threshold of "near death experience" weeks before. Her recovery was a true miracle—the result of prayer and healing hands.

She asked me to take the roses home with me on the day she was being transferred to a rehab center, where she was to continue her already-lengthy recovery and rehabilitation. As I often do, I asked the Divine Feminine, Mary Magdalene, to bless the roses as I laid them on my altar. They continued to blossom there alongside my pictures of Mary and Jesus for nearly a week.

My dear friend Carolyn Quan, a photographer, was at my home for a dream group on the same evening that I had brought the roses home. I was naturally excited to show her and the other members of my group the splendor of the roses on my altar. Carolyn, with her fine eye for detail, noticed the anomaly of twin buds at the center of the rose that stood front and center in the bouquet. We were all amazed at and in awe of this unusual and splendid rose. Carolyn pulled her digital camera out of her purse in excitement. To our dismay, the display on the camera read "low battery." She had an awful time getting the picture to stay on the viewer so she could snap some shots. I prayed again, this time asking Jesus and Mary to bless Carolyn and her camera. The camera suddenly came on and she was able to get three shots before the camera failed.

Carolyn e-mailed me the photo of the rose within a few days and I gazed into its center several times that hour, marveling at its beauty and rarity. The third time I pulled the image up onto the desktop of my computer, my eye was pulled into the center of each bud, where for the first time I noticed two figures, male and female. I gasped in recognition of them.

What the photo reveals is astonishing—two tiny figures, each nestled within the two buds at the center—Jesus, recognized by dark hair and a chin beard, sitting beneath three palm branches (left bud) and Mary Magdalene, recognized by a long head veil, the customary attire seen in biblical images of women of Judea during the time of Christ, (right bud). The outer petals of the left blossom unfold forming an angelic figure with wings facing right at the center of the rose and the outer petals of the right bud reveal yet another figure whose arms embrace Mary.

The imagery within the rose appears to convey a story in which the transfigured angel, Jesus Christ, emerges from beneath palm branches and redirects his pose to stand before his beloved in recognition of the divinity of their union. Mary sits in repose embraced from behind by the arms of what appear to be an emanation of the Holy Spirit.

Does the rose represent a divine apparition, or is it merely anomaly of nature being subjected to the overly imaginative wanderings of an intuitive mind? The picture presents what was captured in one miraculous moment of divine communication through the lens of an ordinary digital camera. The rose cropped-photo on the left was not artistically produced or altered. The one on the right has been artistically enhanced to point out the location of the tiny figures of Jesus and Mary Magdalene.

What does this miracle manifestation and communication from the Divine suggest?

It suggests to me a confirmation that Mary Magdalene and Jesus were twin souls and beloveds, forever bound in beauty, love and devotion, qualities symbolized the rose.

I have lovingly named the photo on the cover Magdalene's Rose.

The anomaly of the twin-centered rose in and of itself can be appreciated for its beauty, rarity and perfection. Its blossoms unfold to form a trinity-matrix design of complex unity and symmetry. The full singular outer blossom houses a mystery in its center: two symmetrical unfolding bud centers unified together to resemble the yin-yang symbol of balance and unity of opposites. The two within the one, a sacred trinity, expresses the unification of opposites within the totality of the One, as well as the unification of twin souls in the bridal chamber of the heart.

Symbolically, the ordinary red rose represents a complex symbol of heavenly perfection and earthly passion. It is often depicted at the center of the crucifix in Christian iconography as an emblem of divine love. Rose gardens evoke the paradisiacal location of the mystical marriage between Adam and Eve. In mythology, the red rose is associated with the passionate beauty of the love Goddess Aphrodite (Venus) and its redness with the blood of Adonis. Interestingly enough, this mythological association of the rose reflects the mystical union of the God and Goddess archetypes and is the underlying mythology of the sacred union between Mary Magdalene and Jesus. Today, red roses are bestowed as gifts of love, appreciation and devotion by lovers everywhere on Valentine's Day. Roses also adorn altars to the Divine Mother.

What the camera lens captured was a divine imprint of meaningful imagery. The imagery within the twin-centered rose encapsulates a story of spiritual evolution between Jesus and Mary Magdalene, as sacred bride and bridegroom. Jesus is depicted beneath what appear to be palm branches, symbolic of Jesus' personal glory, righteousness and victory. Palm leaves were used in several celebrations, one of which is the Feast of the Tabernacle to the glory and triumph of the Israelites. We know that upon entering Jerusalem on Nisan 10, the day for the selection of the Pascal lamb to be sacrificed for the Passover supper and days before the Crucifixion and Resurrection, crowds waved palm branches as Jesus rode into Jerusalem on a donkey. The crowds waving palm leaves celebrated him as the true King of Israel. Some authors, such as Lawrence Gardner, suggest that Jesus deliberately made his entry into Jerusalem on that day to enact the prophecy of Isaiah 53, which would have solidified his claim to the Davidic legacy. It is logical to interpret the pose beneath palm branches in the left bud as a snapshot of Christ's glorified state just before the Resurrection.

Did Jesus, in seeking recognition as the true King of Israel, turn away from his beloved Mary for a time?

The imagery conveys that while Mary was turned toward her beloved, Jesus had turned away from her, perhaps in favor of his personal quest for self-realization and the fulfillment of his individual destiny as the Son of Man. Perhaps he lacked appreciation of Mary's worth to his spiritual unity with God and it wasn't until his transfiguration that he realized her divine connection to him through an initiation in the bridal chamber of his Stellar Heart. The imagery of the spirit form of Christ, emerging from the bud and standing in front of his beloved, remarks on this spiritual transformation that turned him toward his twin complement again in recognition and in love. He appears to be ready to reveal his heart to her and embrace her as his sacred bride. The imagery almost reminds us of the resurrection scene that occurred when Mary arrived at the tomb after the Crucifixion to anoint the body of Jesus. He appeared to her in the sepulcher on Easter morning as an angel, and it wasn't until moments later that he identified himself to her as Jesus.

Looking closely at the right bud, we see that Mary is adorned in head veil and is seated in repose. She humbly faces her beloved as if expecting him to rise to the power of love. The image certainly denotes her divinity in connection to Jesus. Looking closely, we notice that she is embraced by another figure whose arms appear to cradle her. These arms seem to emerge from a larger-than-life feminine deity situated behind Mary in the outer folds of the right bud. This figure might very well represent the feminine aspect of God, the Holy Spirit, supporting Mary's spiritual evolution and healing her from the shame of separation to resurrect her soul to its divinity.

The unfolding story in the photo represents a remarkable spiritual revelation, pointing to the divinity of the relationship between Jesus and Mary Magdalene. As a focal point in the right bud of the rose, Mary reconciles the split between God and Goddess, inspiring us to venerate her and bring her out of the shadows of obscurity and perceived irrelevance to Jesus' life. It cannot be denied that what was captured by the camera was meant to be regarded as a divine communication, understood for its intrinsic truth and preserved for its spiritual value in helping us to appreciate the divine union between Mary Magdalene and Jesus Christ after centuries of misconception.

APPENDIX II
The Gospel of Thomas

Translated by Thomas O. Lambdin

These are the secret sayings which the living Jesus spoke and which Didymos Judas Thomas wrote down.

(1) And he said, "Whoever finds the interpretation of these sayings will not experience death."

(2) Jesus said, "Let him who seeks continue seeking until he finds. When he finds, he will become troubled. When he becomes troubled, he will be astonished, and he will rule over the All."

(3) Jesus said, "If those who lead you say to you, 'See, the kingdom is in the sky,' then the birds of the sky will precede you. If they say to you, 'It is in the sea,' then the fish will precede you. Rather, the kingdom is inside of you, and it is outside of you. When you come to know yourselves, then you will become known, and you will realize that it is you who are the sons of the living father. But if you will not know yourselves, you dwell in poverty and it is you who are that poverty."

(4) Jesus said, "The man old in days will not hesitate to ask a small child seven days old about the place of life, and he will live. For many who are first will become last, and they will become one and the same."

(5) Jesus said, "Recognize what is in your sight, and that which is hidden from you will become plain to you . For there is nothing hidden which will not become manifest."

(6) His disciples questioned him and said to him, "Do you want us to fast? How shall we pray? Shall we give alms? What diet shall we observe?"

Jesus said, "Do not tell lies, and do not do what you hate, for all things are plain in the sight of heaven. For nothing hidden will not become manifest, and nothing covered will remain without being uncovered."

(7) Jesus said, "Blessed is the lion which becomes man when consumed by man; and cursed is the man whom the lion consumes, and the lion becomes man."

(8) And he said, "The man is like a wise fisherman who cast his net into the sea and drew it up from the sea full of small fish.

Among them the wise fisherman found a fine large fish. He threw all the small fish back into the sea and chose the large fish without difficulty. Whoever has ears to hear, let him hear."

(9) Jesus said, "Now the sower went out, took a handful (of seeds), and scattered them. Some fell on the road; the birds came and gathered them up. Others fell on the rock, did not take root in the soil, and did not produce ears. And others fell on thorns; they choked the seed(s) and worms ate them. And others fell on the good soil and it produced good fruit: it bore sixty per measure and a hundred and twenty per measure."

(10) Jesus said, "I have cast fire upon the world, and see, I am guarding it until it blazes."

(11) Jesus said, "This heaven will pass away, and the one above it will pass away. The dead are not alive, and the living will not die. In the days when you consumed what is dead, you made it what is alive. When you come to dwell in the light, what will you do? On the day when you were one you became two. But when you become two, what will you do?"

(12) The disciples said to Jesus, "We know that you will depart from us. Who is to be our leader?"

Jesus said to them, "Wherever you are, you are to go to James the righteous, for whose sake heaven and earth came into being."

(13) Jesus said to his disciples, "Compare me to someone and tell me whom I am like."

Simon Peter said to him, "You are like a righteous angel."

Matthew said to him, "You are like a wise philosopher."

Thomas said to him, "Master, my mouth is wholly incapable of saying whom you are like."

Jesus said, "I am not your master. Because you have drunk, you have become intoxicated from the bubbling spring which I have measured out."

And he took him and withdrew and told him three things. When Thomas returned to his companions, they asked him, "What did Jesus say to you?"

Thomas said to them, "If I tell you one of the things which he told me, you will pick up stones and throw them at me; a fire will come out of the stones and burn you up."

(14) Jesus said to them, "If you fast, you will give rise to sin for yourselves; and if you pray, you will be condemned; and if you give alms, you will do harm to your spirits. When you go into any land

and walk about in the districts, if they receive you, eat what they will set before you, and heal the sick among them. For what goes into your mouth will not defile you, but that which issues from your mouth - it is that which will defile you."

(15) Jesus said, "When you see one who was not born of woman, prostrate yourselves on your faces and worship him. That one is your father."

(16) Jesus said, "Men think, perhaps, that it is peace which I have come to cast upon the world. They do not know that it is dissension which I have come to cast upon the earth: fire, sword, and war. For there will be five in a house: three will be against two, and two against three, the father against the son, and the son against the father. And they will stand solitary."

(17) Jesus said, "I shall give you what no eye has seen and what no ear has heard and what no hand has touched and what has never occurred to the human mind."

(18) The disciples said to Jesus, "Tell us how our end will be."

Jesus said, "Have you discovered, then, the beginning, that you look for the end? For where the beginning is, there will the end be. Blessed is he who will take his place in the beginning; he will know the end and will not experience death."

(19) Jesus said, "Blessed is he who came into being before he came into being. If you become my disciples and listen to my words, these stones will minister to you. For there are five trees for you in Paradise which remain undisturbed summer and winter and whose leaves do not fall. Whoever becomes acquainted with them will not experience death."

(20) The disciples said to Jesus, "Tell us what the kingdom of heaven is like."

He said to them, "It is like a mustard seed. It is the smallest of all seeds. But when it falls on tilled soil, it produces a great plant and becomes a shelter for birds of the sky."

(21) Mary said to Jesus, "Whom are your disciples like?"

He said, "They are like children who have settled in a field which is not theirs. When the owners of the field come, they will say, 'Let us have back our field.' They (will) undress in their presence in order to let them have back their field and to give it back to them. Therefore I say, if the owner of a house knows that the thief is coming, he will begin his vigil before he comes and will not let him dig through into his house of his domain to carry away his goods. You, then, be on your guard against the world. Arm yourselves with great strength lest the robbers find a way to come to you, for the difficulty which you expect will (surely) materialize. Let there be among you a man of understanding. When the grain ripened, he came quickly with his sickle in his hand and reaped it. Whoever has ears to hear, let him hear."

(22) Jesus saw infants being suckled. He said to his disciples, "These infants being suckled are like those who enter the kingdom."

They said to him, "Shall we then, as children, enter the kingdom?"

Jesus said to them, "When you make the two one, and when you make the inside like the outside and the outside like the inside, and the above like the below, and when you make the male and the female one and the same, so that the male not be male nor the female female; and when you fashion eyes in the place of an eye, and a hand in place of a hand, and a foot in place of a foot, and a likeness in place of a likeness; then will you enter the kingdom."

(23) Jesus said, "I shall choose you, one out of a thousand, and two out of ten thousand, and they shall stand as a single one."

(24) His disciples said to him, "Show us the place where you are, since it is necessary for us to seek it."

He said to them, "Whoever has ears, let him hear. There is light within a man of light, and he lights up the whole world. If he does not shine, he is darkness."

(25) Jesus said, "Love your brother like your soul, guard him like the pupil of your eye."

(26) Jesus said, "You see the mote in your brother's eye, but you do not see the beam in your own eye. When you cast the beam out of your own eye, then you will see clearly to cast the mote from your brother's eye."

(27) <Jesus said,> "If you do not fast as regards the world, you will not find the kingdom. If you do not observe the Sabbath as a Sabbath, you will not see the father."

(28) Jesus said, "I took my place in the midst of the world, and I appeared to them in flesh. I found all of them intoxicated; I found none of them thirsty. And my soul became afflicted for the sons of men, because they are blind in their hearts and do not have sight; for empty they came into the world, and empty too they seek to leave the world. But for the moment they are intoxicated. When they shake off their wine, then they will repent."

(29) Jesus said, "If the flesh came into being because of spirit, it is a wonder. But if spirit came into being because of the body, it is a wonder of wonders. Indeed, I am amazed at how this great wealth has made its home in this poverty."

(30) Jesus said, "Where there are three gods, they are gods. Where there are two or one, I am with him."

(31) Jesus said, "No prophet is accepted in his own village; no physician heals those who know him."

(32) Jesus said, "A city being built on a high mountain and fortified cannot fall, nor can it be hidden."

(33) Jesus said, "Preach from your housetops that which you will hear in your ear. For no one lights a lamp and puts it under a bushel, nor does he put it in a hidden place, but rather he sets it on a lampstand so that everyone who enters and leaves will see its light."

(34) Jesus said, "If a blind man leads a blind man, they will both fall into a pit."

(35) Jesus said, "It is not possible for anyone to enter the house of a strong man and take it by force unless he binds his hands; then he will (be able to) ransack his house."

(36) Jesus said, "Do not be concerned from morning until evening and from evening until morning about what you will wear."

(37) His disciples said, "When will you become revealed to us and when shall we see you?"

Jesus said, "When you disrobe without being ashamed and take up your garments and place them under your feet like little children and tread on them, then will you see the son of the living one, and you will not be afraid"

(38) Jesus said, "Many times have you desired to hear these words which I am saying to you, and you have no one else to hear them from. There will be days when you will look for me and will not find me."

(39) Jesus said, "The pharisees and the scribes have taken the keys of knowledge (gnosis) and hidden them. They themselves have not entered, nor have they allowed to enter those who wish to. You, however, be as wise as serpents and as innocent as doves."

(40) Jesus said, "A grapevine has been planted outside of the father, but being unsound, it will be pulled up by its roots and destroyed."

(41) Jesus said, "Whoever has something in his hand will receive more, and whoever has nothing will be deprived of even the little he has."

(42) Jesus said, "Become passers-by."

(43) His disciples said to him, "Who are you, that you should say these things to us?"

<Jesus said to them,> "You do not realize who I am from what I say to you, but you have become like the Jews, for they (either) love the tree and hate its fruit (or) love the fruit and hate the tree."

(44) Jesus said, "Whoever blasphemes against the father will be forgiven, and whoever blasphemes against the son will be forgiven, but whoever blasphemes against the holy spirit will not be forgiven either on earth or in heaven."

(45) Jesus said, "Grapes are not harvested from thorns, nor are figs gathered from thistles, for they do not produce fruit. A good man brings forth good from his storehouse; an evil man brings forth evil things from his evil storehouse, which is in his heart, and says evil things. For out of the abundance of the heart he brings forth evil things."

(46) Jesus said, "Among those born of women, from Adam until John the Baptist, there is no one so superior to John the Baptist that his eyes should not be lowered (before him). Yet I have said, whichever one of you comes to be a child will be acquainted with the kingdom and will become superior to John."

(47) Jesus said, "It is impossible for a man to mount two horses or to stretch two bows. And it is impossible for a servant to serve two masters; otherwise, he will honor the one and treat the other contemptuously. No man drinks old wine and immediately desires to drink new wine. And new wine is not put into old wineskins, lest they burst; nor is old wine put into a new wineskin, lest it spoil it. An old patch is not sewn onto a new garment, because a tear would result."

(48) Jesus said, "If two make peace with each other in this one house, they will say to the mountain, 'Move Away,' and it will move away."

(49) Jesus said, "Blessed are the solitary and elect, for you will find the kingdom. For you are from it, and to it you will return."

(50) Jesus said, "If they say to you, 'Where did you come from?', say to them, 'We came from the light, the place where the light came into being on its own accord and established itself and

became manifest through their image.' If they say to you, 'Is it you?', say, 'We are its children, we are the elect of the living father.' If they ask you, 'What is the sign of your father in you?', say to them, 'It is movement and repose.'"

(51) His disciples said to him, "When will the repose of the dead come about, and when will the new world come?"

He said to them, "What you look forward to has already come, but you do not recognize it."

(52) His disciples said to him, "Twenty-four prophets spoke in Israel, and all of them spoke in you."

He said to them, "You have omitted the one living in your presence and have spoken (only) of the dead."

(53) His disciples said to him, "Is circumcision beneficial or not?"

He said to them, "If it were beneficial, their father would beget them already circumcised from their mother. Rather, the true circumcision in spirit has become completely profitable."

(54) Jesus said, "Blessed are the poor, for yours is the kingdom of heaven."

(55) Jesus said, "Whoever does not hate his father and his mother cannot become a discile to me. And whoever does not hate his brothers and sisters and take up his cross in my way will not be worthy of me."

(56) Jesus said, "Whoever has come to understand the world has found (only) a corpse, and whoever has found a corpse is superior to the world."

(57) Jesus said, "The kingdom of the father is like a man who had good seed. His enemy came by night and sowed weeds among the good seed. The man did not allow them to pull up the weeds; he said to them, 'I am afraid that you will go intending to pull up the weeds and pull up the wheat along with them.' For on the day of the harvest the weeds will be plainly visible, and they will be pulled up and burned."

(58) Jesus said, "Blessed is the man who has suffered and found life."

(59) Jesus said, "Take heed of the living one while you are alive, lest you die and seek to see him and be unable to do so."

(60) <They saw> a Samaritan carrying a lamb on his way to Judea. He said to his disciples, "That man is round about the lamb."

They said to him, "So that he may kill it and eat it."

He said to them, "While it is alive, he will not eat it, but only when he has killed it and it has become a corpse."

They said to him, "He cannot do so otherwise."

He said to them, "You too, look for a place for yourself within repose, lest you become a corpse and be eaten."

(61) Jesus said, "Two will rest on a bed: the one will die, and the other will live."

Salome said, "Who are you, man, that you ... have come up on my couch and eaten from my table?"

Jesus said to her, "I am he who exists from the undivided. I was given some of the things of my father."

<...> "I am your disciple."

<...> "Therefore I say, if he is destroyed, he will be filled with light, but if he is divided, he will be filled with darkness."

(62) Jesus said, "It is to those who are worthy of my mysteries that I tell my mysteries. Do not let your left (hand) know what your right (hand) is doing."

(63) Jesus said, "There was a rich man who had much money. He said, 'I shall put my money to use so that I may sow, reap, plant, and fill my storehouse with produce, with the result that I shall lack nothing.' Such were his intentions, but that same night he died. Let him who has ears hear."

(64) Jesus said, "A man had received visitors. And when he had prepared the dinner, he sent his servant to invite the guests.

He went to the first one and said to him, 'My master invites you.' He said, 'I have claims against some merchants. They are coming to me this evening. I must go and give them my orders. I ask to be excused from the dinner.'

He went to another and said to him, 'My master has invited you.' He said to him, 'I have just bought a house and am required for the day. I shall not have any spare time.'

He went to another and said to him, 'My master invites you.' He said to him, 'My friend is going to get married, and I am to prepare the banquet. I shall not be able to come. I ask to be excused from the dinner.'

He went to another and said to him, 'My master invites you.' He said to him, 'I have just bought a farm, and I am on my way to collect the rent. I shall not be able to come. I ask to be excused.'

The servant returned and said to his master, 'Those whom you invited to the dinner have asked to be excused.' The master said to his servant, 'Go outside to the streets and bring back those whom you happen to meet, so that they may dine.' Businessmen and merchants will not enter the places of my father."

(65) He said, "There was a good man who owned a vineyard. He leased it to tenant farmers so that they might work it and he might collect the produce from them. He sent his servant so that the tenants might give him the produce of the vineyard. They seized his servant and beat him, all but killing him. The servant went back and told his master. The master said, 'Perhaps he did not recognize them.' He sent another servant. The tenants beat this one as well. Then the owner sent his son and said, 'Perhaps they will show respect to my son.' Because the tenants knew that it was he who was the heir to the vineyard, they seized him and killed him. Let him who has ears hear."

(66) Jesus said, "Show me the stone which the builders have rejected. That one is the cornerstone."

(67) Jesus said, "If one who knows the all still feels a personal deficiency, he is completely deficient."

(68) Jesus said, "Blessed are you when you are hated and persecuted. Wherever you have been persecuted they will find no place."

(69) Jesus said, "Blessed are they who have been persecuted within themselves. It is they who have truly come to know the father. Blessed are the hungry, for the belly of him who desires will be filled."

(70) Jesus said, "That which you have will save you if you bring it forth from yourselves. That which you do not have within you will kill you if you do not have it within you."

(71) Jesus said, "I shall destroy this house, and no one will be able to build it [...]."

(72) A man said to him, "Tell my brothers to divide my father's possessions with me."

He said to him, "O man, who has made me a divider?"

He turned to his disciples and said to them, "I am not a divider, am I?"

(73) Jesus said, "The harvest is great but the laborers are few. Beseech the Lord, therefore, to send out laborers to the harvest."

(74) He said, "O Lord, there are many around the drinking trough, but there is nothing in the cistern."

(75) Jesus said, "Many are standing at the door, but it is the solitary who will enter the bridal chamber."

(76) Jesus said, "The kingdom of the father is like a merchant who had a consignment of merchandise and who discovered a pearl. That merchant was shrewd. He sold the merchandise and bought the pearl alone for himself. You too, seek his unfailing and enduring treasure where no moth comes near to devour and no worm destroys."

(77) Jesus said, "It is I who am the light which is above them all. It is I who am the all. From me did the all come forth, and unto me did the all extend. Split a piece of wood, and I am there. Lift up the stone, and you will find me there."

(78) Jesus said, "Why have you come out into the desert? To see a reed shaken by the wind? And to see a man clothed in fine garments like your kings and your great men? Upon them are the fine garments, and they are unable to discern the truth."

(79) A woman from the crowd said to him, "Blessed are the womb which bore you and the breasts which nourished you."

He said to her, "Blessed are those who have heard the word of the father and have truly kept it. For there will be days when you will say, 'Blessed are the womb which has not conceived and the breasts which have not given milk.'"

(80) Jesus said, "He who has recognized the world has found the body, but he who has found the body is superior to the world."

(81) Jesus said, "Let him who has grown rich be king, and let him who possesses power renounce it."

(82) Jesus said, "He who is near me is near the fire, and he who is far from me is far from the kingdom."

(83) Jesus said, "The images are manifest to man, but the light in them remains concealed in the image of the light of the father. He will become manifest, but his image will remain concealed by his light."

(84) Jesus said, "When you see your likeness, you rejoice. But when you see your images which came into being before you, and which neither die not become manifest, how much you will have to bear!"

(85) Jesus said, "Adam came into being from a great power and a great wealth, but he did not become worthy of you. For had he been worthy, he would not have experienced death."

(86) Jesus said, "The foxes have their holes and the birds have their nests, but the son of man has no place to lay his head and rest."

(87) Jesus said, "Wretched is the body that is dependant upon a body, and wretched is the soul that is dependent on these two."

(88) Jesus said, "The angels and the prophets will come to you and give to you those things you (already) have. And you too, give them those things which you have, and say to yourselves, 'When will they come and take what is theirs?'"

(89) Jesus said, "Why do you wash the outside of the cup? Do you not realize that he who made the inside is the same one who made the outside?"

(90) Jesus said, "Come unto me, for my yoke is easy and my lordship is mild, and you will find repose for yourselves."

(91) They said to him, "Tell us who you are so that we may believe in you."

He said to them, "You read the face of the sky and of the earth, but you have not recognized the one who is before you, and you do not know how to read this moment."

(92) Jesus said, "Seek and you will find. Yet, what you asked me about in former times and which I did not tell you then, now I do desire to tell, but you do not inquire after it."

(93) <Jesus said,> "Do not give what is holy to dogs, lest they throw them on the dung-heap. Do not throw the pearls to swine, lest they [...] it [...]."

(94) Jesus said, "He who seeks will find, and he who knocks will be let in."

(95) Jesus said, "If you have money, do not lend it at interest, but give it to one from whom you will not get it back."

(96) Jesus said, "The kingdom of the father is like a certain woman. She took a little leaven, concealed it in some dough, and made it into large loaves. Let him who has ears hear."

(97) Jesus said, "The kingdom of the father is like a certain woman who was carrying a jar full of meal. While she was walking on the road, still some distance from home, the handle of the jar broke and the meal emptied out behind her on the road. She did not realize it; she had noticed no accident. When she reached her house, she set the jar down and found it empty."

(98) Jesus said, "The kingdom of the father is like a certain man who wanted to kill a powerful man. In his own house he drew his

sword and stuck it into the wall in order to find out whether his hand could carry through. Then he slew the powerful man."

(99) The disciples said to him, "Your brothers and your mother are standing outside."

He said to them, "Those here who do the will of my father are my brothers and my mother. It is they who will enter the kingdom of my father."

(100) They showed Jesus a gold coin and said to him, "Caesar's men demand taxes from us."

He said to them, "Give Caesar what belongs to Caesar, give God what belongs to God, and give me what is mine."

(101) <Jesus said,> "Whoever does not hate his father and his mother as I do cannot become a disciple to me. And whoever does not love his father and his mother as I do cannot become a disciple to me. For my mother [...], but my true mother gave me life."

(102) Jesus said, "Woe to the pharisees, for they are like a dog sleeping in the manger of oxen, for neither does he eat nor does he let the oxen eat."

(103) Jesus said, "Fortunate is the man who knows where the brigands will enter, so that he may get up, muster his domain, and arm himself before they invade."

(104) They said to Jesus, "Come, let us pray today and let us fast."

Jesus said, "What is the sin that I have committed, or wherein have I been defeated? But when the bridegroom leaves the bridal chamber, then let them fast and pray."

(105) Jesus said, "He who knows the father and the mother will be called the son of a harlot."

(106) Jesus said, "When you make the two one, you will become the sons of man, and when you say, 'Mountain, move away,' it will move away."

(107) Jesus said, "The kingdom is like a shepherd who had a hundred sheep. One of them, the largest, went astray. He left the ninety-nine sheep and looked for that one until he found it. When he had gone to such trouble, he said to the sheep, 'I care for you more than the ninety-nine.'"

(108) Jesus said, "He who will drink from my mouth will become like me. I myself shall become he, and the things that are hidden will be revealed to him."

(109) Jesus said, "The kingdom is like a man who had a hidden treasure in his field without knowing it. And after he died, he left it to his son. The son did not know (about the treasure). He inherited the field and sold it. And the one who bought it went plowing and found the treasure. He began to lend money at interest to whomever he wished."

(110) Jesus said, "Whoever finds the world and becomes rich, let him renounce the world."

(111) Jesus said, "The heavens and the earth will be rolled up in your presence. And the one who lives from the living one will not see death." Does not Jesus say, "Whoever finds himself is superior to the world?"

(112) Jesus said, "Woe to the flesh that depends on the soul; woe to the soul that depends on the flesh."

(113) His disciples said to him, "When will the kingdom come?"

<Jesus said,> "It will not come by waiting for it. It will not be a matter of saying 'here it is' or 'there it is.' Rather, the kingdom of the father is spread out upon the earth, and men do not see it."

(114) Simon Peter said to him, "Let Mary leave us, for women are not worthy of life."

Jesus said, "I myself shall lead her in order to make her male, so that she too may become a living spirit resembling you males. For every woman who will make herself male will enter the kingdom of heaven."

REFERENCES

Baigent, Leigh, and Lincoln. *Holy Blood Holy Grail*. New York: Dell Publishing, 1983.

Baigent, Michael. *The Jesus Papers*. New York, NY: Harper Collins, 2007.

Berry, Jean. *Les Petites Heures de Jean, duc de Berry*. Paris. Bibliothèque nationale de France, Ms. Latin 18014, circa 1372-1390.

Comfort, W. W. The Quest of the Holy Grail. Cambridge, Ontario: Old French Series, 2000.

Crossan and Reed. *Excavating Jesus*. New York: Harper San Francisco, 2001.

Crossan, John and Wright, N.T. *The Resurrection of Jesus*. Minneapolis: Augsburg Fortress, 2006.

Crossan, John Dominic . *Who Is Jesus? Answers to Your Questions About the Historical Jesus*. New York, NY, Harper Collins, 1996.

Daniel-Rops, Henri. *Bernard of Clairvaux: The Story of the Last of the Great Church* Fathers. New York, NY: Hawthorn Books, Inc., 1964.

Dart and Riegert. *The Gospel of Thomas: Unearthing the Lost Words of Jesus*. Berkeley, Calif.: Seastone, 1998

France, James. The Cistercians in Medieval Art. Kalamazoo, Michigan: Cistercian Publications, 1998.

Freke and Gandy. *Jesus and The Lost Goddess*. New York: Three Rivers Press, 2001

Frale, Barabara. *The Templars :The Secret History Revealed*. New York: Arcade Publishing, 2008

Gardner, Laurence. *Bloodline of the Holy Grail.* Dorset, Great Britain: Element Books Limited, 1996.

Gardner, Laurence. *The Magdalene Legacy.* San Francisco, Ca.: Weisner Books, 2005.

Graves, Robert. *The Greek Myths: Combined Edition.* New York: Penguin Books, 1992

Hall, Manly P. *The Secret Teachings of All Ages.* New York: Jeremy P. Tarcher/Penguin, 2003.

Kenyon, J. Douglas. *Forbidden Religion: Suppressed Heresies of the West.* Vermont: Bear and Co., 2006.

MacDonald, R. Dennis. The Homer Epics and the Gospel of Mark. Connecticut: Yale University Press, 2010

McLaren, Fiona. *Da Vinci's Last Commission.* Edinburgh and London: Mainstream Publishing, 2012

Malory, Thomas. *Le Mort D' Arthur.* New York: New American Library, 2001.

Matarasso, Pauline. *The Cisterian World: Monastic Writings of the Twelfth Century.* New York: Penguin Books, 1 993.

Murphy, Wallace Tim and Hopkins, Marilyn. *Custodians of Truth.* Maine: Red Wheel-Weisner,LLC, 2005.

Nabarz, Payam. *The Mysteries of Mithras: The Pagan Belief That Shaped the Christian World. Vermont: Inner Traditions, 2005.*

Newman, Sharan. *The Real History Behind the Templars.* New York: Berkley Books, 2007.

Pagels, Elaine. *Beyond Belief: The Secret Gospel of Thomas.* New York: Random House, 2003.

Picknett and Prince. *The Templar Revelation*. New York: Simon & Schuster, 1997

Robinson, J. Armitage. *Two Glastonbury Legends*. London: Cambridge University Press, 1926

Robinson, James M. *The Nag Hammadi Library*. New York: Harper San Francisco, 1990

Rudolph, Kurt. *Gnosis: The Nature & History of Gnosticism*. New York: Harper San Francisco, 1987

Skeat, Walter W. *Joseph of Arimathie: The Romance of Seint Graal or Holy Grail*. London: N. Tubner & Co, 1871.

Starbird, Margaret. *The Woman with the Alabaster Jar*. Vermont: Inner Traditions, 1993.

Starbird, Margaret. *Mary Magdalene, Bride in Exile*. New Mexico: Bear and Co., 2005.

The Holy Bible: King James Version

Taylor, William John. *The Coming of the Saints*. England: The Covenant Publishing Co. LTD, 1969

Williamson, Marianne. *Enchanted Love: The Mystical Power of Intimate Relationships*. New York: Simon & Schuster, 1999

Voragine, Jacobus de, *The Golden Legend: Readings on the Saints*, trans. William Granger Ryan, Volume 1, Princeton: Princeton University Press, 1993, 375.

Woodman, Marion. *The Ravaged Bridegroom*. Toronto: Inner City Books, 1999

INDEX

Aaron, 14, 21, 95, 105, 207

Adam and Eve, 9, 22, 86, 275

Adonis, 4, 6, 10, 16, 82, 92, 94

Adonis and Aphrodite, 6, 9, 10, 12, 16, 52, 93

Adonis-Aphrodite myth, 22

afterlife, 138, 156, 187, 188, 189, 211, 236

Against the Heresies, 252, 253

Aix en Provence, 181, 183

Anahita, 5, 9, 52

Andre de Montbard, 148, 150, 151, 153, 156, 157, 158

androgyny, 190, 257

Angers Book of Hours, 238

Aphrodite, 6, 10, 11, 13, 16, 22, 47, 52, 71, 93, 146, 216, 272

Apocryphon of John, 260

Apostles, 13, 39, 67, 100, 116, 117, 126, 189, 221, 224, 226, 245, 257

Aquarius, 52, 68, 69, 72

Archers of Leuven, 197

Ark of the Covenant, 156, 159, 160, 165, 166, 167

Arrest of Christ, 250, 251

astrology, 5, 28, 51, 67

Avalon, 102, 109

Baldwin, 148

Bernard Clairvaux, 152, 153, 154, 156, 157, 159, 161

Bernard de Montbard, 151

Blanche de Castile, 161

bloodline, 177, 183, 189, 205, 207, 213, 217, 220, 263

Book of Revelation, 156

Bridal Chamber, 19, 27, 33, 34, 35, 37, 38, 39, 40, 41, 42, 43, 44, 45, 46, 47, 48, 107, 112, 121, 124, 136, 138, 139, 186, 228, 254, 272

bride and bridegroom, 1, 32, 39, 44, 47, 107, 157, 186, 204, 208, 240, 272

Bride of Christ, 94, 111, 183, 184, 189, 194, 209, 217, 229, 230

bridegroom, 13, 14, 40, 41, 43, 45, 131, 209, 217, 259, 272, 287

Canonical Gospels, 3, 4, 19, 90, 130, 148, 250, 256

Capetian kings, 149, 176

Capricorn, 52, 58, 59, 60, 61, 71, 72, 80

Caravaggio, 210, 213, 214, 215, 216, 217, 220, 266

Carrying the Cross, 231, 233

Caterina, 189

Cathars, 35, 103, 221, 222, 246

Chartres Cathedral, 155, 160

chrism, 39, 42, 43, 228, 257

Christ self, 38

Christendom, 120, 121, 147, 148, 154, 155, 161

Christian Orthodoxy, 12

Christology, 4, 209, 245, 246, 253

Ciborium, 166, 208, 209

Cinderella, 21, 31

Cistercian, 4, 114, 115, 116, 120, 159, 160, 161, 162

Cistercian monastery, 154

Coptic texts, 125, 139
cornerstone, 112, 133, 134, 135
coronation, 175, 176, 183
Count of Champagne, 149, 151
cross, 4, 17, 34, 35, 36, 39, 86, 89, 90, 93, 105, 107, 108, 121, 135, 150, 161, 181, 197, 205, 209, 219, 223, 231, 240
Cross of Provence, 181
Crossbowmen, 197
crucifixion, 3, 8, 11, 17, 55, 62, 86, 89, 90, 91, 93, 97, 100, 108, 116, 127, 160, 182, 193, 235, 240, 246, 272
Crucifixion Trinity, 241
Crux decussata, 35
cypress tree, 182
Da Vinci Code, 186, 194
Davidic legacy, 150, 203, 272
Dennis R. MacDonald, 97
Deposition, 160, 162, 197, 198. 203, 204, 210, 211, 240, 245
Desposyni, 143
Didymus Judas Thomas, 128, 138
divine communication, 271, 273
Divine Complement, 28
divine destiny, 55, 77,123
Divine Emanation, 270
dreams, 1, 2, 53, 65, 89, 100, 108, 114, 142, 144, 171
Druid, 34, 37
Duke and Duchess of Cambridge, 143
dynastic marital contract, 14
Ecclesia,119, 160, 261
Elohim, 219, 260

enlightenment, 6, 32, 46, 114, 130, 152, 156, 256
Entombment, 93, 97, 233, 235, 236, 237
Eucharist, 39, 42, 121, 166, 257
Fiona McLaren, 168, 170
First Crusade, 148, 149, 157
fleur-de-lis, 35, 147, 174, 175, 176
Francesco Melzi, 193
Freke and Gandy, 12
Galilee, 4, 34, 56, 68, 248, 249
Garden of Eden, 268
Gaul, 2, 7, 8, 9, 95, 96, 100 101, 102, 111, 113, 117, 129, 175, 181, 183, 185
George Alexander Louis, 143
Georges le Tour's *Penitent Magdalen*, 210
Gerbhard Flatz, 220
Gherghe Tattarescu, 64, 65
Gilead, 104, 117, 152, 165, 166
Glastonbury, 101, 102, 103, 104, 109
gnosis, 1, 150, 226, 229, 230, 241, 245, 250, 252, 256, 257, 261, 263, 267, 269
Gnostic Church, 34, 254
Gnostic Holy Trinity, 244, 260
Gnostic Mary Magdalene, 221, 237, 260, 267
Gnostic path, 231, 267
Gnostic stream, 186, 260, 264
Gnostic tradition, 5, 115, 222, 223, 230, 241, 242, 254, 260, 263, 264
Gnosticism, 236
God self, 32
Godfrey Bouillon, 149
gods and goddesses, 9, 10, 56

Golgotha, 182, 183
Gospel of Judas, 242, 243
Gospel of Mark, 3, 20, 115, 248
Gospel of Philip, 34, 40, 41, 42,
   43, 222, 228, 233, 249, 256,
   257
Gospel of Thomas, 8, 16, 17 ,
   18, 19, 39, 40, 125, 126, 134,
   137, 158, 187, 222, 255, 276
Gothic cathedrals, 182
Grail Church, 116, 117, 121,
   185
Grail legends, 104, 112,
Grail Table, 114, 115, 117, 118,
   185, 186
great secret, 4, 5, 151, 158, 159
Greek Orthodox tradition, 219
Green Man, 182, 183
Hasmonean, 14, 67, 68, 95, 104,
   176, 187, 204
Heliopolis, 3, 94
Hellenistic era, 4, 6
Henry Lincoln, 14, 53
heretical secrets, 169, 194
Holy Blood, Holy Grail, 14, 88
Holy Grail, 104, 105, 107, 113,
   114, 115, 142, 152, 158, 165,
   186, 198
Holy of Holies, 25, 42, 155, 157
Holy Place, 42
Holy Spirit, 18, 34, 39, 111,
   165, 166, 224, 226, 227, 228,
   229, 241, 254, 256, 257, 264,
   271
house of figs, 268
House of Stuart, 143
Hughes de Payen, 149, 150,
   151, 156, 157, 158, 159
Hundred Years' War, 263
Hylic, 242, 245

iconography, 35, 90, 107, 160,
   226, 236, 237, 272
Imperishable Aeons, 249, 250,
   263
Iona, 110, 111
Isaiah, 9, 15, 16, 91, 94, 95, 99,
   180, 184, 205, 207, 219, 272
Isis Knot, 213, 214
Jacquemart de Hesdin, 225
Jacques de Molay, 163
James Ussher, 109
jataka vicara, 28
Jean de Berry, 224, 225, 228,
   247, 262, 264, 265
Jean le Noir, 224, 225, 237, 265
Jerome Cardan, 52
Jerusalem, 46, 86, 94, 98, 101,
   126, 148, 149, 150, 151, 152,
   153, 154, 156, 157, 158, 159,
   166, 226, 227, 272
Jesus, 51
Jesus Maria, 103, 232
Jesus' ministry, 4, 21, 22, 71,
   117, 118, 229, 230
Jewish Gnosticism, 222
John Debate, 254
John the Baptist, 170, 172, 173,
   177, 179, 180, 183, 184, 187,
   189, 193, 203, 212, 222, 254,
   256, 261
John's gesture, 178, 179, 244,
   276
Joseph de Marmore, 111
Joseph of Arimathea, 7, 47, 96,
   97, 98, 99, 100, 101, 102,
   103, 104, 105, 107, 108, 109,
   110, 111, 115, 116, 121, 122,
   152, 158, 185, 202, 208, 216
Judaic tradition, 17, 27, 72,
   121, 146

Judaism, 127, 134
Judea, 4, 6, 14, 15, 16, 22, 68, 82, 96, 98, 104, 125, 180, 181, 271
keys to the Kingdom, 18, 46, 105, 137
Keystone, 38, 133, 134
King Arthur, 46, 105, 109, 112, 165
King David, 9, 16, 42, 104, 110, 112, 118, 155, 166, 186, 207
King John the Good, 224
King Louis VII, 152
King Merovee, 146
Kingdom of God, 19, 40, 47, 48, 114, 132, 137, 156, 187
Kingdom of the father, 114, 132
knighthood of Christ, 149
Knights Templar, 107, 109, 110, 117, 120, 121, 148, 149, 150, 151, 152, 153, 154, 155, 157, 158, 159, 170
kundali milan, 28
La Queste del Saint Graal, 5, 7, 114, 115, 116, 120, 152, 158,161 165, 186
Lamb of God, 57, 90, 177,180, 183, 256
Languedoc, 35, 150, 217, 221, 263
Last Supper, 47, 90, 105, 107, 108, 113, 116, 150, 158, 169, 173, 185, 186, 193, 197, 213, 250
Laurence Gardner, 5, 14, 53, 146, 216
Lazarus, 20, 44, 89, 95, 96, 101, 102, 195, 196
Leo, 52, 72, 73, 83, 85

Leonardo Da Vinci, 170, 179, 180, 189, 197, 213, 256, 259
Leonardo's dream, 190
Les Saintes-Marie-de-la-Mer, 89
Little Mermaid, 31
Logos, 37, 229, 242, 245
Luke, 48, 67, 90, 98, 99, 124, 125, 135, 223, 248, 252, 2556
Lynn Picknett, 180
Madonna and Child with John the Baptist, 170, 181, 189, 193
Madonna Litta, 174
Madonna with Carnation, 172
Magdala, 34
Magdalene's Rose, 271
Mandaeans, 180, 256
Mani, 126
mantle, 172, 203, 205, 226, 227, 231, 232, 235, 236, 237, 263
Margaret Starbird, 5, 44, 147, 176, 186, 236
Maria Ecclesia, 261
Mariology, 157, 176, 230, 263, 264
Mark, 3, 4, 20, 41, 67, 97, 98, 107, 115, 116, 126, 127, 133, 151, 186, 248, 253, 268
Marseilles, 89, 95, 96
Martha, 20, 21, 89, 95, 96, 101, 102, 157, 196, 266, 267
Mary and Martha, 266
Mary Magdalene, 67-74
Mary Magdalene and Jesus, 77-87
Mary of Bethany, 14, 44, 205, 266
matrix, 30, 33, 272

Matthew, 3, 18, 51, 90, 116, 125, 126, 132, 133, 216, 248, 152

Merovingian, 143, 144, 145, 146, 147, 148, 151, 157, 175, 176, 263

Mithra, 4, 9, 12, 51, 52

Mother of Sorrows, 237

Museo del Prado, 197

mystical marriage, 34, 107, 229, 257, 272

mythic blueprint, 6, 11, 89

mythologizing, 186, 248

mythology, 9, 10, 2, 13, 22, 52, 53, 57, 92, 141, 171, 183, 186, 192, 228, 230, 232, 246, 260, 272

Natal Chart, 50, 51, 54, 57, 63, 66, 68, 69, 77, 86

Nazarene, 29, 96, 99, 248

Nazareth, 3, 50, 66

New Dispensation, 119, 156, 167

Nicodemus, 100, 202, 205, 237

Nile Delta, 94, 95

Noli Me Tangere, 211, 240

Northrop Frye, 171

obelisk, 2, 3, 94

oblique cross, 34

Onias, 94

optical, 170. 171, 182, 187, 188, 192, 194

Orantes, 236

pagan, 35, 90, 101, 110, 146, 175, 182

palazzo, 267

paralysis, 184, 188

Parsifal, 46, 47

Passion of Christ, 99, 224

Passion scene, 67, 90, 91, 96, 97, 98, 99, 240, 246, 264

Passover, 62, 89,90, 108, 185, 250, 272

Penitent Mary Magdalene,, 67, 218

Pentecost, 166, 224, 225, 226, 227, 229, 231, 233, 246, 261, 264

Perceval, 117, 120, 121, 123, 142, 166

Persephone, 10, 11, 67, 93, 103

Persians and Medians, 9

Peter, 16, 17, 79, 219, 223, 231, 252, 253

Petites Heures, 221-265

Pharisees, 15, 20, 42

Phoenician trade, 95

Pieta, 238, 240, 265

Pisces, 51, 52, 56, 57, 59, 60, 61, 61, 69, 71, 74, 80, 81, 86

pomegranate, 204, 217

Pont de l'Ama, 144

Pope Paul V, 177

prayer heart, 202, 214

pregnancy, 203, 204, 205, 208, 211, 267

Prince Harry, 141, 142

Prince Philip, 143

Princess Diana, 141, 144, 145

Priory of Sion, 5

prophesies, 9, 16, 156, 252

pseudo-myth, 4, 6, 292, 230

Ptolemy, 94, 187

Puecell, 223

Pyrenees, 2, 222

Queen Elizabeth, 143

Queen of the Heavens, 45, 176, 177, 183, 227

Quentin Matsys, 210

Ariadne Green

reconciliation of the fall, 6, 9,
20, 22, 47, 229
Red Cross Shield, 105, 107,
108 115
Rembrandt, 195, 196
Renaissance, 5, 170, 182, 202,
209, 210, 213, 217, 219, 226,
235, 237, 240, 266
Rennes-le-Chateau, 5, 35, 36,
217, 218
Resurrection, 1, 4, 6, 9, 10, 12,
34, 39, 42, 52, 62, 67, 86, 89,
90, 91, 92, 97, 98, 121, 122,
124, 125, 158, 182, 183, 195,
211, 220, 246, 248, 249, 257,
272, 273
Rhone Valley, 95, 102
Robert Boron's, 113, 116
Robert Brydon, 150
Round Table, 153, 158, 165,
166
sacrament, 39, 121, 208, 257,
258
Sacred Bride, 1, 13, 46, 96, 183,
186, 231, 240, 272, 273
sacred marriage, 12, 13, 31,32,
35, 41, 43, 44, 46, 113, 187,
230
Sadducees, 15
Sainte-Victoire, 181
Salome, 89, 101, 248
Sauniere, 220
Scotland, 110, 139, 150, 157,
170
Second Coming, 47, 95,110,
156
sensus communis, 188
Sethian Gnostics, 240
Sigmund Freud, 171

Sir Galahad, 104, 105, 108, 114,
117, 152, 153, 165, 166
Sleeping Beauty, 31, 81
Son of God, 3, 6, 30 46, 53, 60,
90, 94, 111, 124, 131, 269
Son of Man, 18, 19, 21, 256,
273
Song of Songs, 44, 45, 157, 217,
231
Sophia, 67, 125, 134, 135, 147,
184, 222, 226, 228, 229, 230,
231, 241, 242
spiritual mastery, 69, 79, 85
split soul, 12, 19, 30, 37. 41, 45
St. Andrew, 35
St. Baume, 103, 110, 181, 219
St. Irenaeus, 99, 121, 252, 259
St. Maximin, 95, 181
St. Venture, 181
Star of David, 35, 43,187
Stations of the Cross, 224, 240,
261, 264
Stella Maris, 157
Stellar Heart, 19, 29, 33, 35, 37,
38, 47, 48, 107, 112, 125, 257,
259, 269, 273
Stellar Promise, 7, 20, 22, 32,
47, 85, 86, 131, 138
*Study for the Head of Mary
Magdalene*, 173, 174
Sun and Moon, 72, 74, 83
Sun god, 3, 190
Synagoga, 160
synastry, 28, 54,56, 63, 77, 78,
85, 86, 123
Temple Church, 150, 152
Temple Mount, 148, 149
Temple of Jerusalem, 94, 95
The Bloodline of the Holy Grail,
100

The *Gospel of Mary*, 124, 222, 229

The Templar Revelation, 180, 214

The Tripartite Tractate, 242

The Vulgate Cycle, 119, 120, 155, 166

Theopharastus, 176

three chief tables, 116, 117

Titian, 219, 240

tree-cross, 219, 220

trinity, 37, 38, 119, 181, 241, 242, 260, 272

tri-unity, 7, 32, 37, 41, 124, 131, 138, 254, 257, 260

Twin Flames, 9, 20, 34, 68, 202

unified intelligence, 29, 30

Valentinian Gnostics, 35, 228, 242, 256, 258

Vatican, 96, 121, 160, 177, 226, 227, 237

Venus, 52, 71, 72, 73, 82, 83, 123, 135, 216, 272

Vincent Van Gogh, 195, 196

Virgin birth, 6, 12, 53, 228

Virgin Mary, 61, 100, 103, 172, 175, 177, 205, 216, 227, 232, 237, 240, 245, 261

Walter Map, 114, 120, 152

Waterhouse, 24

wedding feast, 13, 14, 46, 47, 209, 230

wedding ring, 202

Weyden, 198, 200-210, 213, 217, 219, 220

white flower, 266

White Friars, 154

Yahweh, 229

Yaldabaoth, 260

Yolande of Flanders, 223

Zoroastrians, 99

ABOUT THE AUTHOR

Ariadne Green is a dream, soulmate and mythology expert and the author of *Ariadne's Book of Dreams*, Warner Books, 2001, *Divine Complement*: *The Spiritual Terrain of Soulmate Relationships*, Palm Leaf Press, 2006 and *Divine Complements Forever*, 2012.

Ariadne Green holds a Masters degree in Educational Psychology from Cal State Hayward and completed two years of doctoral coursework in Consciousness Studies and Philosophy of Psychology at Saybrook Institute in San Francisco. She studied under the mentorship of Stanley Krippner, world-renowned expert on the paranormal and dreams.

In addition to her books, Ariadne has written and published over one hundred articles on a variety of spiritual topics such as: soulmates, mythology, dreams, self-help, Gnosticism and religion. Ariadne has also completed writing her first screenplay titled: Gilead's Dispensation, an adaptation of Jesus Mary Joseph.

For more information visit Ariadne's other websites at:

http://www.jesusmaryjosephbook.com

http://www.ariadnegreen.com

http://www.dreamthread.com

Made in the USA
Middletown, DE
22 April 2019